THE A

John Jacob Astor ═══ m. ═══ Sarah Todd
(1763 – 1848)

William Backhouse Astor ═══ m. ═══ Margaret Armstrong
(1792 – 1875)

William Backhouse Astor Jr. ═ m. ═ Caroline W. Schermerhorn
(1830 – 1892)

Ava Willing ═ m. ═ John Jacob Astor IV ═ m. ═ Madeleine Force
(1864 – 1912)

William Vincent Astor
(1891 – 1959)

John Jacob Astor VI
(1912 –   )

m.

Ellen Tuck French

William Backhouse Astor
(1935 –   )

* Not a complete Astor genealogical chart.

THE
ASTOR FAMILY

Other Books by John D. Gates

THE DU PONT FAMILY

THE ASTOR FAMILY

John D. Gates

DOUBLEDAY & COMPANY, INC., GARDEN CITY, NEW YORK
1981

Library of Congress Cataloging in Publication Data
Gates, John D
    The Astor family.
    Bibliography.
    Includes index.
    1. Astor family. I. Title.
CT274.A86G37   973'.009'92 [B]
ISBN: 0-385-14909-3
Library of Congress Catalog Card Number: 79-6580

For Snooze

ACKNOWLEDGMENTS

The Astor family is not an easy one to get to know. The American branch of the family is rather publicity shy, with the exception of a few distant cousins, and the English branch, while impeccably polite, steers a wide berth around any controversy. More importantly, a majority of the major Astor ancestors, from Vincent all the way back to the original John Jacob, had a habit of destroying personal and business documents—the stuff of primary source material. There is no indication that any Astor was afraid of what such material might reveal. It simply had lost its usefulness and therefore its right to exist. In the first John Jacob's case, a fire over which he had no control apparently did the damage. Given his vision and desire for recognition from posterity, he is virtually alone among the Astors in being unlikely to have built a bonfire of personal or business papers. Among the living, Mary Jacqueline Astor, Winthrop Aldrich, Allen W. Betts, Laura White, Christopher Phillips and several others who requested anonymity were kind or curious enough to see and talk with me. They were all immensely helpful, although one or two might deny that statement as being too self-serving on my part. The fact is that, even though some of our meetings were not of long duration, all were rewarding.

Several books deserve special mention. Kenneth Wiggins Porter has done the definitive work on the original John Jacob, while Lately Thomas is the expert on the Chanler family, although unfortunately his published work ends with the turn of the century, the further saga being intended for a later book. Michael Astor's *Tribal Feeling* is a thoughtful insight into the English branch of the family.

John D. Gates

PART I

PART I

CHAPTER 1

John Jacob Astor was not yet twenty-one when he first stepped off his ship at Baltimore in 1784 and felt American soil beneath his feet. The War of Independence had been over just a few months; the American Constitution would not be framed for three more years. America as a land of opportunity had not yet become a cliché.

During the next sixty-four years Astor helped write the cliché, one that only in recent years has grown tired. This German butcher's son took a handful of flutes and $25, parlaying them into a fortune so vast that upon his death in 1848 estimates of the value of his estate ranged all the way from $8 million to $150 million. The numbers awed the minds of those days. Stephen Girard, the Philadelphia banker, was said to have left an estate of $7 million. No one else came close. Peter Chardon Brooks, a grandfather of Henry Adams and reputedly the richest man in Boston at the time, died the same year Astor did and left an estate of $2 million. The generally accepted figure for Astor's worth at the time of his death is $20 million.

More than any other man, Astor laid the groundwork for the men who would become known as the "robber barons" of the post-Civil War era. Astor's American Fur Co. was the first of the great trusts. By the time he got out of the fur business in 1834, the American Fur Co. was the largest business enterprise in the United States, and yet the vast majority of the wealth he accumulated came not from furs but from real estate. It was Astor who first personified successful capitalism and the free enterprise system—their inherent dangers as well as their limitless opportunities.

Later generations would make the Astor name synonymous with "Society." Indeed, the irony here is that social distinction was something few Astors cared about or sought; their wives made the Astors social lions, not infrequently against their wills, and the Astor who qualified as a member of the socially elite because of attributes other than wealth was a rarity. John Jacob Astor was never endowed with the charm, wit or grace that allow lesser men to penetrate the upper reaches of society, but he was a far more complex and remarkable man than James Gordon Bennett, publisher of the old New York *Herald*, gave him credit for when he called Astor "a self-invented money-making machine."

Around such men as Astor grows a crust of myth and legend that is often difficult to cut away, but clearly, whatever else he may have been, Astor was a man of great vision and tenacity. The latter came first.

It is safe to assume that the birth of John Jacob Astor on July 17, 1763, was attended by little fanfare even within his family. Although he was named after his father, he was the youngest of four sons. His mother died when he was still a boy, leaving two daughters as well. His father, the butcher in the small village of Walldorf, near Heidelberg, was content to be buffeted by fate, drinking when he could, just scraping by most of the year and enjoying the six weeks of harvest during which he prospered modestly. A butcher in Walldorf then was not the fellow behind the meat counter at the local supermarket; he was the man who traveled around to the neighboring farms slaughtering the animals chosen to provide the farm's meat supply. It was not full-time work.

When John Jacob's mother died, his father soon remarried. The stepmother provided the family with six more children and, as far as John Jacob was concerned, little else. His older brothers left home. George went to England and found work with a musical instrument company in London. Henry went to the United States and became a butcher. John Melchior became the steward at the estate of a German nobleman. John Jacob was left to care for his sisters and work, against his will, for his father. It was not an easy life, but chances are John Jacob didn't mind the hardship. After all, in his old age he used to boast he had walked forty-five miles in a day back then just to pick up letters from his brothers in London and New York. The trouble with life in Walldorf, one suspects, was that Astor could see no future there.

The Astors were Protestant in a predominantly Catholic area. Recent research indicates that Astor's forebears were members of the Waldensian sect living in Savoy when Louis XIV persuaded the Duke of Savoy to expel all Protestants. The duke negotiated with some Germanic rulers to give the refugees a home, and the Count Palatine of Heidelberg agreed to take in a Waldensian group whose church elder is now regarded as the first German Astor. He was John Jacob's great-grandfather. It was John Jacob's grandfather who settled in Walldorf. The road on which the Astors found themselves was, from John Jacob's view at least, a dead end. His stepmother's children must have seen things differently. As late as 1978, one of their descendants was mayor of Walldorf.

An invitation to join him in London was proffered by George to John Melchior, who declined. John Jacob, not yet seventeen, decided to take John Melchior's place. Legend has it that John Jacob set out on foot for the sea and while still within view of Walldorf stopped under a tree and made three resolutions: to be honest, to be industrious and never to gamble. His earliest biographer, James Parton, says Astor used to tell this story in his old age.

Astor spent four years in England, learning English, saving pennies and working in the same musical instrument company that employed his brother. He would rise at four in the morning, awakened by nearby bells, and read the Bible and his Lutheran prayer book, although he was probably not deeply religious. Many were the times in his later years when Astor expressed his skepticism about those who professed profound faith in life after death and yet appeared to Astor so unwilling to take the first step in that direction.

History does not relate whether Astor considered London only a stopover on the way to America when he set out from Walldorf, but it did not take him long once news of the peace treaty ending the War of Independence reached him to book passage across the Atlantic, determined to join his brother Henry in New York. He was as unlikely a candidate to become the richest man in America as just about any of his fellow passengers.

Aboard ship Astor became intrigued by what he heard about the fur business. Some have attributed this interest to conversations Astor had with officials of the Hudson's Bay Co. Others suggest that a fellow German aboard who was already in the business convinced Astor of its future. No one mentions this mysterious man's name, but don't forget him, for he is the basis for a remarkable suit against the Astors more than a hundred and forty years later. Since the ship was locked in ice for two months in Chesapeake Bay, Astor had plenty of time for conversation, and it is apparent that by the time he reached New York in the early spring of 1784 he was already thinking fur.

The young man who made his way from Baltimore to New York was not an imposing figure. He was short, stout and square-faced. Were he a dog, he might have been a bull terrier. He spoke English—and would the rest of his life—with a heavy, thick German accent. His granddaughter-in-law, the doyenne of New York society for the better part of thirty-five years, would not have been pleased with him as a dinner partner. But this man burned with an inner fire of ambition whose intensity has rarely been rivaled.

His brother Henry, already a reasonably prosperous butcher, apparently did not have room for his younger brother when the young man showed up, and John Jacob was taken in by George Dietrich, a baker who had known the Astors in Germany. Dietrich needed a peddler boy for his wares, and Astor was it.

Hawking little cakes on the street must not have held much promise for someone already thinking fur, and Astor soon found himself another job. It was hardly glamorous. For two dollars a week and board, he went to work for Robert Bowne, furrier. His main chore was beating the furs at Bowne's place of business during the summer of 1784 to keep the moths away. During the next couple of years Astor apparently worked for several furriers before setting up shop for himself sometime around 1786.

Meanwhile, in 1785, Astor was married to Sarah Todd, a solid woman with sound business and administration sense.

She brought with her a $300 dowry and a connection to the influential Brevoort family. Her older half sister's daughter had married Henry Brevoort.

As time passed, Astor devoted more attention to building his fur operations, but the musical instrument business remained an important part of his commercial activities. About this time he made a trip to London where he established outlets for his furs and became the New York agent for his brother's musical instruments, providing New York with a steady supply of pianos, flutes and violins for the first time. By May of 1786 the Astors had set up a music shop in the home of Sarah's mother, which was a boardinghouse, in two rooms of which lived the Astors.

Over the next several years Astor developed his sources for furs, tramping through the wilderness of upstate New York alone, his trade goods in a pack on his back. He established a reputation that would endure for the rest of his life as a canny trader. Rare was the trapper or Indian who got the better of him. It was also at this time that the first hints Astor was a man of unusual vision appeared. In his old age he would claim to have predicted the development of Rochester and Buffalo, New York, at a time when there were only wigwams at Rochester and next to nothing at Buffalo.

Toward the end of the 1780s, Astor became a frequent visitor to Canada. Montreal was then considered the capital of the fur trade, and it was not many years before Astor was associating with the biggest and best in the business. By the fall of 1788 furs replaced musical instruments as Astor's main business. While he was away wandering in the woods or dealing in Canada, Sarah kept shop. She was very good at it and got better. It has been said that in later years (after 1800) she used to charge her husband $500 an hour to judge furs, a fee he gladly paid.

These were the hardest years, physically, in Astor's life. He did it all himself, buying furs on arduous expeditions, beating them, baling them and loading them aboard ship for sale in London. It is not unlikely that the fragile health that plagued him in later life stemmed from these exertions. Business was good, but if Astor foresaw his future success at this time he apparently kept it to himself. In retrospect, at least, the most significant business transaction Astor made before 1790 occurred on May 18, 1789. From his brother Henry he bought two lots and four half lots of New York City land for £47—his first venture into the business that would make him and his heirs for generations so fabulously wealthy.

His brother also figures in a legendary story concerning a loan to John Jacob, who, it seems, was forever asking Henry if he might borrow a few dollars. Henry grew tired of this and at one point during the early 1790s told his brother, who had just asked to borrow $200, that he would give him $100 if John Jacob would promise never to ask again. The brothers struck a deal.

By this time Astor had set up a web of agents through the upper Hudson Valley to handle his fur-buying operation and was concentrating his own travels in Canada. He had also established a connection with the London firm of Thomas Backhouse & Co. thanks to his acquaintance with a relative of the London Backhouse, the New York merchant William Backhouse. The business was growing, but it was hampered by the fact that the British had retained their military posts along the northwestern borders of what was then the United States and controlled the fur business to the extent that many of the furs Astor bought in Canada had been trapped in the United States. These furs could not be shipped directly to the United States but had to go to London first. In 1794 John Jay negotiated a treaty with the British, a major provision of which required the British to abandon those military posts by 1796. This meant not only that furs could now be shipped directly to New York but also that forts given over to American control would be available for the storage of furs.

"Now I will make my fortune in the fur trade," Astor is said to have told an associate. It was no idle boast. By the turn of the century Astor was worth $250,000. He would say later, "The first $100,000, that was hard to get, but afterward it was easy to make more."

The turn of the century coincided with a turn in Astor's fortunes. He began acting as the middleman between Midwestern fur trappers and London buyers and owned his first interest in a ship going to China. He moved out of his quarters above his store and into a new home at 223 Broadway. Henry Brevoort, Jr., whose family was unlikely to have cherished its liaison with the Astors at the time of John Jacob's marriage to Sarah, began working for Astor, making fur-buying trips into the wilderness. By 1808 Astor's fortune had doubled again, to $500,000.

In 1801 at least five ships arriving in America from Europe carried Astor-ordered goods. In 1803 Astor was the principal owner in a ship sailing for Canton. The fur business was still central to Astor's enterprises, but he was rapidly becoming a factor in the export-import business as well. In a short biography of his great-grandfather, William Waldorf Astor quotes him as liking to reminisce that before the end of the eighteenth century he had "a million dollars afloat" representing twelve ships. The evidence indicates that John Jacob was exaggerating if not the size of his interest at least the timing of it. But the nineteenth century was not very old before it would have been difficult to challenge his boast.

Perhaps no year in his life proved as challenging to Astor's resourcefulness as 1808. Worried that British harassment of American ships would lead to another war, President Thomas Jefferson embargoed U.S. shipping at the end of 1807. In March of the following year an Astor ship returned from India, having left before the embargo. Astor's next move was to sell his interest in another ship—reducing his exposure and his investment in idle ships. Then he looked around for a loophole.

His search ended in July, when Punqua Wingchong, a Mandarin Chinese merchant, showed up in Washington looking to go home because his grandfather had died. The merchant proposed to hire a ship to take him and his property back to China, permission for which was granted by Jefferson, who told Treasury Secretary Albert Gallatin to write a letter allowing about $45,000 worth of specie, furs or other goods to be shipped. When Gallatin learned that the merchant had hired an Astor ship, he suspected subterfuge, but Jefferson said the mission would be good for diplomacy and refused to withdraw his permission.

The rumors began flying. The merchant, they said, was a dock loafer. He had been picked up in a park. He was a sailor, perhaps even an Indian. Astor's fellow merchants were not filled with admiration for his cleverness and wrote an indignant letter to Gallatin, who got it on August 12 and replied on August 17 that Astor's ship had been ready to sail on the eleventh. Actually, the ship didn't leave until the seventeenth. It returned with $200,000 worth of cargo. Not a bad profit for a single voyage.

This was also the year that the American Fur Co. was incorporated. The Jay treaty had not stopped Canadian companies from trapping in the United States, and frequently U.S. traders wound up buying American furs in Montreal. Astor volunteered to put a stop to this practice and in the process care for the Indians then under government jurisdiction. Without knowing the details, Jefferson agreed to the project. At first the company formed to carry out Astor's plan for driving the Canadian trappers out of U.S. territory was to have had ten or twelve partners. The company was to constitute more or less a monopoly because Astor didn't want to deal with fly-by-night operators in for a quick killing. Astor quickly dominated, becoming a virtual one-man partnership. The company flourished. Clearly, by this time Astor had his eye on cornering the United States, and perhaps even the North American, fur business. Before he was through, he had come very close.

But first Astor had to survive what was undoubtedly the biggest disappointment, both financially and emotionally, of his life. History, at least, has given him his share of credit for the vision that helped develop the West and eventually insured that what is today Oregon and Washington would become a part of the United States. It is perhaps going too far to suggest that the map of the country today would be radically different on the West Coast without Astor's great dream, but there are those who would argue so.

The dream was this: Astor wanted to establish on the Columbia River a settlement that would provide a point of embarkation for ships plying the West Coast and would also serve as a terminal for furs going to China brought down to the sea from the western interior of the country. At the time, what is now California was in Spanish hands. Oregon and Washington were largely unsettled. Astor, with approval from the federal government, wanted to stake a claim in the territory. It was to be called Astoria.

Late in 1809, Astor sent a ship around to the West Coast, telling the captain to stop at Spanish ports, trade if he could and find out all he could about what the Russians were up to farther north because Astor was interested in reaching a trade agreement with them. No deal was made. The following June Astor and his partners reached a final agreement to establish Astoria. Astor had eight partners but 50 percent of the stock in the company formed. Two expeditions were mounted, one overland and one by sea.

While these two expeditions worked their tortuous way toward the mouth of the Columbia River, Astor renewed his efforts to make a deal with the Russians, perhaps figuring his cohorts would have all they could handle dealing with the Indians and the North West Co., a Canadian outfit that considered the Northwest its territory and was attempting to enlist the aid of the British to retain domination of the area. He sent his son-in-law, Adrian Bentzon, to Russia, and Bentzon was able to reach an agreement.

Meanwhile, the captain of the ship Astor had sent around the Horn was proving to be a martinet who mistreated the crew and listened to advice with both ears closed. He was Lieutenant Jonathan Thorn, on leave of absence from the Navy thanks to Astor's friendship with President Madison. After a couple of near disasters, generally attributed to Thorn's attitudinal problem, the ship, the *Tonquin*, finally reached the Columbia on May 18, 1811, and the building of Astoria's fort was begun simultaneously with efforts to negotiate for furs with the Salish Indians. Thorn considered the Indians beneath his contempt and sufficiently aroused their ire so that they suggested the trading of furs for knives on a basis highly favorable to the Astoria group, whose members ought perhaps to have been more suspicious. Astor's last advice to Thorn before the ship left was never to let a large number of Indians aboard together, but Astor was a civilian and an immigrant at that. What did he know? Indians clambered aboard with their furs, were given knives in exchange and, when enough of them had made their deals, proceeded to hack the Astorians to shreds. Astoria was then just a month old. Astor took the news of the Thorn debacle in stride, refusing to cancel plans for going to the theater the night he heard of the disaster, explaining, according to Washington Irving, who wrote a book for Astor about Astoria, that he would not cry over an incident about which he could do nothing. In June of the following year the United States declared war on Great Britain. The declaration came while Astor was on horseback riding from New York to Washington to urge the avoiding of war.

The overland expedition was no picnic, either. Its ranks thinned by Indian attacks, a canoeing accident and starvation, the group finally staggered into Astoria to complete the building of the fort. The picture brightened momentarily, and Astor, after twice having failed to do so, finally managed to get a ship out of New York to help defend Astoria from the British. It sailed under pretext of supplying New Archangel. It sailed too late. By October of 1813 the Astorians and the North West Co. had entered negotiations, the former unaware that a ship was en route to relieve them. Astoria had the fort, better supplies and better ties with the Indians despite Thorn. North West had a British man-o'-war on the way.

In retrospect, it is easy to suggest that Astoria could have been saved. William Waldorf Astor, John Jacob's greatgrandson, says the fort could have been defended. Biographer Kenneth Porter argues that the furs could have been moved inland, the fort abandoned and retaken once the British ship left. Astor's view of the situation was that "the plan was right but my men were weak, that's all." Many of them were also Canadian, and a British man-o'-war was an imposing proposition, two factors that weakened the Astorians' will.

At any rate, the Astorians sold out to North West, and

one of Astor's partners joined the firm. The total payment from North West to Pacific Fur Co., the Astoria corporation, was less than $60,000. Astor was furious at the news of Astoria's loss and vowed that, "while I breathe and so long as I have a dollar to spend, I'll pursue a course to have our injuries repair'd." It was one vow he didn't keep. In defense of the Astorians it can be said that the captain of the *Raccoon*, the British ship that reached Astoria on December 12, 1813, and took over Astoria, renaming it Fort George, was unimpressed by the fort. He is quoted as having said, "Is this the fort about which I have heard so much talking? Damme, I could batter it down in two hours with a four-pounder."

A year later the Americans and British signed a peace treaty that returned the Columbia River to the United States, although the fort that represented Astoria was not returned until 1818. Fervent as Astor had been about Astoria, one might have supposed that he would have made more of an effort to re-establish himself there, but in fact the North West Co. continued to operate from there even after 1818. William Waldorf Astor claimed his great-grandfather lost $2 million and was nearly ruined by the Astoria failure.

The facts indicate otherwise. It is true that Astor lost a substantial investment in Astoria, but he was never one to be daunted by occasional setbacks, and the truth is that the net effect of the War of 1812 on his total wealth was probably positive. For one thing, he was a major investor in government loans bought at a 20 percent discount and worth a 20 percent premium a year after the war ended. For another, the war made the cargo of ships successful in eluding blockades especially valuable, and Astor had extraordinary luck in such ventures. Before the war, he owned two ships and had never owned more than five at any one time. At

war's end, he owned nine and part of a tenth. If there is
one overriding reason why Astor did not seriously attempt
a renewal of the Astoria project after the war, it may be
simply that he was too busy with other enterprises.

His great-grandson claimed Astor was inspired in the Astoria venture not by greed but by a grand vision of civiliz-
ing the western United States and bringing it under American control. Parton, his earliest biographer, suggests Astor
loved the planning of vast, far-reaching enterprises. Washington Irving says he sought fame. Porter hints at a man
dreaming of empire. Astor was a man of practical vision.
Astoria was a grand concept, but it was one that made
sense to a man striving to strengthen his grip on the North
American fur trade. Its failure was a matter of historical
bad luck. Without the War of 1812, Astor would undoubtedly have enjoyed huge success whether his goal had been
empire, wealth, fame, helping the United States to gain
control of the West or a combination of these.

A measure of how privy to inside information this underprivileged German immigrant already was by the War of
1812 is that, at its start, he was accused of treason by some
because he was alleged to have told Canada of the declaration of war before the commander of the American Fort
Mackinac on the border found out. This information allowed the fort to be easily taken by the Canadians. It cannot be proved, but if he did tip Canadian officials, it is
highly unlikely that he did so with treason in mind. He
had a substantial investment in furs stored in the fort, and
his only motivation was surely the protection of that investment. At the end of the war, according to William
Waldorf, Astor had a special relay team from Montreal
bring him the news of the Treaty of Ghent and its signing
two days before the American government received official
word. He was quick to share the information with the gov-

ernment. In other words, Astor frequently knew vital information early enough to be considered "an insider" by almost any definition of the term. The one exception to this was perhaps social. While he was a man with whom one had to reckon in business and political circles—and therefore could not be entirely excluded from social consideration—he remained, at least in part of his own volition, an outsider in the social world.

Before, during and after the War of 1812, Astor was constantly involved in negotiations and persuasions that allowed him to overcome or circumvent the rules then governing trade with Canada and Great Britain and the various blockades and embargoes imposed. He talked President Madison into relaxing the rules on importing furs from Canada just before war while the Non-Intercourse Act was in effect. Turned down in his request for permission to send a ship into British territory to bring out furs, he hinted that he might be able to arrange an $8 million to $10 million loan to the government from himself and prominent bankers Stephen Girard and David Parish. Now understanding that Astor had only America's best interests at heart, the government gave its permission for him to send a ship into British waters. At war's end Astor sent out one of his ships immediately, but not before trying to get Secretary of State James Monroe to make the mission a diplomatic one by sending dispatches and news of the war's end on the ship. Monroe declined. Throughout the war Astor was continually using his influence and connections to minimize the effects of the blockades on his commercial traffic. He was one of a very few for whom the war did not dramatically curtail foreign ventures. He continued to send ships to Europe, buying goods for trade with the Indians and selling furs, thereby supplementing the riskier but more lucrative China trade.

By now Astor and his American Fur Co. were starting to dominate the fur business. His markets in the United States were ubiquitous—Albany, New Orleans, Pittsburgh, Philadelphia, Baltimore, St. Louis, New York. His was not yet a monopoly position. Indeed, competition in the Midwest was particularly fierce, but Astor was gaining the upper hand.

His political and philosophical views in this period were, to put the kindest light on them, pragmatic. He supported the political party in power, which required him to change allegiance rather frequently. In 1811 he urged the demise of the Bank of the United States, promising to help the government financially if needed; yet by late 1814 he was saying that a national bank was needed or all was lost. This about-face was the result of his participation in an 1813 private loan to the government of $16 million—the loan he had hinted at earlier. He took more than $2 million himself, and among the three of them—Astor, Girard and Parish—they accounted for more than half the loan. A national bank would help protect Astor's investment.

But if Astor was quick to look out for No. 1, he was also already a firm patriot. He was always willing to help the government however he could, and the then Secretary of the Treasury, Albert Gallatin, noted that Astor's participation in the loan was more than he could comfortably handle, that Astor had gone out on a limb for his country. It was a risk, of course, that was not without its potential rewards.

At the end of the war Astor could write a Russian associate, ". . . I am glad of peace because it puts everything on safe ground & I can always make money if I will be prudent at all events I have enough, since it can make all my children independent, this I however mention only to you." (The capricious punctuation is Astor's.) If he was happy

the war was over, he was unable to resist noting that the timing was less than perfect and that, had it ended either six weeks earlier or six weeks later, he would have been richer by as much as $150,000 because an earlier end would have meant not having to sell some stock in his share of the government loan at a loss while a later end would have meant selling a ship's cargo at wartime prices. No one felt very sorry for him.

In 1815, Astor renewed a partnership agreement he had with some Canadian fur traders for a period of five years, but made sure a clause was inserted in the agreement voiding it should the United States pass a law with which the agreement was in conflict. He then proceeded to urge upon Secretary of State Monroe just such a law. The following year he succeeded, and Congress passed a law that said only U.S. citizens could obtain a license to trade with Indians in the United States. This same law addressed a recurring and serious problem—selling liquor to Indians—and said it couldn't be done. That was fine with Astor. His American Fur Co. favored strict rules. He wanted the Indians to retain their hunting skills. Usually a coalition of Astor and the government was unbeatable, but in this case several factors worked against enforcement of the law.

Liquor was to the Indians of that time not unlike heroin to the drug addict today. The strength of Astor's position in the fur trade made it tough to compete against him within the rules. Astor's strong capital situation made it possible for him to buy quality trading goods for cash, not credit, and therefore, because he paid less, sell them for less. For many fur traders, especially the quick-kill artists, liquor was the only answer. Drunken Indians were more pliable in negotiations, or, to put it more bluntly, easier to cheat. A further incentive was the low cost of the liquor Indians found acceptable. A trader could mix two gallons of liquor with thirty gallons of water, throw in some red pepper and tobacco and sell the concoction for anywhere from $25 to $50 a gallon.

Regulations like the banning of stills in Indian territory, the prohibition of liquor sales by traders to Indians and even a law making it illegal for traders to carry liquor into Indian country were virtually impossible to enforce. Astor, who in 1810 expressly forbade giving or selling liquor to the Indians in the Astoria area, finally found himself in the position of arguing against the spate of laws because they gave the Hudson's Bay Co. in Canada an unfair trade advantage. That company refused to keep liquor out of Indian territory, making only the hollow promise that their agents would be told to keep it out of Indian hands. In 1829 the American Fur Co. tried to make a deal with the Hudson's Bay Co. to ban liquor. The latter smugly told the former the problem was a United States problem. The result was that thousands of gallons of whiskey found their way from the American Fur Co. into Indian country in the Northern area alone. In 1831 a report to the Secretary of War claimed that Astor's company made $50,000 a year just on the sale of lqiuor. When it came to a question of principle versus profit, Astor was a practical man.

One of the major reasons for Astor's success in the fur business was his ability to eliminate the middlemen. He not only worked hard to dominate the business horizontally or geographically but also strove for vertical integration. Independent traders wound up working "for shares," meaning they received a proportion of the profits—or losses —their outfits were able to generate. They had relatively little leverage against the American Fur Co., which provided the trade goods and supplies they needed, not infrequently at prices that made profits scarce for the traders, who also, of course, had to sell their furs to Astor. It was not a good

deal for the trader, but most of the time he could find no
alternative. The men in the field, so to speak, were considered expendable. Once one of Astor's chief agents, Kenneth McKenzie, is said to have inquired after the fate of
the horses, not the men, victimized by an Indian raid.

Astor was equally rough on his smaller competitors. For
the most part, he was able to force them out of business,
after which he would sometimes allow them to work for
the American Fur Co. With the larger competing firms,
Astor was more generous. If they were able to stand up to
his initial onslaught, he would buy into them on terms
highly favorable to them. In 1827, for example, Astor absorbed David Stone's fur company, a major competitor,
after having reached a consolidation agreement with him
four years earlier, and that same year he formed a new partnership with a St. Louis firm. The Columbia Fur Co.,
which was providing formidable competition to Astor's interests in the upper Mississippi region, soon thereafter became another branch of the fast-growing American Fur Co.
tree.

One area where Astor never did overcome the competition was in the upper Missouri and Rockies region, where
the Rocky Mountain Fur Co. gave him fits. McKenzie, Astor's partner in that area, made peace with the Blackfeet
and the Crow, set up trading posts, put a steamboat on
the Missouri to get furs quickly to St. Louis and New
Orleans and even set up stills in the area to get around the
law about bringing liquor into Indian territory. This last
action might have caused Astor to be barred from trading
in the area if Secretary of War Lewis Cass had not inter-
ceded on his behalf. Medals were struck with Astor's like-
ness as presents for the Indian chiefs in the region. And
still the competition raged. The two companies stirred the
Indians against each other's representatives. When the

Rocky Mountain Fur Co. dissolved in 1834, Astor was already getting out of the fur business. He never turned a profit in the area.

But Astor was making tidy profits almost everywhere else. From 1823 to 1827 the American Fur Co., which had been reorganized in 1817 to eliminate even the semblance of partners besides Astor, paid an annual dividend of $100,000. In 1831 the American Fur Co. was employing capital of about $1 million, on which it earned a return of about $500,000. Astor was always claiming the business was profitless. As early as 1825, Astor told an associate, "I may also wish to sell out." Two years later his company sold 550,000 muskrat skins in one day and still had 200,000 remaining. An idea of the potential (at least) profit in the business can be derived from the fact that in the early nineteenth century Astor could buy a gun at wholesale for £1 .7s. and get twenty beaver skins, worth £25, for it. In all, Astor appears to have made at least $1 million and probably closer to $2 million from the fur business in the seventeen years between the reorganization of the American Fur Co. and the time he sold out in 1834, just a year after one of his chief agents, Ramsay Crooks, said of him, "The business seems to him like an only child and he cannot muster the courage to part with it."

Several factors contributed to Astor's withdrawal from the fur trade in 1834, when he sold his interest in the American Fur Co. to some of his agents and partners in various subsidiaries. Furs were believed to be carriers of cholera. Beaver was replaced by silk in top hats. The fur market in China had virtually dried up. But perhaps the crucial factor was that, in 1833, Astor was seventy and suffering from ill-health. The impression the American Fur Co. had created on contemporary Americans varied widely. Zachary Taylor, an infantry officer on the upper Mississippi during the 1820s, once said, "Take the American Fur Co. in the aggregate and they are the greatest scoundrels the world ever knew." On the other hand, writing in 1828, Lewis Cass said, "We are satisfied that the average profits of the fur trade are not in proportion to the risk attending it. We believe it is conducted upon as fair principles as other branches of business in the United States, and we know many of the persons who are engaged in it, who are honorable, intelligent men."

If the American Fur Co. made a significant contribution to American history besides its role in creating America's richest man, it was as a catalyst for westward expansion. Astoria is the most frequently cited example of this, but there are many others. In Bellevue, Nebraska, for instance, the company established a trading post on May 10, 1810, putting up the first building erected by a white man in Nebraska and starting the first permanent white settlement in the Northwest.

While the American Fur Co. was tightening its grip on the American fur market, Astor was also very busy building his export-import business. The China trade was perhaps the most glamorous, spectacular aspect, but legend has tended to make Astor a more important factor here than history justifies. He was neither the first nor the biggest American force in China, and the lucrative era of the China trade was rather short-lived. By 1827, Astor had pretty much lost interest in China. Boston merchants were the first to exploit the China market, although a New York ship that returned from China in 1785 was the first American vessel to make the trip. The Bostonians were also the biggest China traders. The importance of the fur trade in China has also been exaggerated. As early as the 1804–5 trading season, specie accounted for nearly $3 million of the China trade volume, while furs and other commodities

accounted for less than $700,000. By the 1820s, furs had
ceased to be a major factor in the China trade, replaced by
opium, cash and cotton. The other side of this coin was
that by the late 1820s the teas being imported from China
had lost their market edge, at least in part because the
United States had all the China tea it could drink and then
some.

Unlike many of his fellow traders in Boston, Astor found
the money he could make in the opium business not worth
the risks involved. By 1816 the Chinese had started crack-
ing down on opium smuggling, which had been illegal since
1800, a fact that had deterred virtually no one. The Chinese, who had little use for the white man anyway and
called him "fan-kwae" or "foreign devil," were increasingly
disturbed by the addiction of their people to opium and
the havoc the opium trade was wreaking on Chinese bal-
ance of payments. By 1818, Astor had ended the practice
of having his ships stop in Smyrna to load opium cargoes
and there is infrequent mention of opium as cargo on any
ships in which Astor had an interest from then on.

Another cargo for which Astor has received more blame
than he deserves was sandalwood, a product of the Hawai-
ian Islands favored by the Chinese, who burned it as in-
cense. Hawaii was a natural stopover for ships traveling
west to China and was ruled by kings with expensive tastes.
Sandalwood cost them nothing, and they bought lavishly
of the ships that stopped in Hawaii, paying with huge
amounts of sandalwood. Astor participated heavily in this
profitable business, but he by no means had a monopoly.
By 1827, just fifteen years after the start of the sandalwood
boom, sandalwood had become rarer on Hawaii than in
China. Entire forests had been decimated. In February of
1828, Astor sold his last ship to Governor Boki in Hawaii,
who, after declining an Astor offer to sell the ship four

years earlier, apparently finally decided to go into the export-import business for himself.

Once again, as it was so often, Astor's timing in getting out of a business just before it turned down was exquisite. Luck may have played a role, but it is more likely that Astor was simply better informed than most of his competition. For one thing, he had three relatives who were captains of China traders. Then, too, Astor was getting old. His dreams of empire were losing their vitality. He was not, however, through making money. Not by a long shot.

CHAPTER 2

If the Astor fortune was founded on furs and the China trade, it was developed and preserved in land. Where John Jacob Astor acquired the vision that informed so many of his real estate dealings remains a mystery, but that he had it to an extraordinary degree cannot be denied. There is no indication that Astor had any particularly physiocratic notions about land as the source of all wealth or that he had any emotional attachment, any love affair, with land. For him, real estate was a business. No one in history has ever been any better at it. His secret appears to have been simple enough: He saw America as growing virtually unchecked, and he saw New York City as setting the pace. When Astor first set foot in the United States, New York was a town of 25,000 people. About half of it had been destroyed by two recent fires. Its economy had been prostrated by the loss of the royalists who fled at the end of the Revolution. By 1800 the population had doubled, the city boundary had expanded a mile to the north and the economy was bubbling again. Astor better than anyone recognized this vitality as no merely temporary phenomenon.

An oft-told story about Astor has him selling a lot on Wall Street about 1810 for $8,000, a small price for such property even then. The buyer, proud at having put one over on John Jacob, told him rather smugly that in just a few years the lot would be worth $12,000. Astor agreed with that assessment but pointed out that with the $8,000 he would buy eighty lots above Canal Street, and by the time the Wall Street lot was worth $12,000, the Canal Street lots would be worth $80,000. Astor was right. The story illustrates both Astor's vision and his willingness to sell as well as buy. The legend that Astor had a rule about buying and never selling is but a myth. He was a businessman. It may, however, be true that as an old man Astor liked to say he had only one regret: That if he had it all to do over again, he would have bought all of Manhattan.

In the beginning Astor did not limit himself to New York City real estate. He was involved in a number of deals covering thousands of acres in the West, Canada, the Midwest, upper New York State and Putnam County, now one of New York City's bedroom counties. The Western land was primarily for trading posts or was acquired through mortgage foreclosures on traders who bought goods from Astor on credit, using land as collateral. In all, these lands added up to several thousand acres. Astor sold most of this real estate as quickly as he could, much of it at a loss. As early as 1795 he was associated with the head of the Lower Canada Land Committee in a scheme to acquire 2,400 square miles in Canada. Astor put up the front money ($12,000), but nothing came of the project because scandal attached itself to the committee and land grants were suspended.

Astor and two partners bought 37,200 acres in the Mo-
hawk Valley in 1794, a venture fraught with less than spectacular success. The total cost was about $26,000. There
were title problems with some of the land, and by the
time Astor extricated himself from the deal in 1829, he had
received $36,800 on an investment of $10,000, not bad but
certainly not great either, considering the elapsed time involved. Astor's other major plunge in New York State
land came in 1809 when he bought the rights to 50,000
acres in Putnam County for $100,000 from the Morris
family. The government had confiscated the Morris land
after the Revolution because the Morrises were Tories and
loyalists, but the Morrises thus affected were found to have
only a life interest in the property, which was then to re-
vert to their children. At the time Astor bought the property rights, some 700 families were living on the land,
which they had purchased from the government. For more
than twenty years Astor battled with the government over
settling the case. In 1813 he offered to settle for $300,000,
which he claimed was the break-even point, a claim whose
truth was limited to the fact that some partners had
bought into the deal in a minor way late in the game and
would only break even at that settlement price. The state
legislature kept putting Astor off because the original Mrs.
Morris was still alive. She finally died in 1825, and Astor
began pressing his case. In 1827 he won a suit asking for
the ejection of a farmer on part of the land despite an
impassioned defense by the legendary Daniel Webster,
who argued that Astor was using a technicality to steal
land the farmer had worked for years to make worthwhile. The following year Astor and the state legislature
worked out a settlement that required Astor to win three
of five similar suits before he could collect. Overcoming opposition by such famous figures as Citizen Genêt, Astor

won, the final case being decided in his favor in the U. S. Supreme Court in 1832. The end result was that Astor received $520,000 out of the final settlement of $560,000. Biographer Kenneth Porter estimates Astor's suit expenses were $50,000.

In terms of time and capital invested, Astor's biggest real estate project outside New York City was his attempt to establish a town named Astor in what is now Green Bay, Wisconsin. This venture proved to be another of Astor's rarely laid financial eggs. The primary villain in this script was the Panic of 1837, which devastated investors and investments alike across the country, but there were other problems as well, including absentee ownership and a geographically divided management of the project. Astor's age was also probably a factor in that he was less aggressive in seeking solutions to these problems than he might have been at an earlier time. Establishing a steamship route between Green Bay and Buffalo, for example, appeared to be a promising venture both in its own right and as a spur to development of Green Bay, but Astor had lost the drive necessary to see such efforts to fruition.

Astor's first major move into New York City real estate came in 1803 when he and William Cutting bought the 70-acre Medcef Eden Farm for $25,000. The land today encompasses a major portion of the city's theater district around Broadway. The purchase was made in June, and before that summer was out Astor had sold a dozen lots of about an acre each for $7,000 apiece. It was not long before he bought a substantial portion of Cutting's interest in the property. Writing in 1931, Astor biographer Arthur Smith estimated the value of the Eden land at $50 million. Even Astor with his uncanny ability to predict the future potential of what was then rural Manhattan might have been overwhelmed by such development.

Much of the Manhattan real estate Astor accumulated over the years he obtained from important political figures of the day, in whose good graces Astor was adept at remaining. In 1805 he bought a half interest in the Greenwich Village property of George Clinton, former governor of New York, paying $75,000 for 243 lots. He then sold 32 of them over the next decade (mostly between 1806 and 1808) for an average price of $1,000 each. From 1800 to 1819, Astor invested $715,000 in city land, either through outright purchase or by long-term lease. Of this land, half came from Clinton, Aaron Burr and the Protestant Episcopal Church. Leasing was not a major factor. Of the more than one hundred land transfers to Astor during this period, only eight were leases. Seven of those involved land owned by Trinity Church and leased to Aaron Burr.

One of Astor's largest land coups was the purchase of Burr's estate on Richmond Hill in 1804. The estate apparently was heavily mortgaged, Burr being a big spender who was even threatened with debtor's prison while Vice-President. He sold his 160-acre estate to Astor for $160,000 a month before his fateful duel with Alexander Hamilton. Just a dozen years later the land was said to be worth $1,500 a lot.

Astor was not a softhearted landlord, but his reputation for ruthlessness is based more on legend than fact. The advantages he took of those to whom he leased land were standard practice of the day. Lessees agreed to put up a dwelling on unimproved land of at least two stories with a brick front. At the expiration of the lease, the improvements became Astor's property, and during the term of the lease all taxes, duties and assessments were paid by the lessee. On occasion Astor would pay for the buildings when the lease expired, but often he would not. Leases were sometimes renewed. Astor was not prone to make improve-

ments on his land. He much preferred that someone else—a
lessee or the government—undertake those efforts and expenses. He complained about the city building streets
through his property without adequately compensating
him for the land used, even though these streets increased
the value of his remaining land many fold. He balked when
the city asked him to hold up his end of a bargain whereby
the city gave him some water lots—land that was under
water at high tide—in return for his promise to fill them in
and make them usable. But to compare him with the silent film villain in his black suit and smug sneer throwing
poor, defenseless damsels into the cold street at Christmas
for lack of rent money is to overdraw the picture.

Astor did not foreclose on a mortgage until 1813. Indeed, through 1816 mortgages did not play much of a role
in his real estate business. He was involved in only twenty-
four. From 1819 to 1832 there were no foreclosures. In
all, Astor was the holder of fewer than five hundred mortgages and wound up owning property through foreclosure
in fewer than seventy instances. One such instance involved Citizen Genêt himself, who mortgaged some property to Astor in 1816. It is true, however, that Astor's policy was to foreclose if the mortgage interest wasn't paid,
and he acquired his share of cheap land in such a fashion.
Most of the foreclosures came as a result of the Panic of
1837.

Even after his death Astor's mortgage-foreclosure policy
affected some well-known individuals. A year and a half
after his death in 1848, his executors decided to foreclose
on the Washington, D.C., house and lots of Dolly P.
Madison. More than two years later, after considerable
haggling, the executors finally received payment of $3,000
plus $513 interest for the Madison property. In this case, at
least, the Astor interests exercised substantial patience.

Astor's rental income was never astronomical during his lifetime. In 1826 he received slightly more than $27,000 from rents on 174 pieces of property. In 1831 his income was $46,000 from 244 pieces. In 1841, 355 pieces brought him $128,000 in income. His rental income in the last year of his life was $200,000 from 470 pieces. At least in part, this escalating income picture is the result of an Astor policy change around 1820 that downplayed long-term leases and saw Astor concentrate increasingly on short-term leases and yearly rentals. According to Porter, who compiled the income figures above, there were two reasons for this change in emphasis. One, people were able to afford these shorter-term arrangements, and, two, as the value of his property continued to climb, Astor saw no reason not to retain ownership. William Waldorf Astor cited an example of the steep angle of this climb in his biography of his great-grandfather, noting that Astor bought a property in 1811 for $3,500 that was worth $7 million in 1899 with the improvements made thereon.

Hotels held a certain fascination for Astor. In 1828 he bought the City Hotel, then considered the best in New York, for $101,000 at auction. Not satisfied that this represented a ne plus ultra in accommodations, Astor decided to build his own, and in 1834 began construction of the Park Hotel, later renamed the Astor House, on Broadway between Vesey and Barclay streets. Before he was through, the place had cost him about $600,000. Finished in 1836, the hotel contained 300 rooms and 17 bathrooms, an extravagant number in those days. Obtaining the land for the hotel was perhaps Astor's most difficult task, thanks to one homeowner on the block who was not particularly eager to move. Astor wanted that location enough to offer the owner $20,000 more than the value put on the house by a committee of three people, two to be chosen by the owner and one by Astor. In the end, the wife of the owner agreed to accept $60,000 for her house, twice its value as determined by the committee, saying the only reason she was selling was that Astor was such a good friend. The story was one Astor enjoyed telling the rest of his life. Not long after it opened, the hotel was given to Astor's son, William B., for, as Astor put it in the contract, "one Spanish milled dollar and love and affection."

It is interesting, if not mind-boggling, to examine an 1836 inventory of Astor's real estate holdings. If there is a pattern to them, it is that as he moved uptown he leaned west in his acquisitions. Also striking is the fact that a significant portion of the property is already in his son's name. But the most remarkable aspect of the inventory is simply the addresses involved. A random sampling:

The corner of Fifty-sixth Street and Fifth Avenue; Nos. 8, 10 and 12 Wall Street; the corner of Broadway and Exchange Place; Nos. 7 and 9 Pine Street; Fifth Avenue between Thirty-fourth and Thirty-third streets on both sides of Fifth; Madison Avenue between Thirty-fourth and Thirty-sixth streets; a large part of Greenwich Village; the block bounded by Forty-fourth and Forty-fifth streets, Seventh and Eighth avenues; the northeast corner of Fifty-ninth Street and Fifth Avenue; many whole blocks on the upper West Side. Any one of those properties would make a man a multimillionaire today.

Biographer Smith put the Astor fortune at $500 million in 1931, basing his estimate on the $2 million Astor invested in Manhattan real estate. The estimate may not have been far off the mark, but its basis was. As Porter demonstrates, Astor invested slightly more than $2 million in Manhattan property during his lifetime, but he sold slightly more than $1 million, and his net investment was slightly less than $1 million. Only Peter Minuit, who bought all of Manhattan from the Indians in 1626 for $24, ever made a better real estate investment.

While the bulk of his fortune was unquestionably a result of his land acquisitions, Astor made substantial investments in other media as well. He was a director of four insurance companies between 1816 and 1838 and, judging from his son's correspondence, owned an interest at least in several others. Wrote William B. Astor, "Four or five of our insurance companies have lost the whole of their capital, and the rest, with the exception of two or three, have lost heavily. . . ." Astor was probably not investing in insurance companies for profit but primarily for the protection of his other interests. In 1826 he subscribed to a loan of $1 million for the construction of the Ohio Canal, and that same year he owned 500 of the 3,000 outstanding shares in the Mohawk and Hudson Railroad, forerunner of the New York Central. He was a director of that railroad from 1828 to 1831, and of the fifty-one directors' meetings he attended, thirty-eight were held in his house. This was during the construction period of the railroad. By the time it started service in 1831, Astor held only 180 shares, which had risen considerably in value. He was skeptical, however, of the line's future, and in 1834 wrote of lack of public confidence in the railroad. He did not participate in an 1836 bond issue of the railroad and that year sold his remaining stock.

In 1817, Astor bought $200,000 worth of stock in the Bank of the United States and became one of five directors named by the government. He was elected president of the New York branch. He also invested in several upstate New York banks. His largest investments outside real estate were in federal, state and New York City securities. By 1828 he held more than $1 million worth of Ohio obligations. He received New York securities in the Morris land

settlement and owned about $250,000 in Pennsylvania ob-
ligations. His municipal holdings outside New York City
were relatively small and scattered. Toward the end of his
life he had about $2 million invested in state obligations.
In the late 1840s he used many of these various government securities in setting up trust funds for his children
and grandchildren.

By 1830, Astor was New York's only millionaire, but the
signs of this were not outwardly obvious. In his old age
Astor used to enjoy telling a story of how a bank clerk once
questioned him about his worth. Astor asked the fellow to
guess and was amused at the low sum mentioned. He asked
the clerk how much he thought a certain prominent New
York merchant was worth, and the man picked a rather extravagant number out of the air. When Astor told him
that his own fortune was larger than the man's guess for
the merchant, the clerk told Astor he was a fool to work so
hard. While the story has a certain apocryphal ring to it,
the picture of its teller that is revealed fits neatly into the
full portrait of the man.

His accomplishments and acquisitions were considerably
more dramatic than his personality. Astor never shed the
stout, Germanic, peasant aura of his background. The social graces eluded him forever. Although in his later years
he became something of a man of the arts and letters and
displayed a mind and a wit that impressed a number of
contemporaries not easily impressed, his business success
assured his access to the important people of his day without his having to acquiesce to their customs or manners.
He didn't need polish to get along and chose not to acquire
it. One can imagine the anxiety of his hostess when Astor,
in recognition of his financial position, was invited to a formal dinner. He was said to have wiped his hands on the
dress of his dinner partner on one occasion, prompting his

distraught hostess to berate herself for having failed to have a napkin at Astor's place. He dined at the very proper Gallatin home and ate both peas and ice cream with a knife. This incident may well have played part in Gallatin's declining a lucrative partnership offer from Astor in 1815. Astor wrote the Treasury Secretary a letter in October of that year, saying he had capital of $800,000, profits of between $50,000 and $100,000 a year, and the hope that Gallatin would accept a one-fifth interest in the business. Gallatin chose instead to accept the post of minister to Paris.

Outside his family, of which he was inordinately fond, Astor was not a generous man. The stories of his parsimony are legion. His sea captains were frequent victims. He once argued with his top captain about who should pay for a new chronometer for his ship, causing the captain to quit and find himself another vessel, which he proceeded to sail to China and back, unloading before Astor's ship, even though he had set sail two months after Astor's ship weighed anchor. He glutted the market and cost Astor $70,000. Not long afterward Astor saw the man on the street, told him he should have paid for the chronometer and hired him back without an apology. This same captain once saved $700,000 worth of Astor property in China from Chinese expropriation after an Astor agent in Canton died. While Astor verbally acknowledged the service often, the captain was not compensated or even reimbursed for expenses. Another captain and his crew worked two days unloading a shipment of Madeira for Astor, who promised the captain a demijohn of the wine for his troubles. A year passed, and the captain asked Astor one day about his wine. Astor told him it wasn't yet ready. It apparently remained unready; the captain never saw it. The classic captain story, however, has to be the one involving Astor's return from Europe in 1834 aboard the *Utica*, captained by a former Astor employee. The ship ran into bad weather early in the voyage, and a nervous Astor kept telling the captain he'd "giff a t'ousand dollars" to be put ashore. Finally Astor drew up a draft for $10,000, but the captain refused to accept it because it was illegible. Astor refused to sign a draft drawn up by someone else, nerves being an important enough matter but $10,000 being $10,000. The haggling continued until the weather finally broke.

Astor was not very susceptible to charitable appeals during his lifetime, although he could occasionally be cajoled into opening his purse with the right combination of flattery and humor. Biographer Porter tells the tale of how the Henry Clay committee came to Astor in 1844 seeking a campaign contribution. He told its members that he wasn't interested, that he wasn't making money anymore and therefore didn't care what the government did. A committee member likened Astor to Alexander the Great, who wept because there were no more worlds to conquer. "You have made all the money and now there is no more money to make," the man told Astor, who, enjoying the analogy, wrote the committee a check for $1,500.

Others were rather less successful in their appeals. Julia Ward Howe quotes Astor as dismissing a clergyman seeking a donation with the observation that "a person's disposition to do good does not always increase with his means." When Astor offered to give $50 to another supplicant, that fellow thought to increase the offer by pointing out to Astor that his son had given $100. "Ah," said Astor, "but you must remember my son has a rich father."

Even the payment of legitimate bills was an obligation Astor tended to skirt. When John James Audubon asked for the $1,000 Astor owed him for some prints, Astor pleaded penury, a plea finally unmasked one day when

Audubon, Astor and Astor's son William were in Astor's office and the son began rattling off a list of Astor deposits. Audubon was paid on the spot.

There are some indications that Astor was more generous than most gave him credit for. He did, according to Philip Hone, a diarist of the day, give $5,000 of the $20,000 required for a home for old women and made several donations to the Fire Department Fund. But Astor believed that "want" and "fault" were synonymous in the United States of his time, that opportunity was available to all who diligently sought it. Adding to his reputation as a miser was the fact that Astor abhorred waste, no matter how small its manifestation. A great-granddaughter has recalled that Astor used to scold his favorite grandson, Charles Astor Bristed, for taking butter and leaving it on his plate. Joseph Green Cogswell, Astor's paid companion during the final six years of Astor's life, once convinced the old man to hurry along during an outing up the Hudson River by pointing out that the boat they had rented was costing Astor twenty-five cents a minute.

It was Cogswell who badgered and flattered Astor into making his only significant public bequest, although in fairness to Astor it must be said that, had he not already been so inclined, no amount of flattery or urging would have induced him. At any rate, Astor left $400,000 to create a public library, which was combined some years later with two other libraries to form the New York Public Library. Cogswell became the Astor library's first director. Hone called Cogswell in his diary Astor's "train-bearer and prime minister." Cogswell served in a variety of capacities including companion, secretary, nurse and spiritual adviser as well as director designate of the Astor Library.

Cogswell replaced Fitz-Greene Halleck, employed by Astor in 1832, as Astor's man Friday. Halleck was, by most accounts, a minor poet and a major social climber. After he moved in with Astor, he more or less ceased writing poetry, and a number of his friends accused Astor of inhibiting Halleck's poetical talents. Others suggested, with probably more accuracy, that Halleck simply became more interested in the social life of New York, which he could now more nearly afford. Halleck was another victim of Astor's sense of humor in combination with his parsimony. It seems Halleck had once asked Astor of what use all his money was, contending that he, Halleck, would be content with a mere $200 a year as long as he was sure of it. This conversation prompted Astor to draft a codicil to his will leaving Halleck just that. Halleck's friends were outraged at this stingy treatment, but Halleck apparently took it in good humor.

His early years in the fur trade took their toll on Astor. The physical and mental strain under which he operated during the first decade or so of his Americanization eroded his health, and by the time he was thirty illness came often. He was a man of simple tastes and a creature of habit. He enjoyed telling people that he had become a millionaire before anyone realized he was even getting close. A typical day during his middle years saw him leave his office about two in the afternoon. Dinner was at three, followed by a glass of beer and three games of checkers. He smoked a pipe. After checkers, he would ride his horse all about Manhattan looking for land to buy until it was time to go to the theater. Mrs. Byam K. Stevens, a great-granddaughter who was born in Astor's house at Hell Gate, recalled many years afterward that Astor would lean on two men and walk up and down the halls in his last years. She remembered that he used to sit and watch the Boston night boat go by on the river at the edge of Hell Gate and refuse to go in to dinner until it had passed. He was a music lover, and took special pleasure in having his grand-daughter, Emily Ward, sing to him. Astor undoubtedly took some enjoyment as well from making his own music. After all, he sold musical instruments for a number of years. He is also credited with organizing the first orchestra of more than twelve musicians in New York. His love of the theater caused him to join John K. Beekman in purchasing the Park Theater in 1806 for $50,000. It was destroyed by fire in 1820 and rebuilt as New York's best. In 1828 it was worth $150,000. Astor derived perhaps his primary aesthetic joy from the color, shape and feel of fine furs. He more than once chastised his granddaughter-in-law, Mrs. Woodbury Langdon, for sitting too close to a fire while wearing valuable furs. Painting and sculpture were not important to him, although, in a spirit of "keeping up with the Joneses," he had a large if undistinguished collection of both.

Astor's literary interests grew with age. Earlier, his contact with literature was mainly through friends and acquaintances like Washington Irving. As he grew older, he read a good deal, especially in history. The extent to which he developed a personal library is subject to some controversy. His great-grandson, William Waldorf Astor, claims he had "a few thousand choice volumes." His first biographer, Parton, says he did not collect books. This disagreement may arise from the fact that in his last years he sent Cogswell on several book-buying trips to Europe for his planned library and may have kept the books at home.

While Astor was unquestionably a loyal and dedicated American—William Waldorf says his great-grandfather predicted great wealth and power for the country despite its democratic political principles—the tug of his European heritage remained strong throughout his life. Whenever he traveled, it was to Europe, where he spent a third of his life, including his first twenty years. He did little traveling in the United States and none in the Pacific. He spent the better part of the three years from 1819 to 1822 in Europe and in 1824 bought a $50,000 villa in Geneva. His last trip abroad was from 1832 to 1834, a journey from which he returned to find his wife had died. While she, a Scot, did not particularly condone his Germanic, grandfatherly indulgences, they had been married almost fifty years, for the most part happily. He knew relatively little happiness thereafter.

During the 1830s, Astor was subject to fits of depression. They didn't last long, but they were undoubtedly an indication of a deeper malaise. In 1837, Astor finally gave up riding after the second of two falls. He was seventy-four. Anger appeared to act as an anodyne for Astor's ills in his late years. At least that was the opinion of a nephew, Henry Brevoort, who commented on the remarriage of Sam Ward, a former Astor son-in-law, ". . . An untoward event has just happened in his family, which has stirred his ire, a thing which always does him good." Philip Hone wrote of Astor in 1844 that his mind remained sharp but that his body had withered to the extent that a servant had to stand behind his chair at dinner and "watch him as an infant is watched." Continued Hone, "Mr. Astor presented a painful spectacle of the insufficiency of wealth to prolong the life of man." In his last months, Astor could feed himself only at the breast of a wet nurse. He was tossed in a blanket because he was incapable of exercise and his circulation needed stimulating. He lost his capacity for conversation but retained, apparently, his interest in his property, becoming more animated when that subject was broached within his hearing. On March 29, 1848, a little more than three months before his eighty-fifth birthday, Astor died.

He was buried with considerable pomp and some circumstance in an Episcopal cemetery after an impressive Episcopal service arranged by his son. Astor was not an actively religious man. He had been brought up a Lutheran but had become a member of the German Reformed Church in the United States. Porter suggests this may have been a compromise between Luther and the Calvinist attachment of his Scottish wife. In his last years Astor developed insomnia and would often have Cogswell and William, the coachman, stay up with him late into the night discussing immortality. He probably would have been surprised by the degree of immortality history has accorded him. The tone of his obituaries varied widely, from James Gordon Bennett's opinion that he was but "a self-invented money-making machine" to the unequivocally sycophantic encomiums one might have expected. Washington Irving said of him, "He began his career on the narrowest scale, but he brought to the task a persevering industry, rigid economy and strict integrity. To these were added an aspiring spirit that always looked upward; a genius bold, fertile and expansive; a sagacity quick to grasp and convert every circumstance to its advantage; and a singular and never-wavering confidence of signal success."

William Waldorf Astor said of his great-grandfather that he "early divined that the secret of success is concentration." He never asked advice, his great-grandson continued, and possessed an indefatigable industry and "a vein of sentimental sadness. Perhaps this was but a trace of the reverie of one who, grown meditative as the shadows lengthen, and passing the joys and loves and triumphs of a lifetime in review, catches beneath a thousand memories their inevitable undertone of tears."

In an 1850 letter to Horace Mann, then a congressman, Astor grandson Charles Astor Bristed defended his grandfather, rebutting an essay Mann had written comparing Astor and Stephen Girard, the Philadelphia banker who had left almost his entire fortune to Girard College. Bristed argued that the wealthy are automatically subject to bias and suspicion and questioned the justice of the press treatment of the rich. He contended that work is not inherently productive nor idleness necessarily insidious. He might also have pointed out that Girard died childless while Astor's family was substantial.

It took forty-three years to tie up all the loose ends and settle the Astor estate. The last item of business was the disposal of Astor's remaining holdings in Green Bay, an effort concluded on April 16, 1891. Even after this, Astor continued to make news. In 1923 newspapers reported an elaborate hoax that resulted from an 1896 dinner conversation between a member of the prominent Olmsted family and Franklin H. Head, author of *Shakespeare's Insomnia and Its Causes*. The hoax involved a suit by the Olmsteds, owners of Deer Island, Maine, who claimed that a box containing treasures of the pirate, Captain Kidd, had been taken from the island and sold by Astor, who had then invested in New York real estate. Farfetched as this allegation was, enough people chose not to dismiss it so that even today one hears occasional questions about the story that Astor's fortune involved Captain Kidd's treasure.

On May 26, 1928, the New York *Times* carried a page 1 story about a suit brought by nine hundred heirs of a John Nicholas Emerick, claiming that Emerick was the mysterious fur trader Astor had met aboard the ship that brought him to America. Furthermore, alleged the plaintiffs, Emerick had taken Astor under his wing and made him a one-third partner. Emerick had then set up a ninety-year trust with his share of the partnership because he was not fond of his closest heirs and did not want them interfering with Astor's management of the business after Emerick died. The suit contended that Judge Alexander W. Bradford of the Surrogate Court had issued a decree in 1849 upholding the trust, but that the court record books for the years 1847 to 1850 were missing the pertinent pages. The plaintiffs argued that a legal representative of the Astors conceded in 1902 that the trust fund then amounted to $39 million. They said that old Emerick papers substantiating the claim had been discovered the previous April in the lining of a leather chest.

In a book published in 1936, C. I. Hoy, attorney for the plaintiffs, says that the Astors did not contest the existence of the trust, arguing instead that even if it had existed it was void. Thomas D. Thacher, the judge, agreed, saying the court could not rule on the question a hundred years after the fact. Suits were filed in 1930 and 1932 by the plaintiffs in attempts to discover more information. They were dismissed. Intriguing as the case appears on the surface, no one seems to have made any concerted effort to follow it up. The New York *Times* ran several small items during the court session and dropped the story. No one else ever picked it up. New-York Historical Society documents, which include the records of the executors of the Astor estate, make no mention of Emerick, the case or anyone alleged to have been involved, excepting a reference to a Judge Bradford in a totally unrelated matter. There is, however, a reference in those same documents to the fact that the Astors claim to have lost a substantial body of pre-1834 papers in the major fire that swept New York in 1835. The fact that the case was dropped without appeal and has never been exhumed seems to favor the generally held conclusion that the Emerick claim was at best a tenuous one.

It is interesting that Astor frequently expressed his contempt for gamblers and stock speculators, boasting that his money was all made by hard work. The older he grew, the less truth that sort of statement contained. James Gordon Bennett may have exaggerated the case when he claimed that Astor owed half his fortune to the people of New York, whose hard work and prosperity created Astor wealth, but it is surely true that Astor was not a significant developer of the land he owned and could legitimately be accused of aggressive speculation. The only difference between Astor and stock speculators was that he dealt in something with inherent worth that was less easy to manipulate than the paper with which stock market speculators dealt. The major portion of Astor's fortune owed its value and the phenomenal increase thereof to the work and ingenuity of others. As Burton J. Hendrick, writing in the April 1905 issue of *McClure's* magazine, points out, De Witt Clinton and the Erie Canal, the railroads and steamship lines contributed substantially to the Astor fortune. Of even greater importance perhaps were the inventions of the elevator and steel girder construction. All of which does nothing to diminish Astor's genius in the art of buying and selling or his vision, which saw more clearly than anyone else's the future growth potential of Manhattan. The question raised concerns the extent to which Astor contributed to that potential as opposed to simply taking advantage of it.

In the context of the times, Astor's parsimony has probably been overstated. No one would ever accuse him of boundless generosity, but in those days of first-generation wealth, the men who made it usually considered those who didn't to be lacking the proper personal qualities rather than the opportunity. The sense of civic duty and public-spiritedness was undeveloped in those days, and noblesse oblige was a concept scorned by all but a handful of long-established families. When Amos Lawrence died in Boston in 1852, it was estimated that he had given away $700,000 during his lifetime, more than any other American to that date. Both as a dollar amount and more especially as a percentage of his total wealth, Lawrence's benefactions exceeded those of Astor by a wide margin, but the point is that Lawrence's behavior was considered unusual enough to attract wide attention. The tendency to judge the past by today's standards makes Astor a meaner figure than he likely deserves. It helps to give credence and circulation to stories, many of them patently apocryphal, illustrating Astor's miserliness and fosters skepticism about the stories that portray him in a more kindly light.

Astor was no saint, but neither was he the prototype for Dickens' Scrooge.

PART II

CHAPTER 3

Among the tragedies that beclouded John Jacob Astor's happiness none was so dark or enduring as the mental illness that enveloped his eldest son, John Jacob II, who was born in 1791. The father never really gave up hope that his son would somehow be cured. As late as the winter of 1820–21, Astor took his son with him to Paris for the season, but the young man fell into a mental stupor, causing his father untold anguish. The son was finally institutionalized, but in 1838 the father persuaded a man named Dexter Fairbank to become the son's companion, built John Jacob II a home in New York and made sure he would be comfortably provided for as long as he lived.

While Astor hoped for the recovery of his son, he would never have been so sentimental as to stake the future of his business ventures on such a problematic or unlikely event. On the obedient shoulders of his second son—William Backhouse Astor—did the burden of the Astor future fall. William was born in 1792, less than a month after William Backhouse, a prominent New York merchant and

business associate of John Jacob, died. Backhouse's widow
became William's godmother. The boy was sent to a private school in Connecticut when he was eight and to the
University of Heidelberg, Germany, at sixteen. Two years
later, in 1810, William went to the University of Göttingen, whose reputation in physics and mathematics was
unrivaled at the time. Here he was tutored by a noted
scholar, Christian Karl Josias, Freiherr von Bunsen, who
was just a year older than William. Here also William be-
friended the philosopher, Arthur Schopenhauer, a fellow
student who would eventually gain widespread recognition
for his philosophy of pessimism. A great-great-great-great-
grandson, Winthrop Aldrich, speculated not long ago that
if William had had his own way he might have founded a
major university in the United States based on the German
model and therefore differing from most American univer-
sities that evolved in the nineteenth century and were mod-
eled after England's Oxford and Cambridge. By both incli-
nation and ability, William was a scholar, and in his last
years, frequently in the company of his wife's nephew,
James Armstrong, he would escape to his library at Rokeby
on the upper Hudson and lose himself among his books.
From the time William left Göttingen until after the Civil
War, however, he had little time for books, except ledgers
and account books.

Blame Albert Gallatin. When he turned down John Jacob's offer of a partnership, Astor turned to his son. This
time he didn't ask; he ordered. Astor wasn't old at fifty-
two, but by 1815 his health was occasionally shaky and his
business enterprises so widespread as to be difficult for one
man to administer. If Astor had instilled any virtue in his
son, it was filial piety, and when John Jacob sent word for
William to come home, home he came, despite a British

blockade of U.S. ports as a result of the ongoing War of 1812.

Meanwhile, John Jacob's relationship with Gallatin must have become even more strained as the result of Gallatin's invitation to Astor's daughter Dorothea ("Dolly" to her family and friends) to visit in Washington, D.C. She accepted. While in Washington she met Colonel Walter Langdon of Portsmouth, New Hampshire, a man of good family but modest means and limited ambition. Dolly, although she did represent a potentially substantial dowry, was not exactly a ravishing debutante. A Langdon relative described her at the time as "this fat German, Dolly Astor." While her father was bound to disapprove, the colonel probably represented about the best Dolly could hope for. They eloped on September 24, 1812, and, receiving the cold shoulder in Portsmouth, settled in New York, where relative temperatures were hardly less frigid. John Jacob remained unreconciled with Dorothea for something near half a dozen years, until struck by the vague familiarity of a little girl cavorting about at a party he attended. Smitten, he asked her name, learned it was Langdon and told her he would forgive her mother and father for her sake. Generations of Langdons then unborn would owe that little girl a debt of gratitude.

Astor was always a sucker for little children, at least within the family. Cold, tough and stingy as he could be to outsiders, his affection for family was vast and warm. The year 1818 was one of mixed blessings for him. It was the year his first grandson, John Jacob Astor Bentzon, son of his eldest daughter, Magdalen, drowned in Washington, an event that prostrated John Jacob. But it was also the year that William married, making a match that would improve the social standing of the Astors immeasurably. William's bride was Margaret Armstrong, daughter of General

John Armstrong, Secretary of War during the War of 1812, and Alida Livingston Armstrong, whose family credentials were impeccable by anyone's standards. William and Margaret met at the home of Judge Ambrose Spencer in Albany while William was looking after the family interests in a matter of state real estate legislation. Margaret did not possess a beauty capable of making heads turn, but William was taken with her splendid complexion (his private term of endearment for her was "Peachy" in tribute to her skin) and her strong religious beliefs, which he shared. John Jacob was so pleased by the impending match that he chose to overlook the fact that General Armstrong was the author of an atrabilious article accusing Albert Gallatin of treason during the War of 1812 and alleging Astor's conspiracy with his friend.

About this same time Magdalen's marriage to Adrian Bentzon was coming apart at its seams. She was a rather morose, introspective woman to begin with and the death of both her children in infancy had left its mark. Bentzon was flagrantly unfaithful and the situation became intolerably humiliating. Astor arranged a divorce for his daughter, although the era was not one in which divorce flourished. Magdalen managed to find another husband, the Rev. John Bristed, an Englishman, who lasted a little more than a year before retreating to Britain. Henry Brevoort, writing of the incident, remarked, ". . . my well beloved couzen the late Mrs. Bentzon. . . . She is certainly a maniac." Brief as Bristed's tenure was, it was sufficient to father a son, Charles Astor Bristed, whose future became assured when his grandfather took a particular shine to him, putting him through Yale and a stint at Trinity College, Cambridge. Charles wound up marrying Brevoort's daughter, publishing what H. L. Mencken called the first defense of the American language by an American and the "most intelligent brief discussion of the subject ever printed," and inheriting a comfortable fortune from his grandfather. His mother had married his father on March 9, 1820, and Charles had been born on October 6. When his mother died in 1832, Charles was given over to the care of his grandfather. It was not until 1844 that he took Astor for a middle name.

Of all his children, only John Jacob II, William B. and Dorothea outlived John Jacob. Two sons and a daughter died in infancy. Magdalen died when she was forty-four, and his favorite, Eliza, born in 1801, died in 1838. Eliza was the only Astor child living at home after 1818, and John Jacob doted on her, taking her on all his trips. He was determined that she should make the best of marriages, and love was not a part of the equation. Eliza apparently had fallen in love with a dentist, Eleazar Parmly, who was also a pretentious poet, a voracious reader and an able practitioner of the manly art of self-defense. His dentistry wasn't bad, either, and he died leaving an estate worth about $3 million. A reasonable catch for most anyone, even an Astor, but not good enough for John Jacob, who whisked his daughter off to Europe, intent on making her a more appropriate match. The man who best suited Astor's sense of propriety turned out to be a fellow named Count Vincent von Rumpff, a German diplomat in Paris, who was able to get Astor introduced to a variety of royal families and courts, thereby making himself invaluable in Astor's eyes. Von Rumpff and Eliza were married in 1825. Was she happy? The record doesn't say. Romantic legend says that she was miserable and that she died of a broken heart, alone and childless. But a slim volume purporting to be her memoirs by a Robert Baird is a panegyric to the happiness of their marriage and the virtue of Von Rumpff. Somewhere between lies the truth. Eliza did suddenly become deeply religious, funding Sunday schools and entertaining by hosting "religious soirees." Did she find happiness or merely solace in religion?

For a man whose heart was not really in it, William proved a quick study in his father's business and was soon relieving him of many administrative duties and chores, freeing the father to travel with and enjoy his growing family. While John Jacob attended to his health and his family, William attended to business. He was a detail man, meticulous almost to a fault. Soon he could recite the rent rolls by heart. Not, mind you, that William was taking over. All leases still contained his father's signature. William was, in effect, chief clerk, ". . . a very good and trusted one—but an underling, nevertheless," as a friend of his once said. "William will never make any money," his father would predict, "but he won't lose any either."

If he wasn't exactly making it, William was rapidly accumulating money in large chunks. Much of this was, of course, tidbits thrown his way by his father, but in 1833, William's fortune took a quantum leap when John Jacob's brother Henry, the butcher, died, leaving an estate of about $1 million, most of it to William. Along with wealth, William was also accumulating a substantial family, beginning with daughter Emily in 1819. She was followed by John Jacob III in 1822, Laura Eugenia in 1824, Mary Alida in 1826, William B., Jr., in 1829 and Henry in 1830. A seventh child, a daughter named Sarah, was born in 1832 but died before the year was out. A son, Robert, also died an infant. From all accounts, these children must have resulted from a union of duty more than love. Neither William nor Margaret, by all contemporary descriptions, would ever have qualified as sex symbols. Matthew Hale Smith, an acquaintance, pictured William as "a tall, heavy built man, with a decided German look . . . eyes

small and contracted, a look sluggish and unimpassioned
. . . taciturn and unsocial. . . . He was somber and solitary . . . mixed little with general society, and abhorred
beggars." A great-granddaughter, Margaret Aldrich, has described William's wife as a character combining both the
Scottish and Dutch sides of her ancestors, a woman
"serious, inflexible and possessed of an ironic humor."
Mrs. Aldrich used to enjoy telling the story about a family
trip to Italy. William, Margaret and their granddaughter,
Maddie Ward, were staying in a hotel that was ordered
evacuated in the middle of the night because Vesuvius
erupted unexpectedly. William and Maddie were in the
lobby waiting for the unruffled Margaret to come down
from their rooms. Said William, "Your grandmother is a
general's daughter. She cannot be made to feel frightened."
And indeed, she never did come down that night.

For his part, William was nothing if not colorless.
Scribner's Monthly described him after his death like this:
He "used no tobacco and little wine, though when in
health . . . he gave quite pleasant dinners. He seldom was
out late, did not attend theaters, did not get excited nor indulge in profane adjectives, sported not with dogs and
guns (nor do the two sons who are his principal heirs),
never kept a fast horse, never gambled. His whole life was
simple and orderly. He could never be induced to 'take the
chair' or enter into politics, and had small respect for or
confidence in the 'great men' of the period. He minded his
own business." Excepting, perhaps, where family honor
was concerned. At least that's no doubt what Sam Ward
would have said.

Sam married William's eldest child, Emily, in 1838, and
that was fine. His family tree housed a pair of governors,
and his father was a prominent banker. Sam was rich,
witty, lively and worldly. William could boast of only one

of those qualities, but far from being jealous of his potential son-in-law, he was delighted with his daughter's good
fortune. By the time he got married, Sam had settled down
some. After graduating from Columbia, Sam had spent a
lot of time and more money in Europe, where he became
the darling of the social set in most of the Continent's cap-
itals. He knew Franz Liszt and was intimate enough with
Henry Wadsworth Longfellow to call him "Longo." He
was a fluent linguist, a fluid dancer, a writer, a gourmet and
a connoisseur of good wine. He was also a hard worker by
the time he got married. He and Emily did not take a wedding trip. The truth was that he breathed some life into
the Astor family, relieving the stuffiness with his fresh air.
For three years, bliss was the normal state of Emily's existence. Life was less kind to Sam. Within fifteen months—
from late 1839 to early 1841—Sam lost his father and his
brother. Bottom was struck at the end of this period when
Emily died giving birth to a son, who did not survive. Only
Maddie, their first child, remained to comfort Sam in his
grief, which was clearly deep and genuine, if transitory.
Sam was too ebullient a character to stay depressed forever,
regardless of how appropriate his father-in-law might deem
such a posture. In 1843, Sam remarried. The action was
not a popular one with the elder Astors, either William or
John Jacob, but it was the object of that action the Astors
found particularly galling. Her name was Medora Grimes,
a smoky, rootless, enchanting Creole Sam met in New
Orleans.

Indulging in a bit of what today would be called black-
mail, the Astors demanded the custody of Maddie, imply-
ing without subtlety that if Sam didn't give up his daughter he would be endangering her inheritance. William was
so incensed by the news of Sam's remarriage that, upon receiving it, he rang for the butler and ordered a carriage for

Sam's sister Louisa, who was visiting the Astors and taking care of Maddie. "Miss Ward is leaving," Astor informed the butler—and Miss Ward, who never returned, left on the spot. What seemed particularly to upset old John Jacob was Sam's giving his new bride the house that had once been Emily's. Astor family legend has it that the house had originally been given to Ward by the Astors, but records show that Sam's father had given the house to him.

Relations between Sam and William appeared to improve as time went by. In January of 1850, William wrote Sam a chatty, friendly letter wishing him health and success and promising him that his daughter had sent nine or ten letters to him in San Francisco, not just the three he says he received. Three years later, however, things have deteriorated again, and William is writing a rather curt letter accompanying a check for $500, a court-awarded sum that Astor suggests Sam apply to paying off a note of $2,500 in the future. The following year the check again is sent; the tone of the letter with it is formal but more friendly, and the note is not mentioned. In 1855 the final break came when Astor instituted a suit to sell some New York property belonging to Ward for back taxes. William attempts in a letter to justify the move by saying he is just trying to change what is beyond "possible doubt" a liability of Ward's into an asset. William offers this explanation, he says, to "remove any unpleasant feelings toward me," and adds that he cannot invade Maddie's estate to help Sam, although she can when she reaches her majority. It is apparent from Astor's next letter to Ward, which reiterates his position rather testily, that Sam was not satisfied with Astor's explanation. He never forgave the suit, believing he was being kicked while down. For the rest of his full life, Sam rode a roller coaster that alternated success with failure. He became king of the lobbyists in Washington, start-

ing in the Civil War period, and a prince of entertainers.
He continued to be well known and well loved throughout
Europe, and many were the doors that magically opened to
his grandchildren in later years at the mention of his name.
He died in Italy in 1884.

No doubt fortunately, William had little time for brood-
ing about the inconstancy of his relatives by marriage. The
press of business grew only more intense as the years went
by. By the time of the Civil War, New York City's population had exploded to 700,000, and it was estimated that the
Astors owned about one thirtieth of the city's land. Astor
was constantly involved with painters, carpenters, builders,
architects and others who provide services to landlords.
William was not yet convinced, despite his father's involve-
ment with several insurance companies, of the value of fire
insurance, and since New York's fire-fighting abilities were
not yet fully developed, the rebuilding after fires was in itself a substantial part of his business. During those days
two dollars was considered a fair wage for a day's labor;
William's income was estimated at $6,000 a day. His daily
correspondence reflected a tough man but a fair, even com-
passionate one. His letters were short, almost abrupt. They
were matter-of-fact and revealed a man with confidence in
his opinions and judgments. One letter, for example, accompanied the return of a $7.00 interest check to a fellow
who contended that the money represented early payment,
which he could not afford to make. Astor made it clear
that he had never asked for early payment and had, in fact,
indulged the man in late payments in the past. He was returning the check, he said, out of sympathy for the hard
times the man described. The letters also showed that
Astor could be had for a donation or two. In 1848, for example, he made two contributions totaling $450 to the
Society for Improving the Condition of the Poor, hardly

overwhelming as an indication of largesse but a positive response at least. All told, William is supposed to have given away $500,000 during his lifetime, a not insubstantial amount but one that is somewhat diminished when you realize his income in 1865 alone was $1.3 million—in the days before income tax. In 1870 he paid $2 million in property taxes.

On November 24, 1875, William B. Astor died as he had lived—quietly. That very day he had gone down to his dingy office for a couple of hours. He was quoted in the New York *Sun* as saying, "I might have lived for another year if I had not caught this cold, but I am satisfied to go now. I am 84 [he was 83] years old—long past the allotted time of a man—and at my age life becomes a burden."

The most sympathetic obituary may have been that in the New York *Evening Mail*, which called Astor an enhancer of the land and "a just and liberal landlord. He did his whole duty as a citizen and neighbor so far as regards the improvement of his property." However, said the *Mail*, William B. was not in a class with Peter Cooper, for example. William was "not a hero in the battle of life but a true man and exceedingly useful in his day and generation." Cooper was the inventor and industrialist who dreamed of educating the poor and the man for whom Cooper Union in New York is named. It was he, said to be "a man every way competent to judge," who estimated William Astor's fortune at the time of his death at $200 million, taking the high side of estimates that ranged from a modest $40 million upward. Among the obituaries that chose to be gratuitously disparaging was the London *Spectator*'s. Its author observed that "he [William B.] ought to have been more original, more splendid, more generous, more of a recognized benefactor to his kind."

Astor's wealth, generosity and accomplishment are given

some perspective by the treatment a contemporary, A. T. Stewart, America's first department store tycoon, received when he died the year after Astor. The New York *Times* said Stewart had accumulated more money than anyone in a single lifetime but noted that William Astor's fortune when he died was the largest in the United States if not the world. The *Times*, which estimated Stewart's fortune at between $25 million and $50 million with an income running to $1.5 million a year, was critical of Stewart's lack of significant charitable contributions and the fact that he left nineteen twentieths of his estate to his widow. The year after Stewart died, Cornelius Vanderbilt, known as "the Commodore," with some irony given the fact that his edges were rougher than the original John Jacob Astor's, followed Stewart to the grave and caused the New York *Herald* to deliver the following judgment: "It was a giant they buried: The impression made upon the community by both Stewart and Astor was a faint one compared to the deep mark of Vanderbilt."

It is perhaps appropriate here to note another faint connection between the Astors and Stewart. The story involves the elopement of Louisa Dorothea Langdon, daughter of Dorothea Astor and Colonel Walter Langdon, and was told by a niece, Mrs. Byam K. Stevens, to Margaret Aldrich. One morning in the middle of the nineteenth century Mrs. Stevens' mother and Aunt Louisa went for a drive in the carriage. They came to the old dry goods shop where Stewart had begun his career, and Louisa, claiming an errand to run, ordered the carriage to halt. She went into the store and was next seen by her sister after having become Mrs. De Lancey Kane. Louisa apparently had slipped out another entrance and eluded her sister and the carriage. Colonel Langdon, forgetting, evidently, how he came to be married, decreed that Louisa's name should not again be spoken in the Langdon house.

During his lifetime William Astor became known as "the Landlord of New York." Watching the way in which he managed the Astor properties and nurtured their growth, one begins to doubt the likelihood that, if left to his own devices by his father, he would ever have developed so grand or imaginative an institution as a major university. William was a drone, if not by nature, then by habit. He was fastidious about keeping track of every bit and parcel of Astor land and knew how and where to buy more with the profits the land was generating. But, unlike his father, William was not a man of vision. He didn't build anything; he acquired land and held onto it. Improving it was left to others. The city would provide the roads and later the sewers, water, street lights and subways; tenants would do the building and the maintaining. Astor would collect the rent. The Topsy-like growth of the city during his lifetime assured a surplus of tenants and a healthy—reformers would soon be calling it "obscene"—return on his investment.

The irony of his business was that during his life large tracts of Astor land became tenement sites, which in turn fostered some of the most exploitative, inhuman living conditions ever seen in the United States. William Astor was a highly pious man—and the chief beneficiary of the tenement slums, which by 1860 had a population density the equivalent of 290,000 people a square mile. Immigrants with nowhere else to go were forced to share a single apartment with as many as three other families. Tenements, which looked almost rococo from the front, a meretricious façade, had virtually no light, no ventilation and no plumbing. Getting out of a tenement during a fire would have taxed the genius of Houdini, but it is probably not being too melodramatic to suggest that in some cases a fire would have been welcomed as an escape from an intolerable life. Astor did not see this side of his business. What he knew was that he could make 15 to 20 percent a year off land leased for tenements whereas 7 percent was about maximum for property on the tony West Side. The buildings and their condition were not his problem; he owned only the land. Besides, what could he have done anyway? he would surely have asked. The nasty quarters in the tenements were all those people were able to afford. The care and feeding of the city's underprivileged immigrants were not William's departments. In those days it was still fashionable to believe that sloth was solely responsible for a man's remaining in tenement conditions, that opportunity lay within the grasp of anyone willing to reach for it. That was a belief William might well have found it easy to hold, given his father's example.

While he lived, William demonstrated a clear preference for his daughter Emily and his first son, John Jacob III. His other two daughters and William B., Jr., were more or less short-changed. His wife Margaret and he were both devastated by Emily's early death. Margaret and her other daughters would take a daily walk along Broadway after Emily's death. Laura was fourteen, Mary Alida twelve. The three would wear veils over their faces that hung down to their feet. Etiquette in those days demanded that if they should pass an acquaintance he or she must pause, draw to one side and sigh deeply. But if in life William preferred John Jacob III to William B., Jr., in death he treated them equally. Biographers and historians are about equally divided as to whether William left his residual estate—the remaining fortune after adequate but relatively small bequests to his daughters and others—equally to John Jacob and William, Jr., or whether John Jacob received two thirds to one third for William. The weight of the evidence favors an equal division. While it is impossible to know what disposition William may have made of parts of his wealth prior to his death, his will and the letter books of the executors of his estate clearly indicate an equal division. There are two reasons for the difference of opinion found on this subject. The original John Jacob was a believer in primogeniture, the practice of preserving an estate more or less intact by leaving its bulk to the eldest son, and the assumption has been that William would naturally follow his father's lead here as he had most everywhere else. The second reason is that John Jacob III did a good deal more to inflate his share of the fortune than did William, Jr. They died within two years of one another, and John Jacob III left an estate substantially larger than his younger brother's. The third son, Henry, was another story altogether, of which more later.

If the first John Jacob represented the peasantry and his son William the bourgeoisie, John Jacob III was the family's first aristocrat; or at least he behaved and looked like one. He was six feet tall when the average man was as much as half a foot shorter. He sported an imposing mustache, a ruddy complexion, gray eyes and the polite, reserved manner of one who knew his place and expected you to know yours. He seldom wore jewelry, although many of his contemporaries considered jewelry a badge of their wealth. He usually carried, neatly folded, a fresh pair of gloves and wore a conservative suit of black broadcloth. His father and his grandfather had dedicated themselves to their business; John Jacob III was willing to concede the necessity of devoting some time to business affairs, but, quite frankly, business bored him. Making money or being a success held no particular fascination for him because, from his vantage, money and success were inherited privileges, not things one had to struggle for. Their thrill came in large measure from having experienced poverty and failure, or at least a modest income and mediocrity, experiences John Jacob III would never know.

Whether from lack of motivation or a paucity of innate ability, John Jacob was not an adept scholar, conducting himself without disgrace but without distinction either while at Columbia College. Nonetheless, the family was convinced he should have the Astor education—a stint at Göttingen. All that was needed was a suitable traveling companion for the young man. It was 1839, and Sam Ward was still within the good graces of the family. He suggested "Longo," a suggestion with appeal for the family but with little practicality as Longfellow was not in a position to go chasing around Europe for two years. Grandfather John Jacob's companion, the ever hopeful future director of the Astor Library, Joseph Cogswell, was available, and while John Jacob III dabbled in the groves of academe, Cogswell combed Europe for books for the library. On their return, Harvard was sufficiently impressed to admit John Jacob to its law school for a year. After a year in the law offices of an associate of his father's, John Jacob moved into the family business in 1843. The business flourished, through no major contribution of his, but the fact that it was able to flourish while he was in the office was good enough. He was, at any rate, not a negative influence.

In 1847, John Jacob married Charlotte Augusta Gibbes, a neighbor with whom he had grown up and who was therefore not as subject to his capacity for reticence in public or among strangers. She was from a Charleston, South Carolina, family with a lot of lineage and a lack of wealth. Although the two were virtual opposites in physical appearance—Augusta being small and delicate—the match, arranged by their respective families as was customary, proved a happy one. Until William died in 1875, his eldest son and daughter-in-law lived with a becoming lack of ostentation. One of the first items on their agenda, apparently, was to insure continuation of the Astor line, and before 1848 was over the Astors lost their founder, the original John Jacob, but gained another future heir, named William Waldorf by his parents in a thoughtful effort to eliminate some of the confusion caused by naming first sons either John Jacob or William Backhouse. Her duty done, Augusta retired from the business of parturition, and William Waldorf grew up an only child.

As the years went by and William entered his seventh decade, his eldest son was given increasing responsibilities for the business. He was much like his father in basic business philosophy, although he displayed a bit of his grandfather's vision when he applied himself to making new real estate purchases and was a less callous landlord than his father, a fact that may say more about the changing times than about changing Astors. Despite his success within the business, or perhaps because of it, John Jacob III remained unenthusiastic. That he was among the best of the best socially was of equally little moment to him. Relief finally came to him in the grim form of the Civil War. Despite his father's opposition to war of any kind and the fact that the political party in power in New York at the time was pro-Southern, John Jacob sided with Lincoln. It was a position made easier by Augusta, who, ignoring her Southern heritage, backed her husband completely. When Fort Sumter was fired upon, John Jacob III was the putative first citizen in New York to make a financial contribution to the Northern cause, putting up $3,000 to send a ship to the relief of the fort's garrison. Legend has it that Astor offered $10 million to the Union, but it is most unlikely that he actually gave anywhere near that amount. In the winter of 1861, Astor volunteered his services and was made a full colonel, attached, like many other gentleman soldiers, to the staff of Major General McClellan's Army of the Potomac. He moved to Washington, rented a house and hired a chef, steward and valet. For a while Astor was a recording clerk, essentially, but during one tour of inspection he unexpectedly ran into enemy fire and showed the sterner stuff of which he was made. A witness to the exploit has oft been quoted: "I am only a poor soldier with nothing but my sword, but if I had been the heir of the Astor fortune and estate, I would have run away if I had been hanged for it." Whether that little speech is a tribute to Astor's courage or a bit of self-incrimination is left to the reader. The taste of war was still fresh in his mouth when Astor found himself without a commanding officer. McClellan was in considerable disfavor back in Washington and was relieved of his command. On July 10, 1862, Astor resigned. He had been in military service for eight months. At the end of the war, in recognition more of his financial than his physical contributions to the Union victory, Astor was made a brigadier general. He was happy enough as a colonel and in later years would remember his service as the best days of his life. An acquaintance of his during those days recalled nearly thirty years later that ". . . you never saw a man so intent on learning his duties and carrying them out. You would have imagined him a young subaltern dependent for his future on his prospects in the service."

Augusta and other New York society women were largely responsible for the recruiting of a regiment of black troops, to which Augusta presented the colors with a stirring speech about honor and glory. Southern gentlemen were dismayed by this bold act. It was neither the first nor the last liberal act of this remarkable woman.

The best days of his life having ended perhaps prematurely, John Jacob III returned to the office. For the most part his life was calm, well ordered and dull despite the teeming, virulent city in which he lived and profited. Although he was acquainted with the problems of the city and with its politicians, he was never sullied by them. In one instance, he was a member of a committee to look into New York's slum conditions and was appalled by the committee's findings, which led to the passage of a Tenement House Act and the creation, in 1866, of a city Board of Health. The Tenement House Act could have been a rather drastic measure and a huge expense to the city's landlords if its provisions had been closely adhered to, but the landlords were too powerful to be successfully opposed. While they were generally sympathetic in theory to the plight of the tenement dwellers, they were not prepared to admit responsibility, which clearly belonged to the folks who leased the land from them for the purpose of building tenements thereon. The landlords had no control over what these greedy types might do, and the law was not fair to suggest they did. The landlords worked hard to have the law rewritten and appeared to fail when the only change made was to put administration and enforcement of the law under the city's new Board of Health. The board, however, simply did not carry enough clout to enforce or administer anything the landlords didn't want enforced or administered.

John Jacob III next ventured into the public eye as one member of a six-man commission charged with examining the books of the city administration at Tammany Hall to determine the truth of contentions William M. ("Boss") Tweed was stealing the city blind. Astor's commission gave

Tweed a clean bill of health in a report published just a couple of days before the 1870 elections. But Astor's was just the first of several commissions, and eventually, thanks in large part to a vindictive former city employee who had been fired by one of Tweed's cohorts, Tweed went to jail, where he died. Had John Jacob III perpetrated a neat whitewash? Had he been slipped a doctored set of books? The questions remain unanswered, although it has been argued recently that Tweed's conviction was more a bit of emotional railroading then an example of justice served. In other words, it is just possible that Astor and his five fellow committeemen were right, at least within the context of an era of political permissiveness.

While his real estate business thrived, John Jacob III frequently fell in over his head when he waded out much beyond the safety of terra firma. Most of the time, if he invested in securities, they were of the solid gold variety. When he took a more speculative route, he had a knack for getting lost. He was, for example, a large stockholder in the old New York Central Railroad, for which Cornelius Vanderbilt developed a craving. Vanderbilt had a callous habit of taking what he wanted from whoever had it, and the New York Central proved no exception. Jim Fisk and Jay Gould, attempting to imbue the Erie Railroad with respectability, reorganized the board of directors to make room for Astor, August Belmont and several other men of impeccable credentials. Fisk and Gould then engineered some financial prestidigitation that left them rich and the railroad in bankruptcy.

Astor was all gentleman; he was definitely not all business. If he had not been a serious student in school, he appeared to grow fonder of arts and letters as he aged. A contemporary magazine profile claimed John Jacob III read widely in English, French and German "and at times surprised his friends not only by his familiarity with lighter works of genius but by his mastery of difficult scientific questions." He was fond of music and the opera and collected books, paintings and antiques. A gourmet, Astor had an extensive and expensive wine cellar. Most of these luxuries he acquired after his father's death, not so much because it was not until then that he could afford them but because he believed a simpler existence was more pleasing to his father and therefore more seemly. There was, of course, a suitable period of mourning, but once that ended, the Astors, John Jacob and Augusta, became the primary rivals of John Jacob's sister-in-law, Caroline Schermerhorn Astor, as New York's premier host and hostess. It wasn't really a rivalry, because Augusta wouldn't have dreamed of collecting the stuffy assortment of snobs Caroline considered de rigueur. Augusta's criteria for guests were that they be witty, bright and even provocative. Their lineage was of secondary importance at best and frequently was of no import at all. Many of her guests came from the worlds of art and entertaining, spheres totally foreign to the social philosophy of Caroline. In the days when the noted actor Edwin Booth was suffering public abuse because his brother murdered Abraham Lincoln, Augusta asked him to dinner and sat him on her right. She was as charming as she was liberal—some would even say shocking—and invitations to her soirees were much coveted. She was also not actively above ostentation and would appear at fancy balls sporting jewelry worth $300,000.

If Augusta was remarkable as a hostess, she was even more astonishing as a philanthropist, whether she was helping to build a major hospital with six-figure donations or simply comforting a friend with a problem. What's more, she got her husband involved, which enabled even greater generosity. It is perhaps somewhat paradoxical that John

Jacob could be so free with his fortune for charity and so parsimonious in other ways. For example, he joined his father in opposing the building of a subway line up Broadway because it would require condemnation of some Astor property, and in 1874 he went to court to appeal an assessment of slightly more than $30,000 for street improvements, although those improvements unquestionably increased the value of the property assessed, just as the subway would eventually make the property through which it ran far more valuable. This attitude could not be attributed to a simple business conservatism, because it was John Jacob III who insisted that the Astor office keep a large sum of cash on hand so that he would not miss a good deal for want of having the dollars readily available. Still, Astor turned down a request for a loan of $250,000 from P. T. Barnum in 1877, saying he didn't have the money. Whatever the explanation, John Jacob III and Augusta broke the Astor tradition of skinflintiness and broke it with a flourish, although with a minimum of publicity. While John was attending to Astor obligations to the library his grandfather had founded, Augusta was seeing to it that the Children's Aid Society was adequately funded and that its program of finding foster homes on farms for slum children functioned continuously. Augusta had a genuine, humanitarian concern for the city's downtrodden. Besides her efforts on behalf of slum children, she helped establish a mission for the spiritual care and physical feeding of prostitutes in the quaintly naïve hope that a little prayer and a bowl of soup would reform these ladies of the night. Her largest dollar contribution was for the Astor Pavilion of the New York Cancer Hospital, to which she gave $225,000.

It is thanks to her near-legendary compassion and the paranoid privacy she and her husband both insisted on that the Astor name has never really been associated with the gruesome conditions among tenement dwellers or linked with the suspect dealings of Tammany politicians. Not until a little later were the very wealthy subject to skepticism and worse; they tended to be envied and idolized, insulated from dirt and filth, whether literal or figurative. Augusta's obvious goodness and her and her husband's aversion to publicity made linking either of them with anything unsavory seem gratuitously insulting and assured that the good would live after them, while the bad was interred. Augusta died in December of 1887 after a long and serious illness. The event was recorded on page 1 of the New York *Times*. The praise for her life and good deeds was unanimous.

John Jacob III, whose career had been distinguished enough to elicit an invitation from President Hayes in 1879 to become U.S. minister to England (an offer Astor declined), lingered for two more years and a couple of months after his wife's death. In the fall of 1889 rumor was strong that he would remarry—a Mrs. George P. Bouter, a Cincinnati widow. He was said to be lonely and in need of a mistress for his house. Nothing came of it before his weakened heart gave out. On February 22, 1890, he suffered a heart attack and died, literally in the arms of his only child, William Waldorf, at his home on Fifth Avenue and Thirty-third Street. This time the *Times* pulled out all the stops, and in an obituary that began on page 1 offered this encomium: "Thousands and thousands of God's poor and unfortunate have had their wretched lives brightened because he lived."

One person who was affected by John Jacob's death less perhaps than he should have been was his brother, William, Jr. The two had not been so alienated as to be unable to work together on occasion—in 1884, for example, they both signed a pamphlet sent to the state legislature recommending the expenditure of $43.8 million for city parks over the next twenty-five years and pointing out that New York had only 1,094 acres at the time in parkland while Paris had 172,000 and even Philadelphia had 3,000. But John Jacob disapproved of the carefree, liquid life his younger brother led, and, as one periodical put it at the time, the rift between the two men was wider than the open lot that separated their homes on Fifth Avenue. For appearances, William adopted the posture of mourning, but outside of New York observance of that posture was casual. A cousin, Marion Langdon, accepted an invitation the summer after John Jacob's death to stay with Mrs. William Astor at her Newport cottage, Beechwood, but regretted after hearing how gay life was there and how apparently unconcerned the residents were about showing proper respect for John Jacob's memory. Langdon went and stayed with William Waldorf, John Jacob's son, at his cottage, Beaulieu, instead. At the time, William, Jr., was tramping about in the wilds of Minnesota. The venomous Colonel Mann, publisher of *Town Topics*, chose to "dismiss as idle gossip the rumor that he [William] has been drinking everything in sight."

A telling sketch of William has been drawn by a granddaughter, Mrs. Caroline Drayton Phillips, daughter of Charlotte Augusta Astor Drayton. She saw her grandfather through the eyes of a little girl, but wrote about him in an unpublished memoir many years later:

"Grandfather Astor was rather gruff and frightening. He seemed always to be reading the newspaper and to have a yapping Skye terrier at his heels. My brother was terrified of Grandfather and often cried at his approach, whereon Grandfather would say, 'Turning on the water pipes again. Take him away.' But later on Harry became his favorite because one day he gave each one of us a dollar and asked what we were going to do with it. I answered that I would buy some doll's furniture and Harry said he would put his in a bank. My grandfather then proceeded to give Harry an extra dollar bill because he was thrifty but none to me as I was a spendthrift. I boldly replied that there was no fun having money in a bank. What [good] was it if you could not spend it? . . .

"My grandfather must have been a very trying and disagreeable man. He drank and had affairs with second-rate women. When she gave a dance for her daughters, she [Mrs. Astor] had to arrange with one of Grandfather's friends to keep him playing cards at the club as late as possible, for when he got home and found a dance going on, he would order the orchestra out of the house and send the young people to bed. Aunt Carrie [another of William's daughters] told me that, in Newport after her father had gone to bed, her mother would unlatch one of the french windows in the drawing room and let her out to go to a dance. Then, at a given hour, her mother would come downstairs in the early morning and let her in. But the daughter had to appear for breakfast so that the father had no idea she had been out the night before."

William was a man who played a lot of second fiddle in public. His first performance in this role was one of considerable distinction: He graduated second in his class at Columbia. Despite this, he was made to feel he was more or less a second-class citizen when he darkened the door of the family offices, which he learned early to avoid, accepting a back seat to his older brother. At home, another place he learned early to avoid, he played second fiddle to his wife, the former Caroline Schermerhorn, who would become "THE Mrs. Astor," the ultimate social arbiter in the United States from the 1870s until the turn of the century.

Her title as "Mrs. Astor" was the result of a gradual econo-mizing. First to go was her husband's middle name, Back-house, which the fastidious Caroline considered vulgar in its connotations. When William's father died, the "Jr." went with him. There was a period when Caroline and Augusta would surely have been confused had either at-tempted to become "Mrs. Astor," but by the time Augusta died, even the "William" in Caroline's name had become superfluous. It was all too much for William, who chose not to participate.

Instead, he took to the seas and headed south. What business William dabbled in was conducted for the most part in Florida, where he became interested in natural re-source development, especially around Jacksonville, near which the state of Florida granted him 80,000 acres. A town was named Astor, a lake was called Schermerhorn and another town Armstrong, after William's mother's family. So popular did Astor, or at least his money, become in Florida that he was said to have been offered a seat in the U. S. Senate, which he turned down. William didn't really have time to serve in the Senate, having become a devoted yachtsman either because he loved the sea or, more likely, because the goings-on aboard a yacht are not easily scrutinized or interrupted. Astor soon earned himself a reputation as playboy extraordinary. He was not particu-larly handsome, witty or sophisticated, but the showgirls who boarded his yacht didn't seem to notice much. Wil-liam managed to elude the reality that he usually ran a dis-tant second to his money in the affections of his guests by nipping at the bottle early and often.

Reasons for resorting to the numbing effects of alcohol were not hard to find. Not only was William forced to suffer neglect from the family business and mild indif-ference from an ambitious and ugly wife, he even flirted with failure where failure appeared all but impossible to court. For example, he bought 14,000 acres in Florida's Orange County for the astoundingly modest sum of $7,500, planning to develop the largest orange grove in the world. In that very county have the fortunes of many a citrus grower been made, but William's venture never really got off the ground, which somehow declined in value so that when it was eventually sold in 1938 the land brought less than half what William had paid for it. Typical of his luck is the fact that the land is now, of course, worth many times the original price.

For all his troubles, William could be proud that he was second to no man when it came to yacht ownership. He started out with the *Ambassadress*, a sailing yacht generally considered the finest of its kind in America, and when steam yachts became more reliable and less novel, he bought the largest one in the world and named it the *Nourmahal*, meaning "Light of the Harem," an appellation sure to be deemed appropriate by those who knew William. It was 240 feet long. Besides yachts, William also collected undistinguished art and expensive jewelry.

On April 25, 1892, William died in Paris of heart failure, lung congestion and a ruptured aneurysm. His life may have been less than exemplary, but it was certainly an exception to a description of his generation offered by his future English cousin, Michael Astor, midway through the next century. "Its [the Astor family] members," wrote Michael, "became firmly fixed to their moorings, to their family conventions and to the management of their property: too firmly fixed for their lives to be either adventurous or particularly stimulating."

The publication of his will, like the news of his death, struck most news media as a matter of little consequence. The New York *Times* said, "The interest that attached to

William Astor in this country was due to his wealth rather than his personality." Little had been expected by way of public beneficence and little was delivered. The popular if scurrilous gossip and scandal sheet, *Town Topics*, however, chose to remark upon the will, calling it "one of the meanest testamentary documents ever drawn." Indeed, a comparison of William's public generosity with that displayed by his older brother two years before does not reflect kindly upon William, although friends described him as "quietly generous." He gave the Astor Library $50,000; his brother gave $450,000. He gave $15,000 to St. Luke's Hospital; his brother gave $100,000. All told, William's public bequests were $145,000; his brother's were more than $700,000.

There were two people who could not complain about their treatment in the two wills. Through John Jacob III's will, William Waldorf, his only child, became, according to a *Harper's Weekly* profile, "in all probability the richest man of the civilized world today." His first cousin, John Jacob Astor IV, William's only son, had to settle for fewer millions. His father hadn't made as much as William Waldorf's and he had four sisters and a mother surviving his father. But he had all he could use.

CHAPTER 4

Excepting only the original John Jacob, the person who had the most dramatic and lasting impact on the Astor family was an in-law—Caroline Webster Schermerhorn, mother of John Jacob IV, wife of William Backhouse, Jr., and undisputed ruler of New York (and therefore American) society for the last quarter of the nineteenth century. The contention that she was the most influential woman in America during that period says more perhaps for the status of women in those days than it does for her influence, but within the well-defined boundaries of her kingdom, entry to which was much sought after, she ruled supreme. Her position was so well known and generally envied that imitations arose around the country. Mrs. Potter Palmer in Chicago was but the most conspicuous example. No one in this country before or since has commanded the social clout that Mrs. Astor possessed. Unlike Queen Victoria, to whom she has sometimes been compared, Caroline did not inherit this clout as a birthright, nor did she come by it through marriage. It was a goal reached after a careful political campaign and retained through the most delicate diplomacy. It is mainly because of her career that the Astor name is synonymous with high society in the United States, even today, when the Astor glory has faded. Many have blamed her successful struggle with her nephew, William Waldorf, over whether she or William Waldorf's wife would be known as "Mrs. Astor" for his packing his bags and moving his family to England. If that is true—and it seems a shade simplistic—then Caroline is responsible for the English branch of the family, a concept one suspects the English Astors would view with some consternation.

If Caroline was not born to her social crown, she was at least born into a family thanks to whom her social pretensions would not appear hopelessly ridiculous. She was born on September 22, 1830, to Abraham Schermerhorn, a noted New York attorney, and Helen White Schermerhorn, whose family descended from the very proper Van Cortlandts. The Schermerhorns traced their ancestry back to Jacob Janse Schermerhorn, who settled in New York in 1636, then moved to what is now Albany and opened a thriving trade with the Indians until he was accused by Governor Stuyvesant of selling arms and gunpowder to the Indians. The ensuing troubles Schermerhorn encountered with the government caused the loss of much of his property, but his descendants managed to survive and prosper, marrying into such prominent families as the Beekmans, Ten Eycks and Van Burens. It was said that Caroline's debutante ball was a topic for admiring conversation long after the music stopped. Several years later, in 1853, she became Mrs. Astor. Socially, she might have been said to be stepping slightly downward, but wealth has its own rewards, even if one of them is not necessarily happiness.

The early years of her marriage were only moderately social, for a large part of her life was taken up with domestic chores. She gave birth to four daughters, beginning with Emily in 1854 and encoring with Helen in 1855, Charlotte Augusta in 1858 and Caroline Schermerhorn (Carrie) in 1861. Undaunted by her failure to produce a male heir, she tried one final time, in 1864, and luck blessed her with John Jacob IV. At what precise point in time a vague, intermittent caprice bloomed into an overriding ambition within Mrs. Astor to take over society's leadership no one will ever know. Its first public manifestation did not occur until 1872, the earliest possible moment, assuming the wish to observe good form. That was the year her mother-in-law, Margaret Armstrong Astor, died. Traditionally, her place as social leader of the family would have been automatically taken by Augusta Astor, wife of Caroline's older brother-in-law. But Augusta, while she was a consummate hostess and strong rival for social top billing, insisted on affronting the conservative dowagers of society by refusing to recognize the importance of either lineage or wealth in determining who was to be invited where. Caroline was more willing to play the game by its old rules. She was also preparing to bring her eldest daughter into society and was determined to do so correctly. Finally, 1872 was the year she met Ward McAllister and developed with him a plan whereby her money and social standing would combine with his ideas and unique understanding of society to place her on the throne.

How truly different values and judgments were a century ago may be accurately measured by a look at McAllister and the woman he called his "Mystic Rose" and what they stood for. "The talent of and for society develops itself," McAllister wrote in his unwitting self-parody, *Society as I Have Found It*, "just as does the talent for art." McAllister, the apotheosis of the stuffed shirt, admits he learned the proprieties of a ball supper from the Grand Duke of Tuscany at the Pitti Palace in Firenze and acquired the hang of correct summer living from the Prince Furstenburg of Vienna while at Baden-Baden. On the subject of oenology, Mr. McAllister allowed that the future Emperor William was no judge of wine. "I drank the best," said McAllister, "and he was evidently indifferent to it." His bons mots abound. On fish: Spring and early summer are the only times for hot salmon. "The man who gives salmon during the winter, I care not what sauce he serves with it, does an injury to himself and his guests." On a gentleman's transportation: "A gentleman can always walk, but he cannot afford to have a shabby equipage." To this self-inflated hot-air balloon the future THE Mrs. Astor attached herself, and despite a substantial bulk weighed down on socially important occasions by hundreds of thousands of dollars' worth of diamonds, the result was predictable—up she rose. Between the two of them, they determined that it took three generations to make a gentleman. By happy coincidence, the Astors just made it; the Vanderbilts fell a generation shy. The coup d'état the pair brought off in 1872 was the formation of a subscription dance series known as The Patriarchs. With the tacit approval of Mrs. Astor, McAllister formed a committee that chose twenty-five men to be named Patriarchs. They in turn could invite four women and five men to subscribe, and the two hundred and fifty people thus assembled would constitute the crème de la crème. It was a good start.

What is so remarkable about it all is not the posing of McAllister or the ambition of Mrs. Astor, but the fact that prominent, wealthy, influential people recognized their authority and fought or groveled for invitations to The Patriarchs. McAllister by 1872 had made something of a social mark, but he was hardly in a position to call the shots. Born to a good family of modest means in 1827 in Savannah—he was a first cousin of Sam Ward—he had migrated north as a young man, hovering on the perimeter of society's inner circle and sighing with awe and envy. When he inherited $1,000, he spent the better part of it on a costume for a fancy dress ball, a dandy bit of ostentation his friends and acquaintances did not stop hearing about for the next forty years. But, as Louis Auchincloss once said, "Anyone who tries to play the social game without it [money] is in for a bad time," and McAllister knew that as well as Auchincloss. Vowing—and anticipating a more famous hero of some decades later—"I shall return," McAllister journeyed across the continent to San Francisco where his father and brother had opened a law practice, figuring the gold rush of 1849 would provide plenty of business. Ward was not a lawyer, but he was an irreproachable host. Lawyers weren't allowed to advertise in those days, and McAllister served the family firm well by entertaining prospective clients. In a few years he had made enough money to return eastward. He married a mousy sort of woman named Sarah Gibbons and took the grand tour of Europe. Abroad McAllister studied protocol and society and formed plans for the future. A highlight of the trip was dinner with Queen Victoria's chef, who allowed McAllister a peek at the queen's dinner table before telling him it was time to go. Ward's illusions of grandeur went only so far, and he was delighted with this experience, not offended in the least. Back in the United States, McAllister purchased a farm just outside Newport and began to build his Eastern social reputation as a host with the most by throwing lavish fêtes champêtres, for which he would sometimes hire a flock of sheep or a cow or two to heighten the bucolic effect.

For her part, Mrs. Astor was hardly an imposing or prepossessing figure. First, she was from the wrong branch of the Astor family—having married the No. 2 son in an era still entrenched in the belief in primogeniture. Second, she was neither pretty nor witty, devoid of the dazzling, if superficial, virtues that make one an instant social success. A granddaughter who was especially fond of her recalls, "She was not handsome. She had a strong face, rather thick lips and always wore a dark brown wig." All her life— not, to her credit, just during their childhood before she had achieved her ultimate social rank—Mrs. Astor was supremely loyal and devoted to her family, especially the younger generations—her children and later, her grandchildren. Mrs. Caroline Phillips, one of the latter, recalls in a memoir, "When I knew my grandmother, she was very worldly and quite a snob. She lived for parties, and bought endless Worth dresses and was covered with jewels in the evening, though in the daytime she dressed very simply in black and wore only a handsome brooch or some pearls. . . . She cared especially for children and had a maternal instinct, but a very matriarchal one. She dominated poor little Aunt Carrie [her youngest daughter] completely." These impressions come from about 1890, the height of Mrs. Astor's influence, but all the indications are that she did not change in her ways, which rather became more defined and pronounced.

Mrs. Astor's loyalty and devotion to her family were frequently put to the test by her daughters. The eldest, Emily, came out in the winter of 1874–75, met James J. Van Alen and announced her intention of marrying him. Van Alen was not a bad catch. His father, General James H. Van Alen, had had a cavalry command in the Civil War and invested $300,000 in the Illinois Central Railroad, which had made him several times a millionaire. He was also,

however, a widower whose grief was too well disguised to
suit the Astors. In short, Van Alen had developed a reputation as a roué and was doing nothing to dispel it. Although
the general's wife was a Schermerhorn, William Astor was
heard to mutter, "Damned if I want my family having anything to do with the Van Alens!" Word got back to the
general, who was quick to take offense and challenged William to a duel. Seconds were chosen and a venue sought,
but William was beginning to question the worth of risking
his life over a mere Van Alen. He apologized, the general
accepted, and James and Emily were married in March of
1876, Emily having had a trust of $400,000 settled upon
her. It was all too much for William, who fled south on his
yacht the day of the wedding. Emily's victory in romance
proved pyrrhic when she died during the birth of her third
child in 1881. The general took his grandchildren to London to be put into school not long afterward. While there,
he received word that his son was ill in New York and set
sail at once for America. On board ship he suffered a nervous breakdown, decided his condition was not one a gentleman would impose on his friends, and, dressed as usual to
kill, jumped calmly overboard. His son's inheritance made
him a millionaire even without help from the Astors.

The marriage of the Astors' second daughter, Helen, was
more palatable to her parents. The groom was James Roosevelt Roosevelt, twice over a member of a distinguished if
not dramatically wealthy family. His father, remarrying
after the death of his first wife, James's mother, sired another son, named Franklin Delano Roosevelt after his
mother, who was Sara Delano. Sara, in turn, was the
niece of Franklin Delano, whom Laura Astor, William's
sister, married. The close family ties between the Astors
and the Roosevelts managed to survive even FDR's presi-
dency, during which William's grandson and FDR re-

mained, despite wide political differences, friends. Mrs. Astor was able to swallow her distaste for Democrats, especially after the 1884 victory of Grover Cleveland, which led to her son-in-law's appointment as first secretary to the American legation in Vienna. Even happier was Cleveland's second triumph after a four-year hiatus. This led to Roosevelt's appointment as first secretary to the London embassy. Sadly, her daughter died in 1893, before Mrs. Astor was able to enjoy this connection.

Carrie, the youngest daughter, also tested Mrs. Astor's loyalty and devotion by falling for Orme Wilson, Jr. His father was not a man cleansed by several generations of moneyed leisure or aristocratic lineage. Stripped to essentials, the man was a carpetbagger who had made it big, moved to New York, bought old Boss Tweed's Fifth Avenue manse and stormed the citadel of social respectability. His siege met with unprecedented success. One daughter married a Goelet, one a Vanderbilt and one son, Orme, Jr., married Carrie Astor in 1884. Mrs. Astor's love of Carrie overwhelmed her disapproval of Orme, and the wedding was one of the year's most extravagant social highlights.

The sternest test of Mrs. Astor was provided by her third daughter, Charlotte Augusta, who married James Coleman Drayton of Philadelphia, gave birth to four children and then ran off to Europe with another man. She was eventually divorced and, dropping the man with whom she ran away, married a wealthy Scot named George Haig. Adultery and divorce enjoyed a status in those days akin to rape today, and the scandal received extensive coverage. The New York *Sun* got first crack at the story and published a five-column, page 1 exclusive with appropriate pictures on the affair on March 18, 1892. The man with whom Mrs. Drayton had run off was Hallett Alsop Borrowe, son of an insurance company vice-president and a man of first-rank background. Drayton wanted a duel, but Borrowe was reluctant. Meanwhile some shameless cad had sold Mrs. Drayton's passionate letters to a newspaper. There have been many conflicting reports and charges over the affair and the conduct of the Draytons. One thing is sure: Mrs. Astor stuck by her daughter, even after Mr. Astor wrote the poor girl out of his will. In Newport, Mrs. Astor gave a tea party at which she received with Mrs. Drayton at her side. The ensuing divorce was, however, more than even Mrs. Astor could make society swallow. Her daughter had become something of a pariah.

One of the Draytons' children, Mrs. Caroline Phillips, in her unpublished memoirs, recalled her parents: "I often wonder why he [her father] and my mother ever married. She was very flirtatious and I am told quite pretty and a good dancer, but a very immature character, brought up in complete ignorance of the facts of life and the education of her day, French and German, playing the piano, good manners, good handwriting and reading and arithmetic. My father was a very nervous, high-strung man with a violent temper, a love of art and reading and travel, very sociable, but also a lover of solitude, keen about riding, hunting and shooting, and by training and profession a lawyer. He was very impulsive and had the old sensitive Southern tradition of 'honor,' sometimes much exaggerated.

"My mother used to irritate him beyond words by inane remarks and a certain amount of nagging, and I think she found him very difficult also. I remember when we lived at Bernardsville [New Jersey] that my father tried to get her to ride with him, bought a very quiet and gentle horse and had her led around the fields and then took her on one or two rides, but she would not go on with it. It was too strenuous for her. . . . She was vaguely interested in her flower garden and her housekeeping, but I remember her only as

sitting in the drawing room reading a novel, eating choco-
lates, playing on the piano, or entertaining neighbors. My
father, who was interested in local politics, . . . could not
get any help or interest from my mother. He was always a
devoted father and spent a great deal of time with his children. He took Saturdays and Sundays off all summer, and
we went on picnics with him to which my mother occasionally came. . . . My father's occasional outbursts of
temper used to terrify me, but he never lost it with us, and
never punished us in anger. I was always conscious of a certain tension between my parents, and when I was eleven
years old we went to England and a real rift ending in divorce began. I remember Uncle Jimmy Van Alen coming
to see my father to try and stop the divorce and my father
being very angry with him. My mother cried a great deal
and asked me to help her, but if I spoke to my father he
would not let me continue and said he would not discuss it
with me.

"I remember one night in a rented house at Wimbledon
my mother had gone away and also my beloved old
Scottish nurse, Amy Martin, and I was crying alone in my
bed. My father came and told me my mother had left us. I
cried all night and was terribly unhappy. As I have heard
the story, my mother had an affair (whether serious or only
flirtatious, I have no idea, but from my mother's character
I would say only flirtatious) with a neighbor. My father
took it very seriously and challenged him to a duel, which
he very sensibly declined. In any case it ended by a divorce
granted to my mother, but the custody of the children was
granted to my father. Later on Uncle Jack [John Jacob
Astor IV] offered my father a million dollars if he would
give my sister Alida, then a baby, to my mother, but he refused. . . . I did see my mother from time to time until
she married George Haig . . . and then I believed that

such a marriage was adultery and that it would not be fair
to my father to visit her while she was living with another
man. My father was quite bitter against my mother and all
her family and I am sure that he prejudiced me. I had always been closer to my father than to her and tempera-
mentally we were more alike. It is a sad thing to remember,
and I have often reproached myself for my unkindness to
my mother. I think and hope she felt we were reconciled
before she died."

Factually, this account is reasonably accurate as far as
can be determined. The divorce was granted Drayton, not
his wife, and the affair was clearly more than flirtatious,
but otherwise, and accounting for the childlike quality of
the recollections, it is all there. While corroboration is
missing, it is quite possible Uncle Jack, with his mother's
encouragement, offered the million. No sacrifice was too
great where keeping the family together was concerned.
Mrs. Astor's happiness depended on two things—the close-
ness of her family and the unrippled, smooth, ordered
function of society as she and McAllister wished it to run.

The success secret of Mrs. Astor and McAllister was actually simple enough. In a world peopled with men and
women who couldn't be bothered, more or less regardless
of the cause or occasion, Caroline and Ward exercised
an aggressive will, filling what had been a vacuum of
indifference. The pair imposed a system upon what was
becoming a chaotic situation because of the sudden wealth
being accumulated by the post-Reconstruction entre-
preneurs—later and perhaps more appropriately dubbed
"robber barons"—and the quiet condescension of the old
New York aristocracy. Mrs. Astor and her "prime minister" became the arbiters of the system they set up, showing people where within the newly rigid social structure
they belonged. They automatically had the support of

those placed in the top echelon, of course, and if some squawked at being left out, they were a minority and thus subject not only to the tyranny of Mrs. Astor but also to the tyranny of the majority. What enabled Mrs. Astor— and, to a much lesser degree, McAllister—to remain on top of this social heap was an uncanny ability in the practice of diplomacy. She knew precisely what stance or action would fly and what would fall and refused to compromise only where her immediate family were concerned. More accurately, she would compromise her own social principles for her family's sake, and would quickly risk incurring society's displeasure in support of them, whereas, were the family not involved, she would avoid as much as possible any controversy.

Mrs. Astor had two cardinal virtues—unswerving loyalty to her friends, of whom she had rather few, and to her family, and the firm belief, which she practiced as well as advocated, that if you had nothing nice to say about someone silence was appropriate. To these she added ambition to lead, if not to rule, society and a systematic approach not only to accomplishing her goal but also to the very living of her life. She lived life on a schedule. Breakfast was at eight-thirty, even on the mornings after her big entertainments, and by nine-thirty she had finished reading the paper, particularly the editorial page. At that point it was time to see the servants and present the orders for the day. Before getting down to the major chore of the morning— the mail—she spent an hour with her grandchildren, if any happened to be in residence. She used to say that was her favorite hour of the day. The mail was a project for her and her companion/secretary, a Miss Simrock. Many of the letters were simply requests for an entree into society, to which Mrs. Astor was generally sympathetic but strict, if not rigid, regarding the necessary qualifications. Because she ate sparingly at regular meals and not at all when she went out to dinner parties, Mrs. Astor developed a reputation as something of a gastronomic spartan, but her granddaughter, Mrs. Phillips, says, "She had the digestion of an ostrich, and loved to eat chocolate caramels and marrons glacés, but she ate sparingly, for when I stayed with her . . . she always ate a light supper with a milk pudding before going out to dinners where she ate nothing at all." Mrs. Phillips remembers her grandmother's companion as "a forlorn old German . . . called Miss Nimrock [sic] whom she [Mrs. Astor] bullied cruelly." In her later years Mrs. Astor had eye trouble and was unable to read. Mrs. Phillips says her grandmother once told her that Miss Simrock occasionally would read novels aloud to her. Mrs. Astor would always get the characters "frightfully mixed up and was greatly bored by them."

The Vanderbilts did not present any sort of challenge to the social dominance of the Astors until Alva Murray Smith married William K. Vanderbilt, a grandson of the old Commodore. Alva's ambition, which was given free rein, was to dazzle society not just into acceptance but into submission. Her opening gambit was to hire Richard Morris Hunt, give him $3 million and order the most elaborate palace in New York. Taking his inspiration from the Château de Blois and a fifteenth-century mansion at Bourges, Hunt complied, starting a trend in ostentation that Louis H. Sullivan, a founder of functionalism in architecture, appeared alone in opposing. It was impossible for Vanderbilt to live in his new home, said Sullivan, "morally, mentally or spiritually . . . he and his home are a paradox, a contradiction, an absurdity, a characteristically New York absurdity; . . . he is no part of the house, and the house no part of him." No matter. In the winter of 1882–83, Alva let it be known that she would throw a ball to mark the official opening of her new residence. Social New York was abuzz with anticipation for six weeks before the affair. One designer employed 140 dressmakers for five weeks making 150 costumes at a cost of $30,000 for the ball. Alva was dressing as a Venetian princess. Mrs. Bradley Martin was going as Mary Stuart; Mrs. Paran Stevens resembled Queen Elizabeth. Carrie, the youngest of Mrs. Astor's daughters, and a group of her friends organized a "Star Quadrille" and were practicing diligently when, not long before the big event, Mrs. Vanderbilt quietly let it be known that of course she could not possibly invite Mrs. Astor or her daughter because she had never been properly introduced to either of them. This was a calamity Mrs. Astor could have survived with equanimity, but Carrie was desolate, and Mrs. Astor's family loyalty overcame her disapproval of the Vanderbilts. She summoned her carriage and rode up Fifth Avenue to the Vanderbilts' where her footman delivered her calling card to the Vanderbilt butler. The ice was broken; Mrs. Astor had given her stamp of approbation to Alva, who quickly issued Carrie and her mother invitations to her ball. The following January, the Vanderbilts were seen among the guests at Mrs. Astor's annual ball, the one whose guest list determined who was in and who was out of society at the time.

Mrs. Astor's recognition of Alva Vanderbilt was, besides being a conciliatory gesture for her daughter's sake, a capitulation to the inevitable. The days when proper social behavior and status were clear matters of record whose ignoring was simply not tolerated had begun to give way to a more open, mobile society. The young swell, formerly a minor irritant at the periphery, was becoming, with McAllister's blessing but without Mrs. Astor's, a central element in society. Some fragmentation was going on, with Augusta Astor leading a set that viewed wit and accomplishment as important qualifications for inclusion while Mrs. Astor attempted to hold together the old guard against an insistent youth and a crass nouveau riche crowd. Accepting the Vanderbilts meant enlisting them on her side, and Mrs. Astor realized she might need them, quite probably sooner than later. Mrs. Astor was the type who would wholeheartedly have approved of Mrs. Alexander Hamilton and her treatment of President James Monroe after he had failed to show at the altar for his wedding to Nannie Brown, a friend of Mrs. Hamilton's. Some thirty years later Monroe had bowed to Mrs. Hamilton and been ignored. He had explained that he was President James Monroe, to which information she had replied, "Are you?" When he pressed her for an explanation, she told him she did not care to know the man who had stood her friend up at the altar. Those were sentiments to which Mrs. Astor could easily relate. But she also recognized that her position was not so secure that she could indulge her every sentiment, that diplomacy and principle could not always peacefully coexist, and that in some instances diplomacy was the more prudent course.

It required a certain kind of person to take society seriously, even in those days, and Mrs. Astor ascended to her throne as society's ruler at least in part because the competition was not extensive. She combined just enough virtue and good intentions to forestall derision with the snobbishness necessary to a conviction that worth is genetic and not always manifested by success or attractiveness. "If you find them very slow, it's not my fault," wrote a cousin of her husband, Charles Astor Bristed, about New York's upper social crust in 1852, striking a note that still rang true thirty years later. Much of the writing of Julia Ward Howe, Sam Ward's well-known sister, was an attempt to portray and explain society. The reason "women of fashion" are uneducated, she wrote in 1880, is that they have no need to be, enjoying as they do ". . . the happy tact which often enables women to make a large display of very small acquirements." As the turn of the century loomed nearer, Mrs. Astor's society was becoming both anachronistic and paradoxical—a stuffy bastion of respectability and reverence for form amidst a growing and restless class of iconoclasts and hedonists. The paradox was that Mrs. Astor's crowd professed themselves good, God-fearing people whose attendance at church was regular and willing but who yet blithely paid no heed to one of the Bible's most familiar strictures: "Ye cannot serve both God and mammon." There was certainly no one in the Astor coterie who forsook worldly riches. Nor did any of the folks more newly arrived and hoping to break into the group. It was said, for example, that both Ogden Mills and Elbridge T. Gerry could, at an hour's notice, put on dinners for a hundred people at their homes without having to send out for a thing.

But perhaps the most telling attribute of a member of society, what made society's essence form without substance, was the requirement that "the man of fashion should have no business," as McAllister put it. Life was too easy to contain very much meaning for this crowd, and the trivial took on distorted importance in this vacuum. Among the few famous quotations from the usually platitude-prone Mrs. Astor was her explanation of why A. T. Stewart, the first of the department store tycoons, was not being invited to one of her fancy affairs. Just because she bought her rugs from the man, she said, was no reason why he had to come and walk on them. Like so much else in the United States of those days, society was informed by America's youthful exuberance and lack of tradition, which allowed social arbiters to copy and exaggerate European aristocratic customs with a minimum of ridicule, for a while, at least. Mrs. Astor, who shunned most of the excesses, was a far more secure fixture than McAllister, who survives to this day only in caricature despite having held a position of considerable power and influence in his heyday as Mrs. Astor's major-domo. The primary reason for McAllister's loss of stature was his penchant for pronouncement, which was seriously weighed in his day but which is simply ludicrous by today's standards.

It is to McAllister that the world owes a debt for creating four hundred as the number limiting society. In March 1888 he told a scribe from the New York *Tribune:* "Why, there are only about 400 people in fashionable New York Society. If you go outside that number you strike people who are either not at ease in a ballroom or else make other people not at ease. . . . When we give a large ball like the last New Year's ball for 800 guests, we go outside of the exclusive, fashionable set and invite professional men—doctors, lawyers, editors, artists and the like." The popular legend is that McAllister picked four hundred because that was the number Mrs. Astor could comfortably fit in her New York ballroom when she lived in the mansion where now the Empire State Building stands. It is just as likely that McAllister picked the number straight off the top of his head. At any rate, the number became magical, and for years afterward, even when his own magic had become elusive, McAllister was hounded to produce a list of the four hundred people who constituted real society. For Mrs. Astor's New Year's ball of 1892, McAllister finally produced for the New York *Times* a list of slightly more than three hundred people, a list that was essentially the two hundred and fifty names on the invitation list for The Patriarchs leavened with a smattering of eligible visitors from other United States cities and abroad. The list made a far smaller

splash than did the earlier announcing of the number. Part
of the reason was that McAllister's fortunes were declining,
largely because he had contracted a severe case of foot-
in-mouth disease. The first hint of his decline came in
1889, the year of the Centennial Ball in New York, for
which McAllister had some heady plans. The ball
committee—Hamilton Fish, Elbridge Gerry and Colonel
William Jay—vetoed the plans, causing Stuyvesant Fish to
remark to a reporter, "McAllister is a discharged servant.
That is all." The principal vehicle of his undoing was his
autobiographical *Society as I Have Found It*, as comically
outrageous a collection of lorgnette observations and smug
epigrams as ever saw print. It was clear McAllister had un-
wittingly changed roles, from prime minister to court
jester. The public began to wonder how anyone could ever
have taken such a fellow seriously.

Still, McAllister continued to be quoted in newspapers,
even in eclipse, up to about the middle of 1893. It was
probably safe enough, he opined, to visit the World's Fair
in Chicago, provided one associated solely with Chicago's
moneyed folk. In May the New York *Times* quoted him
on the front page as opposing a ball to honor the Infanta
Eulalie of Spain when she visited the following week.
McAllister suggested a fête champêtre as more appropriate
and requiring observation of fewer solemn social rules.
What is too easy to lose sight of today is the fact that
McAllister was the epitome of an important fringe segment of the population and was by no means alone in the
absurdity of his posturing. Again from the *Times* of 1893,
an entire article on page 2: "W. Bayard Cutting has just
shipped two carloads of magnificent rhododendrons from
his conservatories at Islip [Long Island] to the horticul-
tural department of the World's Fair. They were greatly admired on their trip over the Long Island Railroad." People

took such things seriously. About the same time, Mrs. O. H. P. Belmont, the former Alva Vanderbilt, said, "I know of no profession, art or trade that women are working in today as taxing on one's mental resources as being a leader of society." She meant it. Mrs. Astor about this time let it be known that she was effecting another of her famous compromises and was going to throw a bohemian party in recognition of the new importance of art, wit and accomplishment coupled with an anti-establishment irreverence. To provide the bohemian atmosphere she would, she said, invite J. P. Morgan and Edith Wharton (whose maiden name had been Jones, of "keeping up with the . . ." fame), two personages who would appear better suited to Bohemia than society only to someone so thoroughly enmeshed in society's center that she could no longer see beyond its inner circle.

In her glory days, Mrs. Astor was perhaps most in her element on Monday nights at the Metropolitan Opera, where she reigned from Parterre Box 7. Almost without fail, she would arrive at 9 P.M., at the end of the first act. The opera was a social event as much as a musical one, for Mrs. Astor's appearance in her box always caused a great stirring and buzz that lasted most of the first intermission. During the second intermission, Mrs. Astor would hold court and receive visitors. Then, not waiting for the end of the performance, she would rise and depart for whatever ball she was giving or attending later that evening.

Only on the Monday night in January that she gave her annual ball did she skip her visit to the opera. It was to this affair one aspired to be invited if he or she desired to be known as "fashionable." Here society's cream rose to the top, despite the fact that, in the eyes of some, not all the cream had remained sweet. Mrs. Astor was always loyal, however, and her old friends could be seen at the annual ball even if they appeared nowhere else the remainder of the season. In December, Mrs. Astor invariably gave a series of dinners. The heights to which one had to have climbed before receiving an invitation to dine with Mrs. Astor were above even the imagination of ordinary mortals. That is not to say these gastronomic treats were necessarily scintillating. One seldom sat down before 8 P.M. or arose before eleven. Course after course—up to nine—was served with a liveried footman behind every chair. Terrapin and canvasback duck, being considered special delicacies, were seldom absent from the menu. From the commentary that has survived, it is not hard to imagine that the stifled burp was more frequently heard than the witty word. An Astor relative, Mrs. Winthrop Chanler, viewed great New York dinners as "extremely unrewarding. Nothing was done for the guests' entertainment beyond providing them with a vast amount of elaborate food, often served on silver or silver-gilt plates, and with many varieties of wine. . . . One was rarely amused by one's neighbor." Mrs. Chanler invented a secret insurance company with whom she would take out a policy against bores before going to dinner. She soon drove the company into bankruptcy, so often did she collect on those policies.

Mrs. Astor was not alone in offering such occasions. Having attended Mrs. Hamilton Fish's dinner, Julia Newberry, a young lady from Chicago, wrote in her diary: "Thursday evening last I went to my first dinner party and never in my life was I so bored. I had the illustrious Mr. Hamilton Fish, who in spite of having a grandfather is little less than an idiot."

During most of her life Mrs. Astor received alone, standing under a very flattering portrait of herself she had commissioned from Carolus Duran, which hung from a place of honor in both her house on Thirty-fourth Street and the later mansion at 840 Fifth Avenue. For a quarter of a century—between the time of her youngest daughter's debut and a party given two years before her death—no one could recall an occasion when someone else had received with her. On the latter date, Mrs. Astor broke with her tradition to receive with a young woman who was engaged to her grandson, Henry Coleman Drayton. Although society had been aghast at the scandalous behavior of the young man's mother some years earlier, no one questioned the propriety of Mrs. Astor's action, so firm was the grip in which she held society's reins even this late in her life. Although her parties frequently went on through the night, Mrs. Astor seldom stayed up much past eleven, retiring after dinner and leaving the guests in the able hands of her daughters. Ritual was nearly as important to her as her family and sticking to a prearranged schedule was a central part of the ritual by which she lived.

Early each March, Mrs. Astor booked passage aboard an ocean liner and sailed to London. After a short visit there she would go to Paris where she was one of but a handful of American women ever to be fully accepted in the aristocratic salons of the Faubourg Saint Germain, in which district she kept an apartment. In the late spring she would take the waters at a quiet resort or spa before returning for another brief visit to London in the last week of June. As July started, Mrs. Astor would sail for home, resting for a day in New York before going up to Newport for the remainder of the summer.

The active influence Mrs. Astor enjoyed over society peaked in 1891. The following year her husband died, and she went into mourning, more in the interest of good form than in sorrow or bereavement. She and William hadn't spent much time together over the recent years, which had caused more than one guest at her parties to ask, either in thinly veiled contumely or genuine surprise, where William was. Regardless of the questioner's intent, Mrs. Astor was always gracious, replying that her husband was cruising on his yacht, the sea air being particularly good for him, and adding that it was certainly sad she was so poor a sailor, for otherwise she would love to accompany him. William did, however, show up for important occasions, allowing his wife the luxury of remarking on her luck in having married someone so good to her. The death in 1893 of her daughter Helen Roosevelt kept Mrs. Astor out of social circulation for yet another year. Upon her return she found society much changed—grown larger and more fragmented. A younger generation, led by her daughter-in-law, Ava Willing Astor, was no longer willing to accept the credentials of Mrs. Astor's older circle. Once again she mustered her vast reserves of tact and discretion, managing to retain at least the vestiges of her old authority through artful compromise.

About 1895 she demonstrated her loyalty to old friends and her flexibility by breaking her long-standing rule against eating in public. Two old friends, one of them Mrs. Stuyvesant Fish, had caused quite a stir by dining at Sherry's in low-cut gowns and no hats, flouting, some said, good form. Mrs. Astor caused all chattering to cease when she appeared soon afterward at Sherry's for dinner with Harry Lehr, an even more outrageous version of Ward McAllister, in a small hat and a "coquettish raiment of white satin." Lehr and Mrs. Fish were less loyal, choosing to lead a more frivolous segment of society away from Mrs. Astor's domain. Mrs. Astor came as close as she ever did to saying an unpleasant word in public when she hereafter referred to Mrs. Fish. Mrs. Astor considered Mrs. Fish's coterie the "circus set" and told a magazine reporter, "Some New York women seek only notoriety." If this was as mean as Mrs. Astor ever got in words, in deed her meanest moment may have come in 1894 when she refused to cancel a dinner party on the night of her nephew's wife's funeral in London. Why she did this has never been satisfactorily explained, but chances are she was expressing her view of her nephew, not his wife. The social leadership quarrel she had was with him, after all, with his wife playing only a reluctant supporting role.

Public tolerance of the snobbery and ostentation that enveloped Mrs. Astor's social circle reached its nadir the night of February 10, 1897, when one of society's grandes dames, Mrs. Bradley Martin, gave a fancy dress ball for 900 at the Waldorf. America was in the throes of a severe recession, and its people were not amused at Mrs. Martin's explanation that she felt such a party would help stimulate the economy by providing work for dressmakers, caterers and the like. What the party, to which Mrs. Astor wore a $200,000 diamond tiara, did was show the yawning gap between the haves and the have-nots, a picture most found not very pretty. The Martins, it was estimated, spent $250,000 on the affair. New York reacted by doubling the assessment on the Martins' real estate for tax purposes, causing the Martins to pull up stakes and follow William Waldorf Astor to England to settle. First, however, the Martins gave themselves a farewell dinner, again at what was now the Waldorf-Astoria, for eighty-six of their old friends. It cost $116 a plate.

The years began to be reflected in Mrs. Astor's face, giving more validity perhaps to one of her lifelong prejudices: She was horrified at the prospect of having her picture taken. The paparazzi were less insistent in those days, and the state of the camera art protected Mrs. Astor from sneak attack because each exposure required proper lighting and a cooperative stillness from the subject. Nonetheless, she carefully avoided daytime weddings, attended the socially prestigious New York Horse Show only once and then only for half an hour, and seldom went out in daylight without a heavy veil over her face or a parasol to use as a shield. In 1904 she gave her final ball. Her last dinner was given in 1907 for H. R. H. Prince Louis of Battenberg, an affair that caused considerable squirming among the socially insecure because Mrs. Astor's guest list numbered only seventy-nine. Among the missing were the Vanderbilts.

In one of her last interviews with a reporter, Mrs. Astor reflected on her duties and philosophy: "Many people think I could have done a great deal in making New York society as democratic as it is in London and open to anyone of intellectual attainments, as it is over there. But one can only do one's best under the conditions. We have to be more exclusive in New York because in America there is no authority in society. Each woman is for herself and trying to outdo the others in lavish display and mad extravagance."

Not much is known of Mrs. Astor's last year of life. She stayed inside her Fifth Avenue home and entertained very few visitors. Many rumors circulated. A granddaughter recalled those days with as much accuracy and insight as perhaps anyone when she wrote that, some time before Mrs. Astor died, "she fell down a long flight of marble steps in her town house on Fifth Avenue and Sixty-fifth and cut her head in seven places. She sat in a chair clutching the arms of it while the doctors sewed up the cuts. They told her that she must be very quiet and rest and give up her trip to Paris in the spring, which was to take place in a week or two. But she paid no attention to their advice with the result that she broke down physically and mentally (she was in her seventies) and had to lead an invalid life until she died, attended always by two trained nurses. Her mind had gone and she lived entirely in the past. She used to think I was my Aunt Helen long since dead and spoke of her mother and sisters as though they were living. She was an old lady then, quite small and shrunken with white hair and a cap. She would not stay in bed and was always running about her rooms very actively. One day she had the idea that she was about to produce a baby, had everything prepared for its arrival and ordered the doctor sent for! She died just after my return from Europe in 1908. . . . We were not alike in our tastes at all, but I have a warm affection for her. She had courage and dignity. . . ."

Some sixteen years after Mrs. Astor's death, May King Van Rensselaer was told by an old man who remembered Mrs. Astor, Mrs. Fish, McAllister and Lehr, "There isn't any New York society today any more than there is a nation called the Confederate States of America. There are survivors from each. And that is all."

CHAPTER 5

If there was an Astor generation whose male members exhibited all the characteristics of the spoiled brat with few redeeming traits, it was the fourth, as represented by William Waldorf, son of John Jacob Astor III, and his first cousin, John Jacob Astor IV, son of William Astor, Jr. William Waldorf was an only child who grew up with nannies and nurses. John Jacob IV was the youngest child and only son, whose father was away most of the time and whose mother was more loving than understanding. Both inherited their fortunes when young enough to use them according to their own motivations and desires. Both resembled their fathers, although each in his own way was a rather paler imitation. With them turned the tide of the Astor fortunes, which had steadily climbed through the first three generations and which would now peak. They were victims of circumstance, more than they were its creators.

William Waldorf was sixteen years older than his first cousin, having been born the same year the original John

Jacob died—1848. As a boy he demonstrated interests, skills and abilities not unlike those of his forebears, soaking up European education, art and belles-lettres eagerly before returning to New York to study law, specializing in real estate law the better to serve the Astor firm. But a fertile imagination and an impulsive quality about his actions must have made his father and his grandfather cringe a bit. William Waldorf was an active young man, adept in the manly arts of shooting, fencing and boxing, and an imposing figure for those days. The Astor office was, not to put too fine a point on it, boring him silly, and before long he was looking around for other action and listening to a cousin tell how easy it was to get into politics. Really, it was just a matter of quietly seeing that contributions were generously and equitably distributed. In 1877, William Waldorf received the Republican nomination to the state Assembly from the Fifth District, where Republican nomination meant election. In Albany, Astor toed the party line, enjoyed the modest acclaim his name and position brought him and yearned for bigger and better things.

The next two years saw William Waldorf married and elevated to the state Senate. By most any measure, the marriage proved a sounder investment than the Senate seat. In the summer of 1877, William Waldorf fell in love with Mary Dahlgren Paul while the two whiled away the lazy Newport afternoons. Miss Paul was from Philadelphia, where her family knew the right people and had enough money to get by. Her brother had just proved all that by marrying a daughter of Anthony J. Drexel, the city's leading banker. Mamie, as Mary was known to her friends, was not a head-turner, but she had dark, shining eyes, raven hair that reached her feet when let down and a manner that was pleasing if not alluring. She was shy and preferred the background to the limelight. Happiest in the bosom of

the family, she was the kind of girl it would have been so
nice to come home to, especially for someone like William
Waldorf, who combined a fragile ego and thin skin with
an arrogance and insensitivity that frequently left him
badly in need of soothing and reassuring.

Offered a return to the state Assembly, Astor declined,
holding out for the thirty-two-man club that was the state
Senate. Although Astor believed his nomination, again in a
safe district, to the state Senate in 1879 was a tribute to his
unflinching loyalty and staunch Republicanism, at least
one newspaper suggested the more likely reason was that
Chester Arthur and the Republicans needed money. Astor,
buoyed by the rise in his political and domestic fortunes,
was a far more controversial figure in the Senate than he
had been in the Assembly. His first major effort was on behalf of legislation to reduce the fare on New York City's
elevated railroad from a dime to a nickel. Astor claimed
the workingman would benefit. His meaner opponents contended Astor was either attempting to bring family real estate holdings on the outskirts of the city into easy commuting range or seeking revenge on former business rivals like
Jay Gould and August Belmont, who were making huge
profits off the elevated's dime fare. The bill was finally
brought to a vote and was defeated, 22–8. Astor's other pet
bill, to eliminate the ugly Croton Reservoir from Fifth Avenue at Forty-second Street, passed the Senate and received
a majority in the Assembly but failed because it did not get
the required 65 percent in the Assembly. This provoked
Astor, who took his revenge by withholding his consent
from bills sponsored by Assembly opponents of the reservoir bill that required unanimous consent for passage. He
made few friends by this maneuver, but he was ready to
move on anyway and expressed his desires to New York's
political bosses, U. S. Senators Platt and Conkling, who

managed to find him a congressional district that was by no means safe but which did contain a large amount of Astor land. Astor carried on an arm's-length campaign in which he spent a lot of money, played the demagogue a bit by delicately stirring racial and religious hatreds but stayed carefully away from the slum dwellers in the district, for many of whom he was the indirect landlord, leasing the land on which the slums were built. His opponent called him a carpetbagger and nipped him in the election by 165 votes out of 23,000 cast. Astor was generally considered to have made a good showing in what was normally a Democratic district. He was returned to the state Senate in 1881.

State and national politics then became rather complex and very virulent. The pot began to boil when Platt and Conkling resigned over a patronage question with President Garfield, who had been a compromise candidate when Republicans couldn't agree on a third term for General Grant, which Platt and Conkling had desired. The New Yorkers had had to settle for Chester Arthur's nomination as Vice-President. Garfield then ignored New York. After quitting, the senators went straight to Albany and demanded to be re-elected by the state legislature. They had underestimated their strength, and when Garfield was assassinated by a fellow claiming he did it so that Arthur could become President, Arthur supporters were linked by association to assassination and lost much face. Platt and Conkling, to whom Astor was faithful to the end, were finished. Astor and Arthur were, however, still alive. The party showed its appreciation for Astor's loyalty by giving him the nomination to Congress from New York's "silk stocking" district, whose representative, the banker Levi P. Morton, had resigned to become minister to France. The Democrats had a hunch Astor might be beatable and quickly replaced their also-ran candidate in the district with a Wall Street broker named Roswell P. Flower who, with some Democratic help, would prove capable of matching Astor, bought vote for bought vote. It was not a pretty campaign, and Astor, who liked to think of himself as epitomizing the concept of noblesse oblige, was left bleeding and bowed by the harsh criticism heaped on him and his campaign by the press. Just a short time ago, he had been lavishly praised for his public spirit in abandoning the lap of luxury to enter the public arena. Now he became the victim of savage attacks against his wealth, his dogged support of Conkling and Platt and his legislative record as well as the flagrant tossing about of money in the current campaign. In vain did Astor cry that his record was being badly distorted, that the charges against him were without foundation. The $20 gold piece became the symbol of the campaign. Flower was no rose of purity, and the contest was generally viewed as a choice between two evils. The outcome was in doubt right up to Election Day. That evening Astor paced his headquarters alone, checking returns and tugging nervously at his mustache. It became clear rather early that Astor had lost. Flower's bought votes had stayed bought. Both men had visited every bar in the district and bought drinks for the house. Both men had proffered their hands to every eligible voter. But Flower had joined the barflies in their drinks and had taken off his glove to shake hands. The friendly New York *Tribune* offered an explanation. "It is always dangerous for men of great wealth to expose themselves to the suffrage," it editorialized. "The passion of envy is the most deeply planted and the most insidious in the human heart." Other journals were less understanding. The *World* described Astor's political career as having "consisted of a demonstration that a man of wealth and education can be as unscrupulous

a machinist and demagogue as the poorest and most ignorant voter."

The election and its result left William Waldorf Astor a
very bitter man. Chances are his reaction would have taken
a more active course but for the fact that President Arthur
recognized his loyalty and his contributions by naming him
minister to Italy. No doctor could have prescribed a better
cure for Astor's ills. The next few years were the happiest
of his life. Mamie was a big hit with Italian royalty. There
were no diplomatic problems to speak of, and the Astors
enjoyed a status in Rome that had seemed irritatingly elusive at home. William Waldorf was able to reacquaint
himself with his old favorites, the Borgias, and even wrote
a couple of novels about their era that were published by
Scribner's and generally well received by the newspaper
critics, probably because of the relatively pleasant surprise
created by the difference between the expectations of re-
viewers and the books, rather than any real, intrinsic merit.
Sforza, a Story of Milan is actually a book that might well
have been published regardless of the author's name, being
passably well wrought although hopelessly nineteenth-cen-
tury stuffed shirt in tone. Astor did receive some adverse
publicity stemming from an incident in which he agreed to
introduce a Tiffany salesman to King Humbert. The salesman had been traveling Europe and had met with stony
resistance at the other embassies and legations.

These halcyon days were interrupted when Astor's old
ally, President Arthur, was unable to hold his party together for the 1884 election and failed to win even the
nomination. Grover Cleveland won, and Astor was recalled. New York held little fascination for him. Rome had
whetted his appetite for the fine arts and titled society, and
New York was simply too raw, too rough, too energetic for
him, especially now that the one career he might have en-

joyed—a political one—was no longer available to him. The
election of Benjamin Harrison in 1888 gave him a flicker of
hope that he might be named to some ambassadorial post,
a prospect on which *Town Topics* could not resist comment. Colonel William Mann, its editor and publisher, expressed the hope that Astor would not receive any new
post, contending that his "diplomatic faux pas" while in
Rome had made him "the laughing stock of the Eternal
City." Mann suggested that someone write a manual for
ambassadors to teach "the gray-haired diplomatists of the
European foreign offices how to behave at the courts to
which they might be accredited." While it is unlikely that
Harrison paid Mann particularly close attention, Astor was
overlooked when the diplomatic plums were being handed
out, perhaps, as Mann hinted, because Astor was known to
have voted for Cleveland.

Meanwhile, for something to do as much as because he
found the project especially appealing, William Waldorf
gave impetus to Pierre Lorillard's efforts to build an exclusive resort at Tuxedo Park in the country outside New
York City. Astor was among the first to build a house
there, complete with lawn tennis court, for the early summer, pre-Newport season. He also, no doubt because of his
obvious literary credentials, undertook to write a history of
the area. Mamie joined her husband's promotion of Tuxedo by donating a silver trophy for the ladies' sailing competition. There were the usual social obligations. In February of 1887, for example, *Town Topics* reported on a
dinner dance given by William Waldorf and Mamie, noting that it "lacked the life and vigor of former ones. The
company was very much upset by young [Raymond] Belmont's death and there seemed a great desire to leave early
in spite of the entrancing music of the Hungarian band
and the general arrangements, which were so well carried

out. Society is not altogether heartless. . . ." During the day, Astor had some minor business obligations, the result of his being a director of several large companies. None of these activities was sufficient to keep him from a sense of drifting, a sense of purposelessness. In August of 1887 he was seen coming out of a Broadway theater after a performance in "an ill-fitting grey suit, a shocking bad straw hat, out of sorts and generally dilapidated and seedy looking." The observer noted that not even the hungriest of the cabbies lurking in the area waiting for the theater to let out approached him as a potential fare.

With the death of his father at the beginning of 1890, Astor became almost incalculably wealthy. One real estate expert of the time estimated that the Astors owned a twentieth of all New York City real estate by value. He was compared to the Duke of Westminster, whose real estate holdings in London make the current duke worth more than $5 billion today. Like his father, William Waldorf was more than six feet tall. He had sandy hair, blue eyes and movements that bordered on the abrupt. He was growing restless. He was, he believed, now the head of the family by birthright. That would make his wife the social head, a position usurped by his Aunt Caroline. Already there had been several delicate social confrontations, so far resolved by diplomacy and compromise. William Waldorf determined to force a showdown. Newport was chosen as the venue. The outcome precipitated the founding of the English branch of the Astor family.

The showdown itself is a story for another section of this book, but one of its results, the building of the Waldorf half of the Waldorf-Astoria Hotel, cannot here be ignored. The Waldorf was a monument to every base emotion William Waldorf felt. Constructed on the corner of Thirty-third Street and Fifth Avenue—on the site of his own for-

mer home—it towered over his aunt's residence just up the
block and eventually forced her to move farther up Fifth
Avenue. The hotel, which opened in March of 1893, was
the ultimate in snob appeal, extravagant fashion and luxury. It was not at all a monument to William Waldorf's
father, although such a monument was generally considered appropriate. The crotchety Colonel Mann believed
William Waldorf was contemplating his pocketbook and
delivered himself of a philippic on the subject that included this: "I do not think I am straining my statement
when I say that a combination of every cent they [New
York's very rich] have devoted to any philanthropic measure whatsoever is so slightly felt by the populace as a whole
that their benevolence is scarcely worth a passing remark."
Whatever one thought of William Waldorf and his motivations, the Waldorf was an instant and huge success. It
was, for one thing, the first hotel whose social function
rivaled its residential function in importance. For the first
time, one could host a fancy dress ball without possessing
one's own ballroom or give an elegant dinner, overseen by
Oscar Tschirky, later to become world famous as "Oscar of
the Waldorf," with all the flair of any home-grown affair.
No service or luxury was spared in caring for the Waldorf's
guests—fresh flowers, bone china, period furniture, even
(unheard of in the United States) room service. William
Waldorf remained in England during the building and
opening of his hotel, leaving the enterprise in the hands of
George C. Boldt, who had impressed an Astor office execu-
tive with his management of Philadelphia's Bellevue
Hotel. Boldt ran the Waldorf—and later the combined
Waldorf-Astoria—for twenty-three years, until his death in
1916. He was extraordinarily successful, becoming a millionaire several times over in his own right. At one point in
1900, thanks to an Astor tip, Boldt bought a piece of New

York real estate for $1.2 million and sold it in 1904 for $2 million. A German immigrant, Boldt developed an obsequious, not to say sycophantic, attitude toward his rich and royal guests that massaged their vanity and endeared the Waldorf to them permanently. He once summed up his view of the hotel by saying he would rather serve a non-profit glass of water to THE Mrs. Astor than the most expensive dinner to a recently arrived member of the rich and social set.

William Waldorf's young first cousin was duly impressed with the success of the Waldorf. At first he had been provoked by his cousin's obvious slap at his mother and had threatened to build a stable on the grounds of her former home next door to the Waldorf. Eventually John Jacob IV simmered down and, after some extended negotiations, reached an agreement with his cousin by which John Jacob would build a twin hotel tower to be operated jointly with the Waldorf. One of the points for negotiation was the design of the second tower so that it could be closed off and operated separately if at some future date the two cousins decided business and blood didn't mix. Another negotiable item was the name for the second tower. John Jacob wanted to name it after his mother and call it the Schermerhorn. William Waldorf was unalterably opposed, and the happy compromise of Astoria was finally settled upon. The new tower opened late in 1897, and the Waldorf-Astoria, already a major social force as the Waldorf, became a truly phenomenal hotel, with a thousand bedrooms and a magnificent ballroom that could seat fifteen hundred people for dinner—and see to it that they were elegantly fed. John Jacob IV had the symbolic last word, for the Astoria was taller than and cast a shadow over its older twin.

It is an interesting if idle speculation to wonder what

would have become of John Jacob IV had he been born into an ordinary family. Growing up as the only son of a doting mother and an absent father, privately tutored until he went away to preparatory school in New Hampshire, a rather sickly youth who was required to spend a lot of time outdoors, the boy was anything but average. If *Town Topics* is to be believed, his youthful pranks appeared to contain more cruelty than fun and were most frequently indulged aboard his father's yacht. One victim was a member of the crew up behind whom John Jacob sneaked one day, prodding the poor fellow with an awl and causing him to jump overboard in his consternation. On another occasion, he caught the cook taking a nap and tied him up. The captain finally complained to the boy's father, who told the captain he could punish the boy as he saw fit but that he had better be careful. William admitted he was afraid to correct the boy himself for fear his son would put something in his coffee. Such tales should be taken as exaggerations at best, given some of the other commentary Colonel Mann aimed in John Jacob's direction. He was, for example, accused of having left Harvard in 1887 because he had been blackballed in his bid for membership in the Hasty Pudding Club. But he graduated from Harvard in 1888. Oddly, Colonel Mann in his very next mention of this Astor acknowledges the graduation while noting that Astor was entering society that summer for the first time "and scheming mothers and mercenary but beautiful daughters are of course on the qui vive." Indeed, the following year his mother gave the young man his own debutante party, after having postponed it for a year in the interests of good form when Augusta Astor, John Jacob's aunt, died. On other occasions, *Town Topics* noted that John Jacob had been known in his earlier schooldays as "Jack Ass" and questioned whether he "could ever earn his bread by his brains." The answer to that question, by all indications, is an unqualified yes. Although in his Astor office business he has been accused of playing follow-the-leader—usually William Waldorf—John Jacob showed signs of having a highly original and inventive scientific mind. He has been ridiculed on the grounds of impracticality and frivolity where his inventions are concerned, largely because he never made any money out of them. But such criticism overlooks the fact that money was not a major concern for Astor. In fact he turned down an offer of $2,000 for his first invention, a patented bicycle brake. He was turned down by the Patent Office when he approached it with an idea for pumping warm, moist air from the earth's surface into the atmosphere to make rain, but a pneumatic road improver was exhibited at the Chicago World's Fair and won a first prize. He also improved the design of a storage battery enough so that he had a large version of the improved model installed on his yacht. He spent many an hour working on marine turbines and acquired several patents, which he donated to the public domain in 1902, expressing the hope that his action would speed the development of the ideal turbine. It did not, but the turbine theory was sound. A few years later he came up with a way to use peat as fuel for internal combustion engines, a project deemed fraught with potential by no less august an authority than *Scientific American* magazine. His last invention was a gadget for securing swivel chairs.

In 1894, John Jacob imitated his older first cousin in yet another endeavor, publishing a novel called *A Journey in Other Worlds*. While the book is largely without literary merit, and as a novel is less successful than his cousin's efforts, the social and scientific imagination it reflects is quite astonishing and acute. A major theme in this science fiction story is a social structure based on the need to con-

serve energy. Astor also makes a provocative attempt to reconcile science and religion and shows himself as essentially
an optimist. One of the scientific notions offered in the
book is the plan whereby the Terrestrial Axis Straightening
Co. will pump water from one pole to the other so that the
earth's axis will remain perpendicular to its rotation. This
would, Astor contends, result in permanent springtime, a
concept that shows the author had his romantic as well as
his scientific side.

In real life, that side demonstrated a devotion about
1890 to one person in particular. She was Ava Willing,
whose last name belied a contumacious spirit she made no
effort to control. Young Jack Astor caused quite a stir when
he appeared at a Patriarchs' Ball with the gorgeous Miss
Willing on his arm. By the standards of the day, she was
generally conceded to be unmatched in beauty. Her Philadelphia family background was the subject of slightly more
controversy. She was, some said, quite plebeian. They said
so, apparently, with more envy and spite than truth. Ava
could trace her descent back to Alfred the Great, and
Henry I, II and IV of England. Her more recent ancestors
bore the names of Philadelphia's finest families. Jack's
mother watched her little boy and this vision of loveliness
during the summer of 1890 in Newport, pronounced her
satisfaction, and the couple became engaged that winter,
married the next year on February 17, 1891.

The marriage was not a happy one. Ava did produce
quickly a son and heir, William Vincent, born in 1891, but
she would not bear another child until 1902, and in some
circles the rumor still persists that Jack may not have been
the father the second time. At any rate, there is little question that Ava treated her husband with more scorn than
affection, while he, for his part, moped about their various
homes, submitting to his wife's acid tongue or indifference

and managing to lead an active life mostly without her. Wherever they were, Ava nearly always kept a thick buffer of guests between herself and her husband. He played tennis; she gave the game up. She played bridge—constantly—a game he could not abide. It became obvious the couple lost little love between them, and, fanned by the lavish entertainments Ava hosted, the sparks of a rumor that she had married strictly for money began to flame.

One suspects Jack welcomed the outbreak of the Spanish-American War in 1898. His title of colonel, which he used for the rest of his life, was honorary and civilian—conferred by New York Governor Levi Morton several years earlier, but he was also given the rank of lieutenant colonel when he volunteered his services three days after war was declared. He financed the mustering and equipping of an artillery battery before being assigned to General William Shafter, who commanded the somewhat scruffy army that invaded Cuba. Astor saw action in the battle of Santiago, was chosen by Shafter to deliver the official terms of surrender to the Secretary of War and was mustered out of the service on November 1, 1898, having compiled a record of which he was proud for the rest of his life. One war correspondent wrote about an incident that bears a remarkable resemblance to a story about John Jacob III, Jack's uncle, during the Civil War:

" 'That's not him,' I heard a corporal mutter incredulously.

" 'Of course it is,' replied his next neighbor. 'I guess I know Colonel Astor. I saw him in Tampa before we left. Say, did you hear he has given a whole battery, guns and all, to the government for use in the Philippines?'

" 'He'll give his life too if he don't get off that knoll,' was the grim reply. 'Fancy a man with his money fighting down here and risking fever. Humph! If I had . . .'

"'Lie down, men!' sternly commanded an officer. The line of heads slowly dropped from sight, but each man, before he vanished in the grass, snatched another glance at the tall erect figure. . . ."

The story smacks of hyperbole, but it is also one more indication of an Astor trait that extended through all generations of the family, forward and back—a combination of strong patriotism and courage under fire.

Upon his return from the war, Astor settled into a rather heavy office schedule. During the winter he generally spent six or seven hours a day five days a week either at his modest office on Twenty-sixth Street near Broadway or at directors' meetings. He was on the board of Western Union, Equitable Life, New York Life, Illinois Central Railroad and a host of smaller companies. The real estate management job required a good-sized staff to collect rents, stay abreast of maintenance work and make new investments. Jack also needed a private secretary who had time for little else except responding to the sixty or more letters Astor received in a given day. A clear half of these were requests for financial help. They varied from demands made without explanation for large sums, like one from Sweden addressed to Mr. John Jacob Astor, Richest Man in all the World, New York, U.S.A.; to offers of a chance to invest in some wild scheme; to modest, tear-jerking appeals for money to help a sick relative, like one asking for $25 to send an ailing wife to the country. That particular one was acted upon, but an investigation showed the return address was that of a saloon.

The colonel was generous in his charitable contributions, but he was no easy touch, as one Astor, named Ludwig, learned to his chagrin. Ludwig, it seems, came to the United States in 1907 after his brother Jacob, seventy-four, died and named the colonel as a relative to notify in case of death. Jacob had claimed to come from the old Astor birthplace of Walldorf, Germany. He had been a cigar-maker by trade, but recent times had been hard, and he had died in the poorhouse. Ludwig, upon arriving in New York, camped out on the colonel's doorstep, announcing he would remain there until he received some financial as-sistance from the colonel. He claimed his grandfather, John Stephen Astor, had helped Colonel Astor's father during a visit to Walldorf. The colonel denied the whole story, despite some rather dubious documentation pro-duced by Ludwig, and had the poor fellow arrested.

It has been argued that Jack was not the businessman his first cousin was. For proof, some have noted that William Waldorf, with as much as three times the property (this is clearly a substantial exaggeration), required only seven clerks while Jack had a staff of twenty. This overlooks the fact that William Waldorf was operating a caretaker busi-ness, while Jack remained active and present. Jack's busi-ness philosophy required perhaps more manpower than his cousin's, too, because he believed in investing in men as well as real estate, a belief that necessitates a careful inves-tigation process. Jack felt that the more a man borrowed for his business, the more investment he had and the more committed to its success he became. The philosophy was not unsuccessful. In 1905, Astor's annual income was es-timated as in excess of $3 million, a tidy sum exceeded—maybe even doubled—by William Waldorf's income.

In the summer Astor had his yacht, the *Nourmahal*, recommissioned. It had been on loan to the Navy during the Spanish-American War. Astor and friends would spend many days aboard this giant steamer, built for his father, cruising in whatever waters the spirit of the moment moved them to cruise. Although his behavior toward yacht-ing and his wife was not nearly as drastic as his father's, the yacht was often used as an escape, Ava rarely, as the years went by, joining her husband. In 1909, Ava finally sued for divorce. She contended through lawyers that she had discovered in 1904 that her husband had other female interests, and evidence gathered by detectives hired by her lawyers corroborated the claim. Jack did not contest the proceedings, and on November 8, 1909, in a three-minute hearing before a judge, an interlocutory decree of divorce was granted. Jack was rumored to have settled $10 million on his former wife. He retained custody of his son Vincent, while Ava kept her daughter Alice. Two days later Jack and his son sailed for the Caribbean with some friends aboard the *Nourmahal*. Ava had not attended the hearing. By mid-November she, too, was at sea—aboard the *Lusitania*.

About the fifteenth of November a hurricane struck the Caribbean, and various conflicting reports began to swirl around the whereabouts of the *Nourmahal* and her passengers. For a week there was no definite word. The rumor-mongers had the *Nourmahal* at the bottom of the sea, safe in a Florida port and unconfirmed in San Juan, Puerto Rico. Communications were rather less sophisticated in those days, and repeated attempts to raise Puerto Rico by wireless met with nothing but static. The New York *Herald* was the first to report an eyewitness' story that the yacht was safe in Puerto Rico, where it had been when the storm first started and whence its captain refused to venture until the storm had abated. Within the family, there was much posturing of relief. Ava received word when the *Lusitania* landed at Queenstown, South Africa. A *Herald* report noted that she seemed relieved but expressed no opinion. Ava continued to make her presence felt in American social circles over the next half dozen years, floating between London, Newport and New York, entertaining lavishly and occasionally posing as the concerned mother.

In 1916 she married Lord Ribblesdale, long considered the prime British catch as a husband. She was looking for the gay life he had so prominently represented for so many years; he was, unbeknownst to her, looking to abandon all the pomp and glitter for a fireside, pipe and slippers life with his new bride. For nine years Ava suffered in silence with her much older husband, who finally died in 1925, allowing her to return in full glory to her social circles, where her gradually fading beauty was slowly being replaced by an eccentricity and an ever acid tongue. She was brutal. Once, in his presence, she described a young writer as "a rhinestone in the rough." In 1940 she returned to the United States and regained her citizenship, lost when she had remarried. She complained a lot, lived to be eighty-eight and died in 1958, leaving an estate of more than $3 million although she frequently had deplored her shabby financial condition.

Meanwhile, it appeared that the colonel had finally decided not to flirt again with the danger of domination by a woman. The lesson of his mother and his wife had been learned. What he did flirt with was a young woman his son's age. She was Madeleine Force. Her grandfather had been mayor of the old and quite proper Brooklyn and had entertained Astors and Vanderbilts in his day. Her mother was highly ambitious for Madeleine and her sister Katherine, grooming them carefully for important marriages. Jack Astor first met Madeleine while he was more or less "slumming" at a party in Murray Hill in 1911. That summer, love bloomed in Bar Harbor, Maine, where Madeleine was something of a tennis star and belle. The colonel parked his yacht in the harbor, entertained and carried on a whirlwind courtship. Madeleine may actually have been in love with another man at the time, but despite the disparity in their ages—she was eighteen, Astor was forty-six when they met—Madeleine knew a layer of golden eggs when she saw one. She was his guest at a ball in Newport to celebrate his return to society after his divorce. The rumors began to fly, and on August 1, Madeleine's father announced the engagement of the couple in the hope of quieting rumors. Astor's recent divorce and the age difference caused quite a stir among the clergy and finding a suitable minister to perform the marriage ceremony was a bit of a problem. The more righteous among society's leaders were aghast, or at least disappointed that the colonel hadn't chosen from among a bevy of more suitable beauties, but who he was proved more important to most everyone than what he was doing, and the marriage took place in Newport on September 9. Said the *Herald*, "Mrs. Astor declined to make any statement, but her beaming face showed her happiness." The colonel had been afraid that the wedding would cause large crowds to gather, but his Newport neighbors bothered him not at all. He and his bride disembarked from the *Noma*, his new yacht, for the wedding at his mother's old Newport mansion, Beechwood, and were back aboard before an hour had gone by. The only interruption to the smooth flow of events was the appearance in the early morning of a deputy sheriff, who boarded the yacht and served an agreeable Colonel Astor with a summons in a $30,000 damage suit brought by the mother of a former Princeton football player. The young man had been killed in an accident while doing some electrical work at Beechwood in the summer of 1910. The wedding was a very small one. Vincent was best man for his father while Katherine was maid of honor for her sister. "Now that we are happily married," Jack told the press after the ceremony, "I don't care how difficult divorce and remarriage laws are made." The destination of the bride and groom was not officially revealed, but everyone knew the couple was headed to Ferncliff, Astor's bucolic but elegant manse on the Hudson River at Rhinebeck, New York.

With the onset of winter, Colonel and Mrs. Astor sailed for Europe and the Middle East, a particularly grand version of the grand tour. From Egypt in late February came word that the Astors were expecting the stork in July and would return to the United States in the spring. As befitted one of the richest men in America and his new bride, a stateroom was secured aboard the most luxurious ship ever built for her maiden voyage across the ocean. The *Titanic* was also billed as the world's safest ocean liner. Of the more than two thousand people on board, a vast majority was more comforted by knowledge of the *Titanic*'s luxury than its safety. Ocean liners simply didn't sink often. On the night of April 14, 1912, or the morning of the fifteenth, depending on which time zone you were accounting by, the *Titanic* hit an iceberg a glancing blow that ripped its hull and caused it to sink in a matter of hours. Colonel Astor was in the majority of those aboard and died; Madeleine was in the minority and survived. Her own account of the tragedy is that she was awakened by her husband in the middle of the night and told she should get dressed because something was wrong with the ship. He assured her the *Titanic* would not sink and left her to get dressed. He came back soon with the news that the ship had struck an iceberg. He looked grave. She dressed quickly, putting on some of her jewelry, and they went to the deck where the lifeboats were. Both put on life jackets. The colonel saw his wife was dressed too lightly for the damp, chill night air and sent for a heavier dress, which he helped her put on. He then wrapped a fur coat around her.

"I got into the next to last boat," Mrs. Astor recounted some days after she had safely reached New York. "Colonel Astor said to me, 'The sea is calm. You'll be all right.

You're in good hands. I'll meet you in the morning." Then he kissed me affectionately and stood smiling down at me as the lifeboat was lowered. I noticed that the ship was settling as we rowed away, and I could make out the figure of Kitty, my favorite terrier, running about the deck.

"Then I saw the *Titanic* go down. We floated seven hours. It was very cold and the icy water was sweeping through the bottom of the lifeboat up to my knees when the *Carpathia*'s men rescued us. I rowed part of the time, as I knew how to handle an oar, and so did Mrs. George D. Widener. We picked up eight or ten drowning men during the night. Our eyes searched the darkness for signs of help, and some thought they could see the lights of a steamship approaching. As day broke we saw we were surrounded by icebergs. Then the *Carpathia* appeared and we were rescued."

The paper that published this report noted that Mrs. Astor did not give it all at once, but bit by bit to her family as her strength permitted. Naturally, the tragic disaster was grist for the media mills of eyewitness drama and human interest. Versions of what had happened were nearly as numerous as survivors. A Philadelphia banker, Robert Williams Daniel, was widely quoted, especially after he had been interviewed by the deeply grief-stricken Vincent Astor. He told Vincent he had seen his father and another passenger, Walter M. Clark, and urged them to jump overboard but they had refused. Daniel did and was finally rescued. In another interview, Daniel was quoted as saying that "wives refused point blank to leave their husbands. I saw members of the crew literally tear women from the arms of their husbands and throw them over the side to the boats. Until I die, the cries of those wretched men and women who went down clinging helplessly to the *Titanic*'s rail will ring in my ears."

Most reports agreed that Colonel Astor had behaved calmly and bravely. He did, apparently, begin to get into the lifeboat with his wife, explaining that she was pregnant, but he also was quick to get out again when told the boat was for women and children only. Every indication is that he was thinking first of his wife. In one version, he gave her a flask of brandy just before the boat was lowered over the *Titanic*'s side, saying: "This will keep you up while you're in the boat."

The news of the *Titanic* hit Vincent like a violent blow to the stomach. He rushed to his father's office as soon as he received the first word and spent the remainder of the night and most of the next morning trying to get some news of his father's fate. At one point he told an operator at the Marconi Co.'s wireless offices he would give all the money anyone could possibly ask for word of his father's safety, but such assurance was not forthcoming. He also visited the offices of the Associated Press. He even tried to contact the *Carpathia* on his own by wireless. It would be several days before he would know with absolute certainty, when his father's body was recovered.

It had only been a few months earlier that Colonel Astor had completed the work on the house at Sixty-fifth Street and Fifth Avenue, taking the two dwellings (his mother's and his own) and combining them into one magnificent palace. The new house had seen one splendid ball and then had been closed while the colonel and his bride toured Egypt and England. Jack Astor, who seemed at last to have found a measure of true happiness with his child bride, was the last of the American Astors for whom money was no object. It was not something one made, or felt guilty about; one simply inherited it. Vincent, to be sure, hardly had to restrain himself from indulging his various whims, but he just wasn't as comfortable with his fortune as his father had been with his. This affinity for wealth was not necessarily a personal thing, a filial difference between father and son, but rather a signal of changing eras.

The first-class passengers who went down with the *Titanic* represented more than $500 million in personal fortunes and an era whose end would be sealed by World War I. Besides the colonel, there was Benjamin Guggenheim, $95 million in mining; George Widener, son of P. A. B. Widener, who made $50 million in the street railroad business; Isidor Straus, $50 million in dry goods; and Colonel Washington Roebling, builder of the Brooklyn Bridge and worth $25 million. The dollar amounts of the fortunes of these men are probably exaggerated by the newspaper accounts from which they are taken, but in any case, they were substantial.

History is seldom very cooperative with historians trying to make neat chronological divisions among epochs and eras, which don't begin or end cataclysmically but flow from one to the next. But in the two decades separating the 1908 death of Mrs. Caroline Astor, the colonel's mother, and the stock market crash of 1929 are contained the handful of events that constitute for virtually everyone the end of flagrant excess in America's choice inner circles. The tinsel dreams produced in Hollywood became more real during the Great Depression than the real, if discreet and cautious, flamboyance of high society. The nation's relationship toward its wealthy class was changing dramatically. The graduated income tax, legislated in 1913, was a symbol of new attitudes.

PART III

PART VII

CHAPTER 6

The banks of the Hudson River as it stretches north from New York City are lined with some of America's most beautiful estates. North of Poughkeepsie, the countryside grows more rugged, more rural, less manicured. At Hyde Park, better known for its Roosevelt connections, begins Astor territory. At one time the east bank from Rhinebeck to Red Hook was largely Astor-family owned. John Jacob Astor I started the Astor association with Rhinebeck and environs, although it was his son William B. whose presence was first felt. The family founder purchased a Hyde Park estate in the 1830s and gave it to his daughter Dorothea. The place belonged to the Langdon family until the 1890s. The Langdons also had a place near Rhinebeck.

Just north of Rhinebeck was the homestead of General John Armstrong, father of William B.'s wife and husband of Alida Livingston, out of whose family's land the Armstrong estate had been cut. The families represented in General John and Alida were as good as America's best and as proud as America's proudest, but the Armstrongs were not wealthy. In Rhinebeck as in most other places where the Astor name has become prominent, money played an important role. The Armstrong place was known as La Bergerie, but Margaret Armstrong Astor, on her honeymoon with William B., read Sir Walter Scott's poem, *Rokeby*, in which Scott described a place much like part of La Bergerie, and Margaret prevailed upon her father to change the name. Rokeby it became and, in 1836, an Astor property it became as well. William B. paid General Armstrong $50,000 for the home and about 720 acres. Family legend, to which one of the present Rokeby residents, Winthrop Aldrich, subscribes, is that the money had been given by John Jacob for the purpose as a wedding present back in 1818. Armstrong was loath to sell, but the Astors convinced him finally that the $50,000 would allow him to live out his life in comfort and free from worry. There would even be money left to leave to his sons. The eldest son, Horatio Armstrong, wasn't too pleased with the way things worked out, having expected to inherit Rokeby for himself. When his father died in 1843, the Astors offered to buy the furnishings and paintings in Rokeby, but Horatio decreed that they be removed and split among Armstrong's sons.

With the death of General Armstrong, William Astor began to make his imprint upon Rokeby. He undertook a major remodeling project about 1858, adding a third floor, a kitchen wing and a library tower to the building and increasing the number of rooms from twenty to forty-eight. The Astors ordered the work and then took off for Europe to wander the Continent until the job was finished. Another change generally attributed to William is the view from the west side of the house out over the Hudson to the Catskill Mountains in the distance. Judging from the soil and the surrounding contour of the land, William had a

hill that had been obscuring the view of the river leveled so
that the land now slopes gently from the mansion down to
the river. In those pre-bulldozer days, such a project was a
massive undertaking, one General Armstrong would never
have thought appropriate as it ruined a good number of
tillable acres by removing all the topsoil. Well, Rokeby
wasn't a farm anymore; it was a summer home for a very
wealthy family—the wealthiest, in fact, in the United
States. Vistas were more important than vegetables. This
was, remember, before the rise of Newport as New York
society's summer place. In William B.'s generation, Rokeby's only competition as the Astor Hudson seat was a
place just downriver bought by the Langdons, his sister
Dorothea and brother-in-law Walter. The Langdon place is
one of the few that did not remain in Astor hands into the
second half of the twentieth century. The Langdons sold it
to Frederick W. Vanderbilt, a grandson of the old Commodore.

As William B.'s children grew to adulthood they began
to spread along the river. Rokeby would eventually go to
William B.'s granddaughter, Maddie Ward, and her husband, John Winthrop Chanler. John Jacob III would buy a
place across the river, one of the other Astor homes that
did not stay in the family for generations. Laura Astor
would marry Franklin H. Delano and move into a place
not far downstream. William, Jr., would start Ferncliff,
which in time would rival and eventually surpass Rokeby
in magnificence. Even the black sheep of the family, as
William's youngest son, Henry, was generally considered,
settled down in the neighborhood, moving to West Copake after a marriage the family tended to view with a
collective jaundiced eye. It was not until the 1850s that
Rhinebeck and its neighboring villages began to thrive as a
desirable area for the second homes of wealthy New York

City families. The railroad was largely responsible. Before it opened service to Rhinebeck in 1851, William Astor had to commute first by sloop and later by steamboat, a hardship that had caused him to write in 1848, responding to an inquiry about his interest in a Canadian estate as a country home, that, as far as he was concerned, Rhinebeck was too far from New York, making a home in Canada out of the question.

As the youngest child of William Astor, Henry spent his first thirty-eight years in relative obscurity. A great-niece of his once said of him that he "never fully developed mentally." That judgment is perhaps too harsh, but he was not a man of particular brilliance or motivation. Following Astor tradition, Henry took a stab at Columbia, a stay that was undistinguished at best, and went on to Europe with a tutor for a couple of years that were less than memorable. On his return, it was clear to everyone that Henry was not going to be a very valuable asset at the family offices. He went back to Rhinebeck where he lived at Rokeby. A hulk of a man with a red beard and a barrel chest, Henry was generally a playful, generous fellow, although occasionally given to violent outbursts of temper. Mornings he would drive a pair of trotters into a lather riding about the estate. He enjoyed playing tag, blind man's buff and more adult pastimes like horse racing, boxing and wrestling. As the income from his share of the Eden Farm property, left to him by John Jacob I, began to mount ($80,000 a year by 1890), he would loan money to neighbors in need, paying little attention to details like interest rates or repayment schedules. He apparently derived his interest in trotting horses from his namesake, the butcher who was John Jacob I's brother. That Henry Astor had purchased the English stallion, Messenger, in 1793. Messenger would sire the even more famous Hambletonian, perhaps the most sought-after stud in trotting in his day.

While Henry, William's son, was not afraid to mix it up himself, one of his favorite occupations was promoting amateur boxing and wrestling matches among his friends and neighbors with five-dollar bills as prizes to the winners. Henry could take a joke and was never one to make very much of his Astor or Armstrong/Livingston heritage. Once he promoted a battle between two farmhands armed with garden hoses only to become entangled in the hoses himself. Before he could untangle himself he was drenched, and for a moment there was some concern that the only thing madder than a wet hen might prove to be a soaked Astor. Then Henry burst into pleasant, hearty laughter.

One thing Henry didn't do too well was drink. One relative put it that Henry couldn't drink without becoming "irresponsible." This relative used to tell an unlikely story about how drinking led to Henry's excommunication from the family. According to this story, some neighboring farmers got Henry drunk one night and made him sign a paper in which he agreed to marry their fifteen-year-old sister. Sometime later the farmers showed Henry the paper he'd signed, prepared to share a good laugh with him over their little joke. Henry, who was thirty-nine at the time, took the whole matter in complete seriousness, allowed as how a gentleman was required to honor his word and proceeded to marry the girl. However it happened, Henry did indeed marry a girl, causing, to put it mildly, great consternation within his family. The concern was twofold. First, the girl, Malvina Dinehart, was a farmer's daughter with none of the breeding, stature or grace usually considered de rigueur for an Astor wife. It was not, after all, Astor money alone that had boosted the family into the top echelon of American society. Equally appalling to the Astor hierarchy was the rumor, soon to be proved fact, that Henry had married the girl without even buying off her dower right with a prenuptial settlement, basic procedure if you were to keep the family fortune more or less intact. Indeed, Malvina was the first woman to marry into the family with her dower right alive. From New York, Henry's brother William was dispatched with alacrity to halt the proceedings if he possibly could. But he arrived to find the deed already done.

The father was furious and wasted no time reducing Henry's inheritance from him to a tawdry $30,000. Henry was not greatly disturbed. His needs were modest and income from the Eden Farm property would satisfy them fine. The property had been put into a trust whose control was no longer Henry's. One story is that the Astors took control after Henry had lost his temper once and struck the four-year-old daughter of a farmer, who later sued him for $20,000 and won. Another version is that Malvina's brothers were not satisfied with Henry's largesse toward them and, when one of them fell playing tag and broke his leg, he sued Henry. The suit was unsuccessful, but its implications frightened Henry's eldest brother, John Jacob III, who determined that Henry's fortune ought to be taken out of his control. Henry's estrangement from his father was virtually complete. A few of William Astor's letter books have survived, and they show William in a very paternal, if somewhat patronizing, attitude toward his youngest son before the marriage. Letters explain the business William has been conducting on Henry's behalf and express warmth and affection. After 1871 there are no more letters to Henry.

While William's judgment may have been a bit precipitous and harsh, Henry was, to be honest about it, somewhat eccentric. His wife's family owned some property near a hamlet called Milan not far from Rhinebeck, and Henry always managed to leave the impression when questioned about his marriage that it had taken place while he was abroad. Frequently when Henry had been drinking the urge to preach would come irresistibly over him, and whether he had been provided with an audience or not, he would bang on a bell with a crowbar and launch into a spirited sermon on whatever biblical warning or advice came to mind. His younger relatives in the Rhinebeck vicinity soon learned to view Henry as one might a freak in a sideshow, with a mixture of awe, curiosity and pity.

In 1874, Henry bought about two hundred acres near Rhinebeck in West Copake and built himself a house. In one room, he had the floor inlaid with silver dollars, which legend and enthusiasm soon turned into $20 gold pieces. Henry had the silver dollars taken up when hotel lobbies and barrooms began to imitate him. He decided the idea had been irreparably cheapened. The Astor estate bankers never were able to break Henry of his habit of taking the checks sent to him by the Astor estate and squirreling them away in his desk until such time as he needed some money. Then he would send in a whole stack of checks. Estate books were constantly teetering on the edge of imbalance, a situation about which Henry could not bring himself to show concern. "Money counts for little in this world compared with love and life," Henry used to say.

As Henry grew older and the century changed and his relatives began falling by time's wayside, money may not have counted for much, but it counted up to a lot. From 1892 to 1914, Henry received more than $2 million income from the Eden Farm properties. From 1914 to 1917, he received more than $750,000. Not bad for a man who was generally considered to have been disinherited. With age, Henry was forced to curb some of his earlier activities, like driving trotters hither and yon about the neighborhood or racing them around the half-mile track he had built. He needed a chauffeur, and while he could have sent to New York for one, he did a typically Henry thing by sending the son of one of his farm employees down to the city to learn how to drive and then using him as his chauffeur. The job was not without occupational hazard, for Malvina became a devotee of mechanical speed and loved to go as fast as the limousine could. To see Henry cooped up in the back of the limousine upset his neighbors, who had, virtually to a man, grown fond of the old boy. His door, until those last few months when he was so ill, had always been open. Friends, neighbors, even strangers had always been welcome. Henry had been a man of action, though, and no one liked to see him unable to do for himself anymore.

In June of 1918, just a month before his eighty-sixth birthday, Henry finally died. He left his estate, estimated to be as much as $1 million, all of it derived from income in excess of what he was able to spend, to his wife, who died just two months later. She in turn left a large percentage to charity—a rather un-Astor-like gesture—and divided the remainder up among her family. But it wouldn't be until almost two years later that the real value of Henry's Eden Farm share was fully realized. Because Henry and Malvina were childless, Henry's residual estate reverted, per stirpes, to great-grandchildren of his father. This required the auctioning of his real estate, which turned out to include the land where stood the Morosco, Bijou and Astor theaters, sixty three- and four-story brownstones, thirty-eight tenements, seven factories, six vacant lots and thirty-nine other parcels. Just before the auction there was much speculation as to how much the Times Square properties would bring. Everyone underestimated. On the day of the auction, March 9, 1920, more than 2,500 people squeezed themselves into the ballroom of the Astor Hotel. The auction took twelve hours. The auctioneer, Joseph P. Day, was perhaps a bit carried away when he called the affair "the greatest sale of improved properties ever held." When the hammer had fallen for the last time, the total of the proceeds added up to more than $5 million.

The estate had been divided into 360 shares—each worth, as it turned out, about $14,000—which in turn were divided among two grandchildren and the great-grandchildren of William B. Astor, except for the descendants of John Jacob III, the English members of the family, who were already enormously wealthy and waived their claim. Each Chanler received 15 shares. The children of John Jacob IV and his oldest sister, Emily, received 8 shares each, the smallest number allotted. Arthur Astor Carey and Charlotte Augusta Drayton Haig, two grandchildren included in the distribution, received the largest number of shares. Carey got 60 while Mrs. Haig got 24. To Vincent, son of John Jacob IV, the inheritance could well have meant simply an increase in the petty cash reserve, but to some of his less well heeled cousins, who received larger shares than Vincent, the money was substantial and the post-mortem blessings heaped upon Henry were undoubtedly many and fervent. Winthrop Chanler, realizing he was receiving a final family legacy called the distribution "the last cookie in the jar."

Henry's sister Laura was the other of William's children who died childless. She was one of three relatives—the others were Margaret Aldrich and Vincent—who had visited Henry after his marriage made him the pariah of the family. In 1844, Laura, twenty, had married Franklin Hughes Delano, whose niece was the eventual mother of Franklin Delano Roosevelt. Delano was a handsome gentleman whose father had made a fortune in the whale oil business. Laura's father approved of the match and gave her a $200,000 trust to celebrate. William also gave the Delanos a piece of Rokeby for their own estate, Stein Valetje, and a New York town house. Delano withdrew from the shipping firm in which he was a partner upon his marriage and indulged his taste for the life of leisure, occasionally taking a shipping venture interest or helping his father-in-law with a real estate deal. The Delanos traveled extensively, collected expensive trinkets like jewelry and porcelain, and eventually moved to Europe. Although they hardly needed it, Laura inherited $1.1 million in real estate and cash when her father died in 1875. Some years later Laura's husband died. To keep Aunt Laura company, the Winthrop Chanlers would send their daughters over to spend a month each summer.

Laura Astor Chanler, who later married the son of architect Stanford White, was Laura Delano's great-great-niece and godchild. In the summer of 1979, at the age of ninety-three, Mrs. White recalled her visits with her godmother. "My father [Winthrop Chanler] dropped the Astor from his name years and years ago because he said it was too expensive," Mrs. White said. "Since I was Aunt Laura's godchild, I kept it. I think it was supposed to help your inheritance prospects. I don't know. Aunt Laura only left me $10,000. It got me to the altar." Mrs. White remembered one time in Lausanne, Switzerland, when her godmother was staying in the royal suite at the best hotel there. The Empress of Austria decided to pay a sudden call on Lausanne, and the hotel manager visited Mrs. Delano, begging her to appreciate his position and give up her rooms for the empress. Aunt Laura would have none of it and refused to budge. Her godchild says she still can see her Aunt Laura sweeping down the staircase at the hotel looking every bit as regal as the empress ever did. It was Mrs. Delano, says

Mrs. White, who gave her goddaughter her first intuitive lesson in social propriety. The two would go for a carriage ride while staying at Aunt Laura's villa in Monte Carlo and Aunt Laura would give Mrs. White a bagful of pennies. "I was supposed to throw them to the beggars we passed. And I did, because you didn't not do what Aunt Laura said, but I just felt that somehow it was wrong."

Laura's younger sister, Alida, has remained remarkably anonymous for a third-generation Astor. Her offspring have been virtually ignored. Alida was born in 1826 and married an Englishman, John Carey, Jr., a man of whom it was said that he had come to America in search of his fortune. If so, he was a success. Being of good family, he was accepted by the Astors, and old William bestowed the usual $200,000 trust on his daughter as well as some $100,000 in other property at the time of the wedding. Like most Americans of property or social distinction, the Astors tended to harbor a favorable bias toward things British, including spouses for their children. In another generation or two this bias would reach absurd heights, with English and other European nobility eager to refurbish decimated family coffers and America's social families vying with one another to capture the biggest title for their own. Alida was blithely unaware of such ramifications, having simply happened to fall in love with Carey. In 1881 she died.

The one revealing story about Alida that survives is that as a young woman she was concerned about the lack of facilities to care for orphaned girls in the Rhinebeck area. She and her mother both urged William to underwrite an orphanage. Her mother was at the same time dropping unsubtle hints about how nice it would be to have a greenhouse. William finally asked which she wanted most—the greenhouse or the orphanage. With Alida acting perhaps as her mother's conscience, that good lady said the orphanage

was most needed. To Alida's delight, William announced
that his wife had given him the right answer and he would
happily provide both. The orphanage, St. Margaret's Home
after William's wife, survived as a family-sponsored charity
until the 1930s.

The Careys had three children—a daughter, Margaret
Louisa, and two sons, Arthur Astor and Henry Astor. The
last is occasionally recalled as the donor of a Harvard sports
building or as a member-elect of the Rhode Island state
legislature when he died in 1893. He had lived in Newport
after his father's death. He is perhaps best remembered
for a bet he made with a cousin just a couple of years before
he died. The cousin, Archie Chanler, was trying to raise
money to send promising American artists to Paris to
study, there being no good study opportunities in the
United States at the time. He talked Henry Carey into
agreeing that whoever died first would leave the project
$25,000. Henry thus became the largest donor to the
Chanler Concours, which eventually helped a substantial
number of student artists reach Paris. In return, the stu-
dents would agree to devote a percentage of their time
after coming back to America to teaching.

For all the attention the Careys have failed to receive,
the Chanlers have more than made up the difference. John
Winthrop Chanler was the son of an Episcopal clergyman. He unknowingly followed an Astor pattern in his education, graduating from Columbia and then touring
Europe. Upon his return, he was admitted to the New
York bar and became interested in politics. He was defeated in a try for Congress in 1860, but in 1862 tried again
and won. Meanwhile, in January of that year, he had married Maddie Ward, daughter of Emily Astor and Sam
Ward. They were a most happy couple and a most prolific
one. Maddie died in 1875, having caught pneumonia dur-

ing the funeral procession for her grandfather, William
Astor. By that time she had produced eleven children, although her eldest daughter had succumbed to scarlet fever
at the age of eight in 1872. Two years after his wife died,
Chanler was playing croquet at Rokeby in bitter weather
one day. He suggested quitting, but his lady opponent ob-
jected and he continued to play. A cold he then contracted
quickly turned to pneumonia and in a matter of hours the
ten surviving Chanler children were orphans.

CHAPTER 7

In Chanler veins ran some rare blood. The combination of Astor, Ward and Chanler genes was bound to produce interesting results, and so it did. A picture in possession of the present owners of Rokeby portrays eloquently the contrast between Chanler/Ward and Astor. It shows Sam Ward holding a wreath of orange blossoms over the head of his bride while she wears the bejeweled headpiece her grandfather gave her to wear at her wedding. Ward had wanted her to wear orange blossoms; the picture was as far as William was willing to go by way of compromise. Having been orphaned when the eldest Chanler child was just fifteen, the family learned early a self-sufficiency. They were a proud, aristocratic bunch in the united front they turned toward the outside, but within the family they were a rowdy, uninhibited, highly verbal and democratic gang. On the death of their father, the older members of the Astor family considered breaking up the Chanler children and distributing them among their Delano, Astor, and Carey relatives. But the children finally prevailed and were allowed to remain together at Rokeby with a large staff to look after them.

Within two and a half months, from late 1882 to early 1883, two of the ten children died—Egerton White from a brain tumor and Marion Ward, yet another victim of pneumonia. That left eight—John Armstrong ("Archie"), born in 1862; Winthrop Astor, 1863; Elizabeth Winthrop, 1866; William Astor, 1867; Lewis Stuyvesant, 1869; Margaret Livingston, 1870; Robert Winthrop, 1872; and Alida Beekman, 1873. Not one of them led an ordinary life. They were all intelligent and in varying degrees, irreverent. In their early years they were tutored. Much later, Margaret would recall how one of her brothers, having failed to master the assigned lesson in French grammar, managed to conceal this oversight by provoking the very French tutor into an argument. Said Margaret's brother, *"Charlemagne était en effet allemand, n'est-ce pas?"* The general attitude of the young Chanlers is summed up by Margaret: "We inclined to the opinion that rich people had saved the world."

Still, there was nothing stuffy about the children, who couldn't abide ostentation or the putting on of airs. When the footmen would bow to Margaret, for example, her siblings would mock the scene, bowing elaborately and snickering facetiously at their blushing sister. Airs and ostentation would have been difficult to maintain regardless of the general attitude because at Rokeby while the Chanlers were growing up there was only one bathroom. The children learned early to share. They also learned to protect their interests from the chicanery of outsiders, which pretty well meant anyone outside Rokeby, blood relative or not. In August of 1882, William Waldorf Astor found himself writing the Chanlers in response to their questioning the large legal bill connected with William Waldorf's with-

drawal as a trustee for the Chanlers. He pointed out that
the legal fee was set by the courts and that there was no
question about the trust's obligation for the bill. America's
new minister to Italy went on to wax diplomatic and generous, noting the good relations between the Chanlers and
himself, expressing the hope that those relations would
remain good and agreeing to pay the bill himself. William
Waldorf signed the letter "with great regard and esteem."
It was Winthrop Chanler who put, perhaps more flip-
pantly than some of his siblings might have, the relationship between the Astors and the Chanlers in perspective. While at Harvard, Winthrop told his friend, Amos
Túck French, "The Chanlers were a very respectable lot of
people in Charleston [South Carolina] until the yellow
splotch of the Astors stained their escutcheon. But you
would have never heard of the Chanlers if it hadn't been
for that yaller stain." He may have been selling his family a
bit short.

The eldest, Archie, began adult life in rather typical
Astor fashion, spending four years at Columbia University and graduating with enough knowledge of the law to
pass the New York bar exam. He was more interested in
adventure than in work, however, and soon abandoned his
law practice to head for New Mexico and the life of a cow-
boy. In 1885 he joined the party of General George Crook
while it stalked the Apache chief Geronimo. After a bit he
went to Europe, then came back to New York where he
turned into something of a night owl. In 1888 he fell in
love with a Virginia woman who soon published a novel,
scandalizing society. The protagonist was clearly Archie.
Amélie Rives—her godfather was Robert E. Lee—came
from one of Virginia's leading families. But she refused to
behave as if she did, and when Archie and she were married, with more Chanlers being informed after than before

the event, family harmony was strained. Winthrop wrote his brother that he would find it rather cool at Rokeby despite the summer's heat. Archie demanded an apology.

Eventually differences were patched and the newlyweds sailed to England, where Amélie ensnared the likes of Lord Curzon, Henry James, Oscar Wilde, Thomas Hardy and George Meredith with her fresh beauty, social charm and literary pretensions that posed no threat to the stature of her new admirers. Archie was probably, although he repeatedly denied it, jealous of his bride's successes. At any rate, the marriage was a stormy one. Amélie was a moody sort with a very fragile emotional stability. In Paris, where next the couple journeyed, the rumor was that Amélie grew inordinately fond of morphine. Archie tried to get his bride to give up writing for portrait painting, for which he was convinced she had exceptional talent. More because Archie asked than for any other reason, Amélie refused. Good old Colonel Mann couldn't resist taking his shot in *Town Topics*, noting that ". . . the intellectually ligneous but auriferous Astors will have at least one person of brains in their select family fold, and the halting and ponderous literary gifts of our ex-minister to Italy will no longer have to bear the burden of rescuing the Astor name from intellectual nothingness." The colonel also promoted Amélie's image as a femme fatale by printing the rumor a year after her marriage that an artist in Paris had committed suicide after having his love scorned by Mrs. Chanler. Amélie and Archie were a pair of headstrong, spoiled children—thinskinned and carrying their emotions near the surface. The marriage didn't have much of a chance, and after a few years of fighting, pouting and making up, the couple were divorced.

Archie's love for his Virginia bride may have cooled but not his love for Virginia. He bought an estate not far from his ex-wife's family seat. There he began to dabble in various fields of psychic and kinetic theory, convinced he had some special powers. The violent arguments he had always had with his brothers while growing up continued now when he met them at board meetings of businesses in which the family was involved. What was healthy intellectual exercise around the family dining table was viewed as rather exotic behavior at the directors' table. One or two of his brothers began to mutter that Archie must be crazy. As Archie found it increasingly inconvenient to leave Virginia to attend to business matters, he was persuaded to give a power of attorney to his friend, Stanford White, the architect. In 1897, White called and asked if he could visit. Archie said no, but White went anyway and persuaded Archie to come back to New York with him. Accompanying them was a physician introduced to Archie as an old friend of White's.

In recent months Archie had discovered a capacity for automatic writing and an extrasensory faculty, which told him among other things that he could change the color of his eyes from light brown to dark gray if he positioned himself in just the right way before a mirror. His eyes changed color, a fact for which there is some independent corroboration by doctors who knew Archie before and after the experiment. It was weird, and White and Archie's brothers were worried. In New York, other doctors showed up. Archie was asked to do his Napoleonic trance and obliged. That did it. He was committed to Bloomingdale, an asylum for the insane just outside New York City. He was thirty-four. Two brothers, Winthrop and Lewis Stuyvesant, and a cousin, Arthur Carey, had signed the commitment papers.

More than two years passed before a court adjudged Archie incompetent to manage himself and his affairs. Dr.

Carlos F. MacDonald testified Archie's was one of the most typical paranoia cases he'd ever seen. Archie was not permitted to attend the hearing. At first Archie had not been particularly concerned about being put away. He figured his family was just being vindictive and that his sanity was self-evident enough to assure his swift release. What is remarkable about the three and a half years Archie spent at Bloomingdale fighting the awful frustration of trying to reason with an indifferent bureaucracy is that the man didn't crack and actually become insane. From every indication, Archie was a volatile, somewhat eccentric and stubborn individual with some unusual habits he did not feel it necessary to hide; he was not insane, or even extraordinarily neurotic. The night before Thanksgiving in 1900, Archie went for his usual walk on the grounds of Bloomingdale and disappeared. For a while the newspapers speculated every time an unidentified body was found. Then Archie surfaced at a Philadelphia hospital, where he had gone voluntarily to have his sanity checked out. He was released as sane, returned to Virginia and obtained a court certificate of sanity. He changed his last name to Chaloner because of what his family had made him suffer through, started a small publishing house and wrote sarcastic, satirical poetry.

In 1909 Archie shot and killed a man named John Gillard. Gillard had come after his wife, who had fled to Archie's house in fear of her husband's drunken rage. The case was considered justifiable homicide, and Archie wasn't even arrested. When the New York *Post* published an article about the temporary insanity defense of Harry K. Thaw, who had murdered Stanford White in 1906 in a fit of jealous rage over the affair White was having with his wife, one sentence read: "The latest prominent assassin had the rare foresight to have himself declared insane before he shot his man." Archie sued and won a $17,500 judgment. His persistent efforts to have himself cleared in New York, where he was still legally insane, finally paid off in 1919. His visit to the city shortly thereafter was more a sad and lonely solo than a triumphant celebration. He was becoming somewhat fanatical about religion at the time, a posture that made people uncomfortable. In 1915 a court hearing had shown his estate to be nearly $1.5 million, with an annual income of $89,000. He didn't need the approval of others. He returned to Virginia and lived out his remaining years in solitude.

If a surviving nephew is to be believed, Archie's latter-day sanity was often more legal than self-evident. This fellow tells tales of Uncle Archie in Virginia, his love of horses and his hatred of automobiles. Archie discovered an old Virginia law requiring drivers of motorized vehicles to keep a careful watch out for horses and to lead a horse past their cars if the rider requested. Archie would patrol his homestead on horseback with a revolver, a klaxon on his saddle and port and starboard lights for night work, forcing compliance with the law on unsuspecting and soon outraged motorists. Among his other foibles, Archie was known on occasion to take binoculars to a restaurant and train them on dilatory waiters. His cane was engraved "Leave Me Alone." He would once in a while visit Rokeby in middle age and grew to love automobiles, but his dining habits remained suspect. His nephew says a satisfactory meal for his uncle consisted of grass clippings and ice cream.

The next Chanler was Winthrop Astor, perhaps the most irreverent of the Chanlers, at least where the Astor connection was concerned. Writing to his family of his impressions as a guest at the wedding of John Jacob Astor IV and Ava Willing in 1891, he noted: "Not one of them

[John Jacob's bachelor friends] would cross the street to shake hands with him for his own sake. But the mother is such a social power and has done so much for them that they are only too glad for the chance." He was forever poking holes in pretense, although he never did much of anything himself except ride and hunt. A granddaughter points out that while Wintie never was disposed to much effort himself, he always knew the most interesting and active people wherever he went, and none of them seemed to mind Wintie's indolence. One of his good friends dating back to his Harvard days was Theodore Roosevelt. They were members of several clubs together and spent a good deal of time hunting, fishing and camping. Wintie didn't charge up San Juan Hill with his friend, but he did play an active role in the Spanish-American War, running guns to the rebels, getting shot in the elbow and generally acquitting himself valiantly.

Two versions of his exploits in Cuba are perhaps worth noting. The official report of the incident in which Winthrop was wounded was written by the senior American officer, who said, in part: "I cannot speak too highly of the gallantry of Mr. Chanler's men, who fought overwhelming numbers until dark when they withdrew . . . with the loss of one killed and seven wounded out of a party of twenty-eight men." Wintie wrote his sister about the same affair: "I got it through the elbow like an ass at Tunas and had to go back. So far I haven't found fighting as amusing as fox hunting."

Winthrop began early to scandalize his family, capping a youthful career with his marriage in 1886 to Daisy Terry, a niece of his grandfather, Sam Ward. She was, besides being a cousin, a Catholic as well, a sin for which it was not easy to be forgiven in the Chanler clan. The Chanlers did try, although elderly cousin Mary Marshall, who had been brought up from South Carolina to help with the rearing of the Chanler children, did decree that Daisy's name must never be mentioned. Expected insult was added to injury when the new couple's first child was christened in 1887 a Catholic. The infant's Aunt Margaret allowed publicly as how the child would have been better off had it died in its innocence but in private could not resist loving the child demonstratively. Her name was Laura Astor Chanler, a bright, gentle, sensitive child who would in later years never quite understand that the screaming and shouting that went on intra-family, sometimes with everyone ganging up on one member, was just healthy Chanler intellectual exercise, nothing to take offense at.

Laura, who would eventually marry Stanford White's son, remembers her parents as liking Colonel John Jacob Astor, although she herself recalls going to a ball he and his wife, Ava, gave and refusing to dance with the colonel because she didn't like his looks. In this light, her father's description of Jack's and Ava's wedding in 1891 merits further quotation. It is from a letter home.

". . . The wedding was really beautiful. The bride is a lovely girl. . . . If she does not make something of Jack, nobody can. Poor girl! They tell me in Philadelphia that she has been perfectly desperate about the whole business. Has left a puddle of tears on every parlour floor in town. Her family, which is very rich and quite the 'fine fleur' of Phil., has forced her into it. Up to the last moment her friends feared that she would rebel and break loose—but she did not. . . .

"Just before time came for the service I went up stairs to see Jack and cheer him up. . . . To my surprise he was not a bit scared or (apparently) nervous. He asked for a Prayer Book just to see 'what he had to say.' I told him it did not matter a single damn what he said now, for the parson

would only and could only understand him in one way.
That seemed to brace him up. Then I went downstairs. . . . Then the service began. After each sentence
that fell from the parson's lips, by some curious coincidence, the crowd of people outside in the street hoorayed
and bawled. Of course the window was shut and the blinds
were down, but the mob yelled as if it were in the room.
The effect was ludicrous in the extreme.

"Jack answered up like a man. The girl whispered her responses below her breath. She trembled and cried a little,
so that I felt as if I were attending a sale in a slave market. . . . Jack never appeared as well. For the first time in
his life he did not behave like a fool. In spite of his ridiculous appearance and manners, he was really dignified and
at his ease. Had a word for everyone, looked happy and
self-possessed. . . . Then came the breakfast. . . . It was
all over by 4 o'clock. At 4:41 my train left and here I am.
Yrs. W."

Winthrop was a very lucky man. Possessed of great
charm and wit, he appreciated life's sensuous pleasures,
which he pursued at will. He had wealth enough for his
needs, which were not unextravagant, and a wife who understood those needs and did not suffocate him or them
with demands on his time or attentions. They traveled a
lot together, and he traveled even more without her, seeking relief for his restless, adventurous spirit. Not only was
Winthrop fortunate in having the means to indulge his
every whim (and have enough whims to stay busy), he was
lucky to escape serious harm without ever being particularly concerned about it. There was, for example, his 1893
escapade in Morocco looking for oil. The project was first
proposed to Winthrop's younger brother Willie, but Willie was getting ready to explore new regions of Africa. Wintie agreed to go along with Stephen Bonsal, a newspaper re-

porter and reckless adventurer. Disguised as sportsmen, the two reached Fez without incident before becoming involved in a running battle with a group of Moslem fanatics stirred up by the city governor. Chanler and Bonsal managed to get away and vowed revenge. They made a pitch to the sultan of Morocco, who nursed no fondness for the governor of Fez anyway. The sultan ordered the governor to apologize publicly to the twosome and pay a heavy fine. A ceremony suitable for the occasion was arranged, and when the governor tried to save some face, Winthrop gave him an impassioned philippic only marginally marred by the fact that when Wintie arose from his chair the move set off a music box, which played German beer-hall tunes. The governor showed his true mettle by prostrating himself before the Americans and paying his fine, but Chanler and Bonsal wisely determined that Fez was probably not too safe a haven and, sustaining themselves with the few remaining bottles of champagne they had salvaged, rode for three days through the desert to the coast. There they learned they had been reported killed. Coffins had been ordered. Samples of the oil they smuggled out were sent to a German and an Englishman for analysis. Both agreed the oil was low grade. The German was sure it came from Germany; the Englishman was just as sure it came from Derbyshire.

Exotic adventures and wars were all right for a change of pace—Winthrop even played an active role in World War I as an aide to General Pershing and as an attaché to the American military mission in Italy—but for daily fare, Wintie had a strong preference for chasing hounds on horseback. He once proposed to his wife that they sell their upstate New York home because the hunt club had been disbanded. She demurred, contending that hunting wasn't the only game in the world, but Winthrop explained that,

to him, it was exactly that. In 1927, Wintie fell off his
horse, went into a coma and never regained consciousness.
His last words before he fell had been, "Let's have a little
canter."

William Astor Chanler was four years younger than his
brother Winthrop, who managed to talk his younger
brother into keeping his middle name and allowing
Winthrop to drop his and thereby clear up the confusion
that had resulted from the two brothers' having the same
initials. Winthrop chortled for years that his hotel bills
decreased by half after he dropped the "Astor" from his
name. In a family famed for its wild adventures, Willie
took a back seat to no one. As soon as he reached his majority Willie dropped out of Harvard and mounted a safari
into British East Africa to explore Mount Kilimanjaro and
Masai country. The trip might be considered a training
run, for in 1892, Willie put together the largest American-
led expedition ever—including a hundred and thirty por-
ters, a dozen guards and seven camel drivers—and returned
for a major exploration party. For a two-year sojourn, there
wasn't much in the caravan to remind Willie of civili-
zation, but he did bring along a few splits of champagne, a
copy of Plutarch's *Lives* and two volumes of Robert
Browning. The bellicose Wamsara tribesmen kept the
party on its toes, except for those who had been felled by
the virulent miasma of the Lorian Swamp. Eventually mu-
tiny, too, decimated the ranks, and William was forced to
turn back before his task was accomplished. He was not allowed too much wallowing in dejection, however, for the
world looked upon his exploits as heroic. He had discovered Chanler Falls, and the Smithsonian Institution classified a number of biological finds, among which were a
new antelope and five new reptiles. Harvard gave him an

honorary master's degree. The Royal Geographic Society in London made him an honorary member.

One night, after Willie had won $20,000 in one sitting at Monte Carlo, Henry Stanley, the man who found Dr. Livingstone in the Congo, approached him and told him that King Leopold of Belgium wanted to see him about leading another expedition. Willie met the king and listened to his proposition but turned him down, afraid that he was being asked to lead a pillaging foray rather than an exploring trip. Later events proved those fears well grounded. Willie returned to the United States and took up politics. After a stint in the war in Cuba as an assistant adjutant general on the staff of General Wheeler, he was wafted into Congress by a Tammany breeze. Before long he lost interest in the Washington approach to adventure and retired from public life.

In 1903, at last apparently ready to settle down, he married Minnie Ashley, a gorgeous music hall actress. The family was as enthusiastic about this patently eccentric mating as it had been when Archie married Amélie Rives. William solved that little problem by moving to Paris, where he entertained explorers, hunted and raised horses and Cain in about equal measure. In 1915 he lost a leg in what was perhaps apocryphally described as a bordello brawl also involving Jack Johnson, the first black heavyweight champion of the world. A New York *Times* report more mundanely attributed the loss of his leg to an auto accident. One of William's nephews has told the story of William lunching at Maxim's sometime after this incident and being in something of a hurry. The waiter was unsympathetically slow, and William finally lost his already loose grip on his patience. He unstrapped his artificial leg, picked it up and hurled it across the restaurant, striking the waiter cleanly—one way to attract the man's attention and, one suspects, keep it.

As he aged, William grew if not senile at least crotchety. He became convinced the world was being taken over by Jews, Catholics and/or communists. He joined the U. S. Naval Intelligence Service but probably wasn't much help as his reports must by then have been mainly concerned with how the Jews controlled the Pope and similar fantasies. In 1934, William died at the age of sixty-seven. He left an estate of about $250,000—perhaps a quarter of his own inheritance—to be shared by his widow and two sons, William, Jr., and Sidney Ashley.

Lewis Stuyvesant Chanler, the fourth of the boys, was alone among the men in the family to understand the obligations and responsibilities that accompany wealth and high birth. He grew up to be a lawyer and devoted his practice to defending the indigent. He did it well and began to develop a substantial reputation. He cut a rather bizarre figure as he wandered among the murderers and pickpockets inhabiting the Tombs. He was always impeccably attired and carried himself in a manner that could have been considered arrogant by those who didn't know him. Lewis had married early—at twenty-one—in part because he chafed a bit at being the fourth brother and therefore something of an also-ran in family councils. He was somewhat stuffy in his righteous attitude toward the law and frequently absorbed brutal ribbings from his siblings.

His extraordinary, if less than lucrative, law practice was cut short by his wife's illness, tentatively diagnosed as typhoid. Lewis packed up his lawbooks, his infant son and his wife and moved to Colorado Springs, where the climate would better suit Alice and give her her best chance of recovery. Unable to remain idle while his wife convalesced, Lewis opened a small law practice, causing caustic Wintie to suggest that his brother probably hired a fellow to shoot another fellow and then paid the second fellow for the privilege of acting as his counsel. Alice's health did improve, and soon the family was on its way back to New York. There Lewis continued to build his law practice until October of 1896, when he startled the local legal fraternity by announcing he would never again practice in New York courts. He gave as his reason the feeling he could not escape that he had been the victim of subtle but intentional affronts and biases from certain judges in the criminal courts who, apparently, felt his pro bono publico work offensive. The situation, Lewis said, had grown intolerable. His announcement stirred a good deal of discussion and substantial sympathy for Lewis, who also had a strong private reason for quitting New York. Alice's health was again fragile, and her doctors were recommending that she try a milder climate. The family had decided to take an extended leave of absence from United States shores and settle in England for a time. Lewis took advantage of the decision to study international law at Cambridge and joined enthusiastically in the debates at the Cambridge Union. Alice's health improved dramatically. Lewis' long affection for the underdog was again aroused, this time by the plight of the Irish nationalists. In the general election of 1897, Lewis delivered an impassioned panegyric on the subject that received widespread notice. His English-by-adoption cousin, William Waldorf Astor, was sufficiently concerned to issue a public denial of Lewis' stated position, emphasizing the fact that Lewis did not represent the Astors in his political views. Lewis' efforts on behalf of Irish nationalism were rewarded with the offer of a seat in Parliament, but Lewis declined, realizing that England would never be a permanent home.

Eventually Lewis made his way back to New York,

where he was soon, despite the clearly inappropriate nature of his heritage, a popular figure among the Tammanyites who ran things political in the state. This popularity led to his nomination for lieutenant governor in 1906 on a slate headed by William Randolph Hearst. At the last minute Hearst lost Tammany's support and the governorship went to Charles Evans Hughes, who would eventually become Chief Justice of the U. S. Supreme Court. Chanler and the rest of the Tammany ticket were elected, even as their leader was defeated. Flushed with victory, Lewis began having delusions of grandeur in which he saw himself following that old family friend, Teddy Roosevelt, into the White House. Things were different in those days, and Chanler's presidential aspirations, encouraged by his older brother, U. S. Representative William Astor Chanler, were plugged into political reality with a $16,000 cash outlay to a professional publicist. In return, Lewis received a handful of newspaper clippings and a bill for an additional $20,000. The publicity proved nugatory, and Lewis' barely conceived campaign was aborted. He was, however, not yet through drinking the heady wine of big-time politics and received the Democratic nomination to oppose Hughes in the 1908 gubernatorial race. Although he acquitted himself well enough to surprise more than one political pundit, he never really had a chance against Hughes. After the loss of that election, Lewis won a seat in the state Senate, which he voluntarily relinquished to help a young neighbor and cousin get his political start. The man was Franklin D. Roosevelt. Lewis then returned, on an erratic basis, to his law practice, taking cases on caprice and charging no fee. In his later years he became a supporter of the pacifist movement, a most uncharacteristic cause for a Chanler to espouse.

Robert Winthrop Chanler, the last of the Chanler

males, was every inch as unconventional as his brothers. At an early age Robert displayed a talent for drawing that was exceptional enough to get him into trouble. Cousin Mary, the redoubtable South Carolina relative brought in to govern the unruly Chanler children, accused Robert of lying when he said he had drawn the horse she was admiring. He was placed in solitary confinement by his family, who at Cousin Mary's command ignored him until brother Wintie happened home, was filled in on the situation and in a fit of rationality suggested that Bob draw another horse, which he quickly did. Before he was twenty-one, urged on by his sister-in-law, Amélie Rives Chanler, he was in Paris studying art and falling in love with Julia Chamberlain, whom he married and divorced within a decade. In 1901 he returned to New York in a badly depressed frame of mind and bought a place near Rokeby where he became a devoted hedonist, entertaining farmers, artists and aristocrats alike. Before long he was bitten by the bug of politics and launched an expensive campaign (legend puts a price tag of $20,000 on it) for sheriff of Dutchess County. He was a big, handsome man, nearly six and a half feet tall with wide shoulders, a thick neck, and a big head covered with blond curls. He must have looked the movie version of a fearless lawman. At any rate, he was elected, did a fine job and became known as "Sheriff Bob" within and without the family. He was the only Democratic sheriff in the county's history.

By 1906, Bob had regained his interest in painting and formed a sudden but rather intimate acquaintance with Gertrude Vanderbilt Whitney, the wealthy sculptress and arts patroness who was married to Harry Payne Whitney. After a visit from him, she confided to her journal:

"Put aside the fact that he is a fraud and a flirt, and he is inspiring. To hear him talk about art, to hear his ideas, to see the great truths coming from him is worthwhile. . . . I am sure that he is a genius and to know such a man and to hear him talk freely and truly about himself, that is an experience and one worth having. . . ."

Soon Robert was back in Paris, where he fell under the spell of a sorceress named Lina Cavalieri, who had recently finished with a prince she had mesmerized and relieved of his fortune. For a week Robert and Lina lived together, time enough for her hypnotic ways to have their effect. Robert signed over his entire fortune to her and when he asked for walking-around money, she told him to get a job. Finally he got a friend to loan him money for the trip back to New York. Luckily, he found his trustees had refused to acknowledge his gift to his new wife. She eventually had to settle for a slice rather than the whole pie, and Bob was soon again divorced. The only family member amused by the whole incident was Bob's eldest brother, Archie, who sent off a three-word wire to Bob: "Who's loony now?"

It would have been easy enough for Bob to beat a hasty retreat into obscurity at this point, but instead he began again to paint and paint with a vengeance. The truth is that Bob was more of a decorator than an artist, but his original, bizarre style—sort of a combination of Rousseau and Gaugin—caught on with New York's social and bohemian groups. Robert bought a couple of places on Nineteenth Street, put them together and came up with what was known as the House of Fantasy, filled with exotic birds, fish and, more often than not, people. It was a place for revelry, day and night. Robert knew how to have himself a good time. He did not simply give himself up to worldly pleasures, however. His painting was becoming ever more fashionable. Gertrude Whitney had him paint murals in the bedroom of her lavish Long Island studio. He developed techniques using a variety of unusual media.

An accident that left him lame for life cramped Robert's energetic style, and he began to put on pounds and wax philosophical. He retired to the country. In 1927, just a day before she died in an automobile accident, Robert was reported engaged to the mysterious dancer, Isadora Duncan. Three years later he himself died, leaving an estate of slightly less than $500,000 to his two daughters.

Especially considering that they lived in an era when women were usually seen but seldom heard, the three Chanler sisters led lives that rivaled their brothers' for originality and excitement. In any event, all three wound up marrying intriguing individuals and displaying a broadness of vision that belied their careful, rather cloistered upbringing. All three grew up under Cousin Mary's strict eye at Rokeby and were sent to England for a final polishing. Unexposed in their youth to the bright lights and glitter of New York, as young ladies they were taken under the wing of their "Aunt Lina," Mrs. William Astor, who ran things social in New York. She saw to it, with the help of a dozen other relatives, that the girls shed their country ways and became comfortable in the company of New York's upper crust. One of the first big social experiences for the girls was not a significant success. Their brother and his wife, Winthrop and Daisy, took a house in New York and gave a sort of coming-out party for the girls. As Winthrop's and Daisy's daughter, Laura Chanler White, recalls, invitations were sent out to the people on her grandmother Maddie Chanler's list. Maddie had been dead for years. She had died young, and therefore many of her contemporaries, on whom she had once called, were still alive. Puzzled but polite, they doddered to the Chanler home at the appointed hour, sipped a cup of tea or a glass of sherry and doddered home again, still puzzled and still polite. As debuts go, this was not a particularly sparkling or auspicious one. Aunt Lina saw to it that whatever shortcomings the girls suffered in their social development were compensated for by her sponsorship.

The eldest of the Chanler women was Elizabeth, who received her English education mostly before her Rokeby one. She was, along with Archie and Wintie, abroad at school when their father died. Already she was promising to become an extraordinary sibling among extraordinary siblings. She was growing pretty, poised and bright when, at the age of thirteen, she was struck by a mysterious disease of the hip. She couldn't walk. She went to the best physician she could find with the help of her guardians, but he offered no help, and she became very depressed. She had most of her life to look forward to, but what sort of life could it be? At this time—it was 1879—her grandfather, Sam Ward, still in disfavor with the Astors, was riding one of the peaks of his roller coaster life and was visiting nobility in England. He prevailed upon Elizabeth's guardians, who harbored a dread that her disease might be fatal, to allow him a visit. Elizabeth would never forget it. Her grandfather was a bright, shiny, promising presence whose enthusiasm for life was infectious. They talked not at all about the disease, the diagnosis or the prognosis. He lavished expensive but thoughtful presents upon his grandchild and renewed in her the joy of living. Elizabeth went to Paris where doctors undertook to prevent a permanent curvature of the spine by strapping her to a board. For the next two years she was virtually a complete invalid, but she bore her troubles with remarkable serenity, developing what a biographer has called "a patient inflexibility that would become her dominant trait." Her courage paid off. She was able to walk with crutches. Then she was able to walk without them. She would never fully recover and on occasion would require a cane, but by 1882 it was clear that she would not be an invalid all her life. She returned to New York, where Cousin Mary reminded her of the futility in challenging God's will. The one step she could not take, of course, was to the altar, and she must never even think about such a move.

As time passed, a situation developed that virtually assured Elizabeth's celibacy. She fell in love with the husband of her best friend. From their first meeting, she and her sister Margaret had formed a close friendship with the John Jay Chapmans, a Boston couple who had moved to New York. Minna Chapman was half Italian, a passionate woman who would seem at first blush to have been Elizabeth's opposite in temperament, but the two immediately became warm friends. John Jay Chapman was a witty, urbane fellow from an exceptional family background who had become deeply involved in municipal government reform and was a principal organizer of the Good Government Clubs that had started springing up in response to corruption gone wild. He was a lawyer by training, but a man of letters by preference. He enjoyed reading aloud and was good at it. One night Margaret watched the face of her older sister and suddenly knew what neither Elizabeth nor Chapman had yet guessed—her sister was in love. The potential for scandal and heartbreak imbedded in that fact was enough to spur Margaret to action. Taking the initiative usually held by Elizabeth, Margaret whisked her sister away for a long trip around the world, featuring stops in India and Japan. The two ladies stopped in England on the way and picked up letters of introduction from important people to other important people, letters that promised the sisters would receive red-carpet treatment wherever they went. Elizabeth allowed herself to be led along and spent hours compiling a massive travel diary. They reached Calcutta, near the end of their India tour, and were met with the solemn news that Minna Chapman had died ten days after the birth of her third child, a son. John Jay Chapman had written the letter with the news and urged them not to disrupt their journey on his account because all his and Minna's friends had rallied around and "done what mortals could do." That exhortation was more than Elizabeth was willing to endure. She swiftly retook her old initiative and had the sisters returning to New York as quickly as she could book passage.

Chapman proved to be in worse shape than his outwardly calm, even cheerful, demeanor indicated. The eldest of his three children was only six. He disliked being a lawyer. He was deeply in debt. And the rock of love to which he had clung was now gone. The return of Elizabeth was followed almost ineluctably by the flowering of their love. The couple made quiet plans to marry. Elizabeth was about to take the biggest step of her life. Not only had she long been steeling herself to life without a husband, she was also falling in love with a man who was surely most difficult to live with. His passion on occasion could exceed all reasonable bounds. As a young man at Harvard courting Minna he had struck a certain young man, imagining the man had slighted his bride-to-be. Upon learning he had been mistaken, Chapman took the offending fist and thrust it into a fire, leaving it there so long that it had to be amputated. But perhaps age had tempered his passion. He was now thirty-six and she thirty-two. They brought a subdued maturity to their love that gave it a chance. They were married in 1898, settled on a farm that was adjacent to the Rokeby estate and spent much time traveling in Europe. Chapman gave up the law and devoted his time to writing essays and literary criticisms. Also letters. No less a literary figure than Edmund Wilson once called Chapman the greatest letter writer in America.

Margaret Livingston Chanler was probably the most like the brothers Chanler of the three sisters. She possessed an independent, pioneer spirit that surfaced early but did not really shine until the Spanish-American War, in which she began as an administrator for a group of Red Cross nurses. The United States has never fought a war for which it was so ill prepared. Everywhere Margaret encountered sloth, indifference and incompetence and everywhere she smote these draconian demons by the force of her will. She combined vast compassion with a strength of personality that had men of much higher rank aquiver. At one point she found herself in Puerto Rico with her twenty nurses running a makeshift hospital ship for soldiers overcome by typhoid and other tropical diseases from which healthy men cringed in terror. Daily an officer would run up the yellow quarantine flag; daily Margaret would have a patient bring it down again because the sight of it so disturbed the patients, many of whom were unaware of the nature of their illnesses. At night the corpses that had accumulated during the day and been stowed out of sight in the lifeboats were rowed out to sea and buried secretly to keep the living patients from panic. At length the ship was ordered to sail for Virginia with the nurses. Margaret was not convinced her work had been finished and since she was under no special orders, slipped ashore before the ship sailed. Of the twenty nurses who had accompanied her to Puerto Rico and sailed back to Virginia, eight contracted typhoid and died.

After asking a great many questions, Margaret finally learned the whereabouts of a putative American hospital. What she found when she got there was plenty of hospital patients, all sardined into a one-room, dirt-floor schoolhouse. This she managed to get closed down, with the patients being transferred to another hospital. Meanwhile she had discovered that officers had no hospital and immediately set about to rectify the situation by renting the largest available house and then overwhelming the landlord, who attempted to cancel the lease after discovering the use to which the house was being put. Margaret took on the duties of night nurse herself. She and a friend, although they did not seek it, began to attract considerable attention with their good works, which continued until the war's end. She returned to New York to discover she was known amongst readers of the Hearst and Pulitzer newspapers as "the angel of Puerto Rico."

One thing Margaret had become an expert on was the nursing of soldiers in the field, and now she began agitating as only a Chanler could for the creation of an army nursing corps. The surgeon general didn't see things Margaret's way and legislation that would set up a nursing corps was running into rumors of exotic behavior by Red Cross nurses in the Philippines. On her own, Margaret determined to see for herself, set sail for Manila and filed a scathing report back to Washington, clearing the nurses and deploring the hospital conditions she found. Her trip carried her to Japan and China, where similar situations existed. She filed similar reports. When she got back, she found that she had stirred up quite a bubbly pot. Her unofficial sponsor, Secretary of War Elihu Root, was embarrassed by the charges of interference being leveled at Margaret by the military establishment and scolded her for not being more discreet and diplomatic in her reports. The nurses' corps legislation was defeated, but Margaret triumphed in the end when Root incorporated such a corps in his general reorganization of the Army, which was adopted.

Margaret went on to become president of the New York Women's Municipal League (predecessor of the League of Women Voters) and to marry Richard Aldrich, music critic for the New York *Times*. She had always felt a special attachment to Rokeby and as it became increasingly apparent that none of her siblings was likely ever to undertake the heavy burden of maintaining the place, she bought out their interest seven years before her marriage and took over Rokeby.

The last of the Chanler women was Alida Beekman Chanler, a lady whose beauty once caught the eye of Nicholas II at a ball in London before he became Russia's last Tsar. Family legend would have you believe that Nicholas was so taken with Alida's beauty that his eventual bride, who became Alexandra, was chosen because she so closely resembled Alida in looks. At any rate, Alida was darkly gorgeous, slightly mystical but generally a quite proper, religious young woman when she fell in love with a young New York lawyer and sportsman, Christopher Temple Emmet, who came from a well-known Irish family involved in the cause of Irish freedom. Her family teased Alida unmercifully, telling everyone she was marrying Temple because he was the first to propose. It was not so; she was very much in love. The wedding took place in the fall of 1896 at Rokeby, which had been transformed for the occasion under the direction of Stanford White, who provided Neapolitan strolling minstrels and a variety of touches that made the affair one to remember. Laura Chanler White, then nine and eventually the bride of White's son, remembers missing the wedding because she was with her parents in Europe and the telegram they received in Paris telling of Alida's impending marriage started out with the news that a young relative had taken his first steps, which so excited everyone that the remainder of the telegram was never read. It is true that Daisy Chanler, Laura's mother, was not at the wedding, having been called to Europe by her mother's serious illness, but

Laura's father, Winthrop, was the man who gave his sister away at the wedding.

Alida was perhaps the quietest of the Chanlers. She did have one rule, according to Mrs. White, her niece. No divorcee could dine at Alida's house. While the rule was not, strictly speaking, broken, Mrs. White recalls a time when her aunt had tea in her house with a divorcee. Mrs. White asked about the incident, and Alida told her that everything was quite proper because Alida had kept her hat on. Alida and Temple were among the few relatives who were sympathetic to Madeleine Astor after she lost her husband in the *Titanic* disaster. The Emmets took the young widow in for two weeks after the tragedy. It was not every day that a Chanler could do an Astor a favor; and in the Chanler household that fact must have galled. The Chanler consensus, after all, had always been that the only thing the Astors had more than they was that filthy lucre—without which the Chanlers would have been a very different family.

CHAPTER 8

Despite their color and excitement, the Chanlers did not contribute much to the power and glory, not to mention wealth, of the Astor family. They were spenders, not accumulators or even conservators. While they are by no means the only Astor story in Rhinebeck today, it is Chanler heritage that predominates, if for no other reason than that quite a number of Chanler descendants have chosen to remain in and around Rhinebeck while few Astors have.

Ferncliff, built in 1874 by William Astor, Jr., and greatly expanded by his son, Colonel John Jacob IV, and his grandson, Vincent, has now become the site of a home for the aged run by the Carmelite Sisters. The main house has been torn down. A new high-rise edifice houses the elderly. The magnificent casino built by Colonel Astor in 1903, one of Stanford White's most successful designs, is now used as a residence for the sisters. The indoor tennis court is decaying and is no longer played on, the area being used as storage space. The indoor pool still functions, a luxury the sisters don't seem to find sinful. The barns, grand stone structures, stand in urgent need of restoration, and the rumors drift about Rhinebeck that the barn area along with a part of the vast acreage of Ferncliff—2,800 acres at one point under Vincent—may be sold to someone demonstrating a viable plan to save the barns. It takes only a modest imagination to picture the almost numinous magic that once was Ferncliff.

To the north, between Ferncliff and Rokeby, lie two small estates. Marienruh is as charming an estate as can be found in the area. Its 100 acres and mansion belonged to Alice Astor, Vincent's younger sister, after her marriage to Serge Obolensky. Marienruh is now owned by a Lutheran organization. One of Alice's daughters by a later marriage, Mrs. Emily Glandbard, now divides her time between more modest Rhinebeck quarters and New York. In Rhinebeck she is considered the closest thing to a real Astor remaining. Orlot is the second estate, modest as estates go but not insubstantial and boasting one of the most glorious views of the Hudson River in the neighborhood. The property belonged to the first Chanler, John Winthrop, who left it to his eldest son, Archie. He in turn left it to his nephew, Lewis Stuyvesant Chanler, Jr., whose son, Bronson W. ("Bim") Chanler, lives there now. Bim is perhaps the most successful of the present-generation Chanlers from a financial standpoint. He recently sold Orlot to a West German financier for a large but undisclosed sum. He is a big, friendly man, a former captain of the Harvard crew.

Stein Valetje, sold by the Delano family in 1959, is next as one travels north along the eastern bank of the Hudson. Then comes Rokeby. Two grandsons of Margaret Aldrich and their families now live there. It is not the same place Margaret knew as a little girl growing up, when singing and music filled the house, with Margaret on the piano, Elizabeth on guitar and the sweet mezzo voices of Alida and Elizabeth. Together they knew perhaps 125 songs. Three grandchildren and a daughter-in-law inherited Rokeby when Margaret died. They also inherited about $50,000 each. That is an amount of money that doesn't last long if one tries to maintain Rokeby. Today the outside of Rokeby bespeaks neglect, although it did get a new $12,000 roof several years back. The paint is flaking, the shutters sag. The 450 acres that make up the estate are not manicured as they once were. Inside, the formal part of the house retains a certain dusty elegance. Much about it is fine.

Winthrop Aldrich, one of the two brothers now living there, works in Albany for the state Environmental Conservation Department. He has become more or less the family historian and has been very active in seeking the preservation of Rokeby. In 1975, Rokeby was placed on the National Register of Historic Places and in recent years Wintie has tried to interest a variety of institutions in restoring the place. It is all he and his brother Ricky can do to pay the property taxes on Rokeby, which were $18,000 in 1980. While Wintie acts as keeper of the history, his brother, who neighbors say borders on genius, speaks a half dozen or so languages fluently but is very shy and seems to prefer communication with nature to conversation with strangers, does his best to farm Rokeby. It is not a lucrative proposition. To spend the night in one of the great, square, high-ceilinged bedrooms and wander the living room, the dining room and the exquisite, eight-sided library is to catch an elusive, fleeting glimpse of past glories, but the two Aldrich families who live there now live not in the lap but under the heel of luxury. It is touching to listen to Winthrop and understand how much of his life is tied up in Rokeby, in fertilizing his roots and preserving the past. Once, a few years ago, some friends stayed at Rokeby while the Aldriches were away. To make the room work more efficiently, they moved the kitchen table—not much, just a bit. It was the first thing the Aldriches noticed and re- marked upon when they returned. They were not angry, just a little puzzled. After all, the kitchen table had always been in that particular spot as long as there had been a kitchen. Moving it was, well, tampering with history.

In a ghastly pink cottage built by his mother for her widowhood lives the Chanler descendant most reminiscent of the original brood—Chanler Chapman, son of Elizabeth and John Jay. The cottage is part of Sylvania Farms, whose lovely mansion house is empty, the tennis court overgrown. Not many years ago the house was rented every summer and provided much-needed income. Chanler Chapman is enough of a character to have warranted a feature story in a 1977 issue of *Sports Illustrated*. Like his father before him, Chanler is a man of letters, publisher and editor of the Bar- rytown *Explorer*, an erratic weekly that contains such Chapman epigrams as, "A sunset may be seen at any time if you drink two quarts of ale slowly on an empty stomach."

Chanler ran a gambling den while he was at Harvard in 1921. Says he and his partners would take in maybe $400 a week. After their customers left around 3 A.M., Chanler would get blind drunk. After college he somehow qualified for a job as a New York *Times* reporter. He spent a year there playing cards and quit. During World War II he volunteered as an ambulance driver for the American Field Service and was on his way to Egypt when his ship was tor- pedoed. Chanler survived after spending a week in a life- boat. He has also worked as a radio interviewer. One time while on vacation in Puerto Rico he interviewed the mayor of San Juan and, for no apparent reason, kept calling him the mayor of Montreal.

In recent years Chanler has been growing cantankerous and eccentric. He frequently totes a slingshot and used to enjoy shooting ball bearings at his cousin Bim Chanler's jeep. In 1977 he bought 600 pounds of gravel for $4.00, figuring he would have a cheap five-year supply of ammunition for his slingshot. His neighbors are probably just as glad Chanler likes slingshots. He once had 115 guns. Chanler enjoys taking verbal potshots, too, especially at relatives. Of Ricky Aldrich he has said that the poor fellow left Poland in 1966 after he was caught selling Italian plastic raincoats on the black market. Of Saul Bellow, who rented a place from Chanler while teaching at nearby Bard College, Chanler is equally scornful. Chapman is supposed to have inspired the protagonist in Bellow's *Henderson the Rain King*, about which Chanler says, "It's his best book, but he is the dullest writer I've ever read." Wintie Aldrich is not spared. Says Chanler, Wintie has "the personality of an unsuccessful undertaker."

Noting that Chapman's son is the postman for Barrytown, Wintie recalls Chapman's father's claim to fame and remarks on a certain continuity of tradition from grandfather as great writer of letters to grandson as great carrier of them. Touché.

The Chanler connection of the Astor family is a fascinating and fitting paradigm of the peak of an era. The eight Chanler children lived in a style—saucy, carefree, self-centered—that was a little reminiscent of Madame Pompadour and her "*Après nous le déluge.*" Their descendants have inherited much of the individualism and charm possessed by those eight but the means and the ambiance are gone. Whether one sees today's clan as quixotic, even pathetic, or noble, defiant and touchingly brave depends not on the family but on one's prejudices. They are faintly anachronistic, probably misunderstood. And, excepting perhaps Wintie Aldrich, don't need or ask for understanding, not, anyway, if privacy must be scarificed for it.

PART IV

PART IV

CHAPTER 9

For nearly a century and a half Newport, Rhode Island, was a quiet, unpretentious summer resort. Its climate was said to cure insomnia, ease the pain for teething children and contribute mysteriously but substantially to longevity. Southerners, particularly families from Charleston, South Carolina, had been going to Newport since 1729. As late as 1852, only four New Yorkers had summer homes in Newport. In 1834, Philip Hone, the New York diarist, described a visit to Newport in which he noted the remarkable popularity of the joggle board or seesaw.

The Civil War decimated the Southern economy, and the annual northerly migration of Southerners to Newport became but a trickle. About this time New York discovered Newport. Mrs. August Belmont is generally considered the first of the major social lights to have settled upon Newport as a summer residence. (The Belmonts were pioneers of a sort. Their move to a Long Island estate in the early 1880s began a trend there, too.) Ward McAllister, well before he became enshrined as society's major-domo, was worming his way into high-class hearts with dazzling divertissements on his Newport farm. By the time Mrs. William Astor puchased Beechwood in 1880, the die had been cast. However the tippy-top of the upper crust of American society chose to live, it would be reflected in the bricks and mortar and the atmosphere of Newport. The world and history have seen comparable extravagance before, but inevitably as tribute to a religion, to a royal family or to death. Newport was a monument to pleasure, an example of architectural one-upmanship, the ultimate statement in an era that believed you were what you spent. By the 1890s summertime Newport along the famous Cliffwalk that skirts the seaside bluff down to which the vast lawns roll was chockablock with Astors, Vanderbilts, Goelets, Belmonts and lesser social luminaries, who nonetheless could blind ordinary mortals with their shine and glitter. The artist, if that is the word, who most perfectly reflected the tastes, if that is the word, of the day was Richard Morris Hunt, an architect who had spent nine years at the Ecole des Beaux Arts in Paris and returned to the United States to copy and elaborate upon European castles and châteaux for the pleasure of his patrons. Price tags of several million dollars were standard. Edifices were constructed that would be impossible to duplicate today at any price, and for the most part that is just as well. Novelist Henry James has been quoted on the subject of Newport's "cottages" and he pulled no punches: ". . . there is absolutely nothing to be done; nothing but to let them stand there always, vast and blank, for reminder to those concerned of the prohibited degrees of witlessness, and of the peculiarly awkward vengeances of affronted proportion and discretion."

The ne plus ultra of all this was a Vanderbilt, not an Astor, monument, built over two years from 1893 to 1895 at a cost that has been estimated at $11 million. Hunt was, of course, the architect. The Breakers, as the place is known, is not a cozy home. The ceiling in the main hall is a staggering 50 feet high. That in the dining room is 45 feet high. The breakfast room is a more elegant dining room than all but a small handful of private eating spaces in the country. The kitchen is as large as an average four-bedroom house. The scale is nowhere human, not even in the bedrooms. Cornelius Vanderbilt, eldest son of William H. and grandson of the old Commodore, was the man who paid the bills. He died in 1899.

Actually, by Newport-cottage standards, the Astor homes are rather modest. THE Mrs. Astor's brother-in-law, John Jacob Astor III, bought Beaulieu, for example, in May of 1879 for $201,000. At that, it wasn't much of a bargain. Even though a Vanderbilt bought it in 1933 and spent $250,000 putting it in shape, it sold in 1958 for $60,000. Beechwood, the home of Mrs. Astor, was an even less impressive structure than Beaulieu, but after a decade had proved Newport more than a fad, Mrs. Astor went to work sprucing up her place. In 1890 she added a stunning ballroom onto the house and made a trip to Europe where she bought a dining room in England and a music room in France. She had them shipped over to Newport, and also hired a host of Italian craftsmen to help get everything back together properly. The availability of these workers is said to have made building the Breakers a much easier and quicker job. By the time Mrs. Astor had finished with them, her husband had spent $2 million. Beechwood was still a mere mansion among magnificent châteaux, but in many ways it was the most tasteful, even exquisite of the important homes along Bellevue Avenue.

While Beaulieu and Beechwood were the principal Astor homes during the halcyon days of Newport, over the years there have been several others. Maddie Chanler, granddaughter of the first William Astor, began spending her summers at Cliff Lawn in the 1860s and may have been

the first of the Astors to make Newport a home away from
home. Her aunt, Alida Astor Carey, also had a big villa
there. James J. Van Alen, a son-in-law of Mrs. Astor, was a
major figure among Newport's socially distinguished. Invitations to his Wakehurst were much prized. John Jacob
Astor VI, the son born posthumously to Colonel Astor
after he went down on the *Titanic*, was the last named
Astor to have a Newport cottage. It was called Chetwode
and burned to the ground some years ago. Several others
within the family had places in Newport at various times.
According to Ward McAllister, who could not help notic-
ing the postbellum changes in Newport and elsewhere, society went European, importing its clothes and its cooks,
not to mention its manners. He pointed out that in 1862
there weren't more than one or two men who spent more
than $60,000 on living and entertaining and not more than
half a dozen chefs in private families. May King Van
Rensselaer, a member in good standing of high society who
came along a generation or so later and therefore had the
benefit of retrospect, arrived at a different and more likely
conclusion. For the last two generations, she wrote in 1924,
money had become the prerequisite for membership in the
exclusive social circles and "birth and breeding, ability and
achievement are minor considerations. . . ." One thing
the Astors had was plenty of money. For instance,
Baroness Boreel, daughter of Dorothea Langdon and therefore a granddaughter of the original John Jacob Astor, died
in 1895 in Nice, France. Her grandfather was not a man
who divided things equally among sons and daughters. He
believed in primogeniture; yet the baroness left a fortune that generated an annual income of $1 million. A lot
of Astors could afford the prices at Newport.

An article in a 1907 magazine details those prices, noting
for openers that Newport was about twice as expensive as
New York. Someone looking to rent a cottage from June to

September might have paid as much as $15,000. People in Newport thought little about spending $100,000 for a stone wall around their home or transplanting a tree it took six weeks to dig up and move. To throw a respectable party required an outlay of about $15,000. Mrs. Cornelius Vanderbilt, Jr., once closed up a Broadway hit musical for two days and brought the entire production to Newport for a performance. Little things like flowers could run up to $1,000 a week. Meat ran about $800 a month, not counting special entertaining. Colonel Astor kept seventeen cars at once, but four were generally deemed sufficient. The *Nourmahal* was not your average yacht, which was a good thing, for it cost $20,000 a month to run. An average Newport staff payroll ran about $23,800 a year, not bad considering one was talking about twenty-four people—the chef, the sous-chef, the private secretary, the tutor, the governess, two nurses, a housekeeper, five maids, a head coachman, a second and third coachman, a chauffeur, a butler, a second butler, a head gardener and four helpers. Here's the way you might break down the average multimillionaire's yearly expenses:

Running the New York and Newport houses	$30,000
Entertainment	50,000
Yacht	50,000
Stable and stud farm (30 men)	40,000
Grounds (20 men)	20,000
Two other pieds-à-terre (Palm Beach, the Adirondacks)	20,000
Clothes	20,000
Pocket money	50,000
Automobiles	10,000
Travel	10,000
Grand total	$300,000

One would think, would one not, that one should be able to make do on that amount with a minimum of complaint, and yet one well-known Newport couple at the time were constantly bemoaning the difficulty of making ends meet on a combined income of $370,000 a year, more than $1,000 a day. What's more, they found plenty of sympathetic ears into which to pour their tale of woe. Not everyone approved, of course. Mrs. Van Rensselaer recalled rather scornfully a dinner James J. Van Alen gave in the late 1880s for a dozen people in which he had great difficulty avoiding the taboo of placing a divorced wife next to a former husband. She also deplored the fact that Alexander Graham Bell spent many summers in Newport completely ignored by society. "It is doubtful," said she, "whether there are more useless and empty ways of spending money in the world than can be found at Newport." A friend of hers described Newport as "a battleground for those who have social campaigns to wage."

In 1892, John Winthrop Auchincloss set Newport abuzz with a sort of non-campaign. This scion of society built Hammersmith Farm not off Bellevue Avenue but on Narragansett Bay, causing no small amount of consternation among some of those who had invested on Bellevue and now wondered whether they had made an egregious error. Peace of mind was not, apparently, one of the things money could buy. Despite the front of solidarity and coziness they put to the public, the nobs and nabobs of Newport were essentially lonely, each left to his own illusions and doubts. Thus could a junior Cornelius Vanderbilt write in 1956 about the 1885 death of William H. Vanderbilt, principal heir of the Commodore, and of the $200 million fortune he left: "Such a staggering fortune made the Lorillards, the Harrimans, even the Goulds and the Astors appear to be very small potatoes indeed." William's two major heirs—Cornelius II and William K.—received $67 million and $65 million respectively, tidy sums but hardly enough to leave William, Jr., or John Jacob III, the comparable members of the Astor family, thinking of themselves as tiny spuds. The Astor/Vanderbilt parallels are striking. Both family founders had namesake sons who were demented. Both had sons named William who preserved and increased the family fortune, which was, in both cases, divided in the third generation.

Besides, in a world of neat distinctions, the Vanderbilts were arrivistes. The Astors still ruled the social roost. If Mrs. William Astor was American society's Queen Victoria, her son-in-law, James J. Van Alen, was the Prince of Wales. Emily, his wife, died during childbirth in 1881, and for the next several decades James was the most eligible widower on the East Coast. He was rich, dashing, elegant, sporting, charming—everything a girl could possibly want, in short, except perhaps constant. The newspapers never tired of reporting his antics. He seldom failed to give them a story, and if he did, they'd make one up, like the New York *World* exclusive saying Van Alen gave $50,000 to Grover Cleveland in 1892, hoping to buy the Italian ambassadorship. He didn't. The most frequent reports speculated on what fortunate female would catch him and tie the matrimonial knot. Usually it was a widow. At various times his name was linked amorously with those of Mrs. George Law, the Countess Fabriocotti, Mrs. William Leeds, Mrs. Henry Redmond, Mrs. Pedar Bruguiere and even Ava Willing Astor after her divorce. If women were susceptible to his many charms, he was no less susceptible to theirs. An oft-repeated reason for his always managing to escape the altar was the dedicated vigilance of his daughter May, who, it was said, even went so far as to develop ap-

pendicitis once to abort one of her father's flirtations that
gave signs of becoming serious.

The other Van Alen exploits receiving newspaper coverage concerned either his entertaining or his outdoor activities. Usually descriptions of his parties dwelt on their
elegance and the prominence of the guests. He divided his
time between his English country estate, Rushton Hall,
in Northamptonshire and his Newport manse, spending
an increasing amount of time abroad after 1919 because,
he said, of the Eighteenth Amendment (Prohibition) and
the resultant "lack of liberty" in America. His shooting
parties at Rushton Hall, at which nobility in droves and
occasional royalty were Van Alen guests, were described
as "princely." Van Alen was equally at home entertaining
children. His lawn party for a grandson in Newport, complete with tents, pony carts and a band, was rated a big success, although some of the adults were suffering visibly
from the effects of the entertainment of the evening before, a housewarming at the T. Suffern Tailers'. If the
parties he gave exuded taste and elegance, those given for
him were not always so decorous. Given the source—
Colonel Mann and his *Town Topics*—the description must
be flavored a bit with salt, but even so, it must have been
quite an evening. Ward McAllister was, says Mann, made
to get down on all fours and was dragged about by his
goatee. The women kept their masks on at this affair, billed
as a surprise party for Van Alen, but they were guilty of
"liberal revelations of other extremities." The servants finished up the wine and cavorted about the lawn while some
among the party decided to go out and paint the town red,
were carried away in their exuberance and wound up paying fines assessed by the local judiciary.

A brief item appeared in the newspaper on May 31,
1910: "James J. Van Alen, son-in-law of the late Mrs.

William Astor, left this morning with a retinue of servants for his annual salmon fishing trip in Canada. He will return in July." Return he did, and the story was a much bigger one. Van Alen had killed salmon totaling 1,869 pounds in about three and a half weeks of fishing. "That the weight is exact there is no doubt," the story said, "as Mr. Van Alen's secretary weighed every one of the fish." Even in those days of lesser environmental damage, that was a lot of fish, and Van Alen's friends were trying to establish that he had set some sort of record.

When he wasn't fishing or partying, Van Alen could probably be found exercising. He was a strong swimmer and was always swimming over from Newport to Gooseberry Island where there was a club to which he was frequently invited for lunch. He would jump in the water, swim the three quarters of a mile to the island, get a rubdown and have lunch. At the age of sixty-two he negotiated the two miles between Bailey's Beach and Gooseberry Island in two hours. The newspaper reported that he used the breast stroke and that, although he had a lifeguard following him in a boat, the precaution proved unnecessary. The water was a chilly 63 degrees. Had he lived today, Van Alen would surely have been a jogger. As it was, he told one newspaper that the secret of good health was open-air exercise and that he walked constantly, morning, noon and night, paced by his chauffeur in the automobile.

Van Alen could, on occasion, clamber to the heights of absurdity. Once, for example, he attempted to blend a black butler and a black chef into his staff at Northamptonshire. His reasoning was unclear. The Louisville *Courier-Journal* suggested he was trying to create an atmosphere of Southern, ante-bellum plantation life, a suggestion that appears on the surface farfetched. At any rate, it didn't work. The other servants harried the two blacks so that they were reluctant to eat or go to bed, and eventually Van Alen was forced to let them go. Another time, Van Alen built a $50,000 wall around Wakehurst and said it was to keep the deer in.

If Van Alen had the most fun at Newport during its heyday, his mother-in-law had the most clout. It is a remarkable tribute to her single-mindedness of purpose that it was a rare social occasion indeed at which she did not find her place at the right of the host despite her plain looks and uninspiring personality. She had a few skirmishes during her reign. Some foolish woman would be egged on to challenge Mrs. Astor's authority, do so and then slip quietly and quickly out of the picture, a victim of the queen's displeasure. To make even a dent in the wall Newport society turned outward toward the public, one needed the approbation of Mrs. Astor, and even if she was favorably disposed toward you, things didn't necessarily open up overnight. Her power was not absolute. There were those who made it even with her disapproval, although few ever stayed on if the disapproval proved more than temporary. One of the gossip columnists' favorite topics was when Mrs. Astor's reign would end and by whom she would be replaced. The reign did not really in any final, absolute or visible way end until her death in 1908, and the truth is, no one can be said to have replaced her.

She was not all tea and socials. A granddaughter recalls: "She must have been quite a sporting young woman. She once told me that she had gone to a prize fight and enjoyed it, and she used to chaperone Margaret Langdon in Newport when she went out sailing in windy weather with nautical admirers, and Grandmother was the only chaperone intrepid enough to go. She was never seasick." Given Mrs. Astor's standard reply when asked where her husband was —"Off on his yacht. If only I were a better sailor . . ."

—that last observation is particularly interesting. But she would always have preferred the little white lie to a truth that was unsettling or unseemly. Good form and appearances may not have been everything to her, but there wasn't very much else.

The challenges to her supremacy—especially during its height from the late 1870s to the late 1890s—came mainly from within the family, although occasionally a Vanderbilt would be said to be awaiting her chance. In more than one instance the challenge was a manufacture of the newspapers more than an active undertaking by the alleged challenger. In this game, of course, Colonel Mann figured excessively if not prominently. In December of 1889, Mann called the gown Mrs. Astor wore to the Assembly Ball the "most costly and superb specimen of the modern dressmaker's art" ever seen in New York and speculated that she was consolidating her position against the likes of Mrs. Cornelius Vanderbilt and Mrs. William C. Whitney. Mann figured the number and cost of the private parties that season was clear evidence of the struggle, adding Mrs. Bradley Martin to the contestants on the grounds that the Martins might well spend $50,000 for an upcoming affair. The Vanderbilts would spend that way too, but Mrs. Astor was never so extravagant, Mann said, noting that the Whitneys had the advantage of a new $125,000 ballroom. One could not, for that matter, dismiss the W. K. Vanderbilts, who were probably the biggest spenders of them all, and had just the year before purchased four acres in Newport for $200,000, outbidding the Astors, who owned the properties on either side. It would be several years before Mrs. Stuyvesant Fish mounted her campaign to take over social leadership. The main challenge from without at this time was from Mrs. Cornelius Vanderbilt, although one could occasionally hear an objection such as, "Yes, but the

Vanderbilts have no great-grandmothers." From within, the challenge was from Mrs. William Waldorf Astor, who was loath to make it but was forced to do so by a husband determined to see her rightful position as head of the family after the death of her mother-in-law established, regardless of how Aunt Caroline viewed their respective places. Aunt Caroline might well have said about her nephew and his wife what she said when asked about young people at her balls: "I like to have them come, but they must look after themselves."

She certainly was capable of looking after herself. In the summer of 1888 a young lady of whom Mrs. Astor did not fully approve persisted in playing Circe to her son's Odysseus. Mrs. Astor quickly demonstrated her grasp of Hera's role, and the would-be siren soon found no one in Newport would talk to her. The rivalry between Aunt Caroline and her nephew's wife, Mary, was inevitable and could have been avoided only with an active effort to do so by Mary. That, given her husband's position on the matter, was impossible. The situation was difficult for others, too, as they tried to do the proper thing. The Centennial Ball of 1889 to mark the anniversary of the United States Constitution was a major affair, and the committee had a host of eligible ladies ready to dance the first quadrille but could choose only sixteen. An Astor surely had to be among the sixteen, but which one? By the tradition of primogeniture, Mrs. William Waldorf Astor was the first lady. Her calling cards were marked "Mrs. Astor," while Aunt Caroline's were marked "Mrs. Wm. Astor." But no one would dare question the social ascendancy of Aunt Caroline. The committee solved the problem by asking them both. It was not long after that that Caroline had her calling cards changed to read, "Mrs. Astor." The lines of battle had been drawn. They were further delineated when Caroline told all her friends to send their letters to her addressed simply, "Mrs. Astor, Newport." The postal confusion became excruciating when her nephew decreed that all mail so addressed should be delivered to his wife.

Naturally enough, *Town Topics* was among the chief chroniclers of the war. Early in 1890, noting that a Sunday newspaper had suggested that Aunt Caroline abdicate her throne in favor of Mary and that the primary reason for this suggestion was that Mary could waltz while Caroline could not, Colonel Mann pointed out what he said everyone knew, that "social leaders are made, not born," and that Mary didn't want the job. Society was, however, getting too big and democratic for a single ruler, Mann opined.

Aunt Caroline must have felt herself besieged, at least at first. She found herself listed against her expressed wishes as "Mrs. Wm. Astor" in the list of patrons for the Casino ball in Newport, one of the season's annual highlights. She denounced the ball committee, withdrew her patronage and refused to speak to the committee members. Mary meanwhile was forced into social retirement by the death of her father-in-law, but the battle raged nonetheless. *Town Topics* reported that the young people in church one Sunday refused to give Caroline more than one seat, forcing her to move to another pew to accommodate her ample posterior. Very rude, Colonel Mann decreed, and a clear sign the young people were siding with Mary.

Maybe so, but the young people didn't count for all that much among the upper strata of Newport society, and it was not too very long before William Waldorf's demeanor had changed once again. At first he had been outraged by his aunt's defiance of his rightful position. Then he became determined. Now he was furious. The propriety of his stance, the righteousness of his character, the straightness of his paths, all should have been obvious to everyone. And here he was the victim of animadversion upon tendentious animadversion. He was misunderstood and underappreciated, and maybe England wouldn't be any better but it certainly wouldn't be any worse as a place to call home. Besides, if a gentleman couldn't count on a fair shake in England, where could he get one? Throughout the late summer of 1890, William Waldorf prepared quietly to abandon "the colonies." He disengaged himself from his public and private commitments, reached an agreement with an old friend, Charles A. Peabody, Jr., who would manage William Waldorf's American holdings, and toward the end of September he and his family sailed for England. The public reaction to the news that America's richest citizen had left the country permanently was largely indifference. There were some who saw the act as a traitorous one; others blamed the country for not demonstrating a greater interest in keeping its leading citizens happy and active. But in general people felt that where William Waldorf went was his own business.

Aunt Caroline was not the sort to gloat in triumph. In her presence, the subject of her nephew's departure for England was seldom broached. Her husband's death in 1892 took her out of circulation and the death of a daughter the following year kept her out still longer. On her return, she resumed her active rule, but society was growing disorderly, democratic and even permissive. Her authority was no longer absolute; her compromises became more frequent. She was still the unquestioned No. 1, but the distance between No. 1 and No. 2 had narrowed, and fewer people cared.

One who cared extremely was Harry Lehr, who took Ward McAllister's place at the fringe of the center social circle and was more court jester than major-domo. For some reason, Mrs. Astor took a liking to this odd young fellow, who dined and dressed and danced with the best while the only visible means of support one could find for him was a modest retainer paid him by an importer of champagnes. Lehr finally coaxed a shy but wealthy, plain but rich young lady into marrying him, unnerving her more than a little when he announced on their wedding night that touching her was out of the question. The poor woman was so stunned, she remained married to Harry for twenty-eight years. Lehr made his first impression on Mrs. Astor when, as a rather young man at a ball to which Mrs. Astor had also been invited, he went up to her—she was bedecked as usual in a fortune's worth of diamonds—and told her she looked like a walking chandelier. She could easily have ended Harry's social ambitions then and there but decided his remark was a clever compliment. He became her pet and before his marriage even lived under her roof in New York during the 1900–1 winter season, an arrangement that ceased when Mrs. Astor's granddaughter began rumors that her grandmother and Lehr were going soon to announce their marriage plans.

Grateful as Lehr was to Mrs. Astor for her patronage, he was really too much of a clown, unable to take high society without a dash of levity, and he and Mrs. Astor were not ideally suited to each other. Mrs. Stuyvesant Fish and Harry were. Together they began a rather radical social revolution. Mrs. Astor thought the whole thing a shame, believing that the circus belonged under the big top. Mamie Fish said, "Mrs. Astor is an elderly woman." The daggers in that remark were thinly sheathed, but even Mrs. Astor's most loyal supporters had to admit the observation was not without its grain of truth.

CHAPTER 10

The one physical reflex that Mamie Fish deplored above all others was the yawn. She could forgive myriad miscues provided she was saved from boredom by them. Harry Lehr was the master of the intentional miscue.

Colonel Mann was not far wrong in describing Newport entertaining in the pre-Fish era thusly: "If Newport women are not the largest eaters in the world, they give a very good imitation in that direction, for they do nothing from one week's end to another but arrange themselves about boards that groan with delectable viands, where they open grateful mouths to everything that comes their way, and this they call social intercourse."

Wintie Chanler, writing home to his sisters of a visit to Newport in 1893, saw things in a different but no less gloomy light: "The poor dear millionaires are trying their damnedest to have a good time, but the wind won't blow for their yachts and it rains whenever there is a particularly good polo game. Internecine strife divides society; many people don't speak, bow or breathe the same air with others. The small fry are all as poor [as], or poorer, than usual. There is no good, cheerful, reeking scandal to comfort the women. The old men are all prophesying 'trouble in the Street.' And yet the same pompous procession of imported carriages, coachmen, harness and clothes meanders up and down the Avenue every afternoon as of yore. . . . The excursionists come in swarms to stare at the nobs, who turn up their noses and snort at the excursionists. Each longs to be having as good a time as the other."

Town Topics was forever taking potshots at Newport and its summer residents. In August of 1887, an issue scolded Newport's women for their vulgarity, lack of breeding and wit and called the younger male generation "putty-headed young imbeciles" who did nothing but drink and talk about money. Newport, Colonel Mann said, would go into swift decline unless something was done to appeal to the younger generations.

The occasionally controversial May Van Alen, who had married Griswold A. Thompson, caused quite a stir when she attempted to disclaim her attachment not only to Newport but to the United States as well. Mrs. Thompson had been living in England for a while and arrived in Boston aboard a White Star liner claiming to be a foreign resident and therefore not liable for the duty usually charged on jewelry and other finery brought into the country. She had no declaration to make, she said about her twenty trunks. Customs officials in Boston chose to question the contention and impounded her baggage, which was finally released under bond pending a hearing on the matter. What was Newport coming to? One answer was surely Mamie Fish's point of view.

At the Fish residence, propriety gave way to variety. Harry Lehr's imagination was allowed to run wild, and the results were often extraordinary, not infrequently in shockingly bad taste, but never dull. The first, and most salutary, change Mrs. Fish and her cohort made was to shorten dramatically the dinner hour. What had been a three-hour gustatory orgy by tradition became comparatively a snack of just about an hour's duration followed by entertainment whose variety, thanks to Lehr, was almost endless. He borrowed an elephant from the circus once and parked it in Mrs. Fish's New York residence for a ball so that the guests could feed it peanuts as they danced by. At one dinner, everyone dressed as a doll and the conversation was conducted in baby talk. At another, the men came dressed as cats and were given white mice to present to their female companions. When human guests got too drearily repetitive, Lehr staged a dinner for a hundred of society's top dogs—literally.

But the ultimate in questionable taste may have been reached on the evening Lehr staged a dinner at the Fish house in honor of the visiting Prince Del Drago. As royalty is wont to do, the prince showed up late. By the time he arrived, the other guests had already assembled at the dinner table. The prince came in on Lehr's arm and was marched down to the seat of honor usually occupied by Mrs. Astor, who was not present that evening. The prince's evening dress was immaculate, which was more than could be said of his table manners. They were pretty good for a chimpanzee, if not a prince, and the monkey was apparently a big hit with most of the guests. Mrs. Astor would not have been amused. Mamie Fish, however, had a different attitude. She thought society ought to be fun. Once she was asked why she served champagne at all her dinners. "You have to liven these people up," she explained. "Wine just makes them sleepy."

Mrs. Fish outlasted Mrs. Astor, but the power of the Astor name in social circles did not wane even with Car-

oline's passing in 1908 and the vast changes society under-
went in the early years of the twentieth century. Evalyn
Walsh McLean—the McLeans of Hope diamond fame—
remembered a dinner party Mrs. Fish gave in 1914 before
Mrs. O. H. P. Belmont's vast Chinese ball in Newport.
Vincent Astor, son of the colonel and grandson of Caroline, had recently married and his new bride and he were at
the dinner, where the decorous Helen Astor and Ned
McLean were not enjoying each other's company. The new
Mrs. Astor sent word to Mrs. Fish, Mrs. McLean said, that
either Ned would leave or she would. Mrs. Fish apparently
told her to go ahead, but the incident touched off a feud
with the Vincent Astors that ended Ned McLean's Newport status as one of the inner circle. Mrs. McLean admitted that it was obvious in the car on the way to the ball
after the dinner that Ned had been overserved; nonetheless, a slight case of inebriation hardly seems adequate
cause for the ostracizing of a man whose Black Point Farm
was among Newport's more elegant dwellings, requiring a
staff of thirty to maintain it. The message was clear: One
did not cross the Astors without paying a price. The fact is
that Ned McLean undoubtedly did not think the price particularly exorbitant.

Things were rather different in Newport after World
War I, as they were all over the globe. Partially it was the
war and the statement it made about some long-lost virtues
and the evils of acquisitiveness. But more it was the arrival
of the graduated income tax and the developing public belief that the rich were automatically suspect, either because
their wealth was ill gotten or because they treated the problems of others with disdain or indifference. The days of
public admiration or envy of all to which the Vanderbilts'
Breakers was a monument were ending. It was becoming
less easy to mistake ostentation for taste, extravagance for

art. The low profile was increasingly the pose wealth struck for the public. In 1924, May King Van Rensselaer saw Newport as "the summer capital of American society, a little too garish, a little shopworn, a little past its prime, as is American society itself." Still, even in those days it took a newcomer three seasons "to get even a foothold" in Newport society, she said.

In some ways, no one better personified the changing Newport than did John Jacob Astor VI. This *in utero* survivor of the *Titanic* sinking began life, said one newspaper article, in a special $10,000 nursery surrounded by eight nurses. "Crowds in Street Pleased When Birth Is Announced" read the headline on another article. An heir to the throne of England would hardly have commanded more notice in the papers. He was born amid sensational rumors, duly reported, that his mother or perhaps her parents would contest Colonel Astor's will on the grounds that she deserved a larger share than the lifetime interest in a $5 million trust the will provided as long as she remained single. Another rumor suggested that, despite word to the contrary, it was likely that the young son would receive more than the $3 million left him in the will and would get it after a friendly out-of-court settlement. The infant, of course, was oblivious to all the hoopla surrounding him. At the age of four, he was reported to need $75.27 a day— $86,034 a year, the story said without explaining the nearly $60,000 added to the daily figure—just to get by. The article explained that pillows were $50 each, which actually doesn't explain all that much.

Jack, or "Jackims" as snippy gossip columnists called him, did not enjoy a run-of-the-mill childhood. He was fatherless, although his mother did soon give up her interest in the Astor trust to marry William Dick in 1915. Dick was an old pre-colonel sweetheart who had recently inherited several million dollars of his own. He was okay as a stepfather, Jack has said, probably better than average but not, obviously, the same as a real father. His mother was a will-o'-the-wisp. She had expected to rule society when she married the colonel. Instead she had been dropped from the Social Register and snubbed in Newport. Her social standing rose significantly when she married Dick. She was even reinstated by the Social Register. This second marriage, which produced two sons, with both of whom Jack got along far better than with his older half brother Vincent, gave some stability to Jack's life, but he grew up without a clear idea of where he was going and with a gnawing sense of having been cheated by fate and Vincent out of fabulous wealth. At his prep school, St. George's in Newport, a fellow student remembers Jack as having had a rather serious constipation problem, which his mother had explained away to the nurse at the infirmary by noting, "Well, you know, his father went down on the *Titanic.*"

By the time he came of age, Jack's $3 million legacy had grown to about $5 million, a modest sum only when compared to the nation's major fortunes. In the Depression-racked early 1930s, Jack's wealth, especially considering the likelihood that much of the public believed he had the same millions as Vincent, was regarded as formidable, and Jack did little to discourage the notion by the manner in which he spent money. He had decided to forgo a college education although what else he might undertake had not been settled on either. In this he was not unlike the heirs to many fortunes. College was, or at least could be, too much like work. Who needed it? Jack traveled and collected and fell in love. He bought a private railroad car, a place in New York City complete with two dozen servants, a yellow Rolls.

He had barely turned twenty-one when he began thinking of marriage to Eileen Gillespie, a great-granddaughter of John Carter Brown, founder of Brown University. Late in 1933 the two became engaged, and Jack gave his fiancée a $100,000 ring and a marriage settlement of $500,000. Not surprisingly for someone deprived of nothing he wanted all his life, Jack was an impetuous sort with an inadequately leashed temper. He and Eileen quarreled frequently and sometimes publicly. The engagement was finally broken in January 1934. Eileen's family, furious at the whole affair, demanded an apology from Jack before Eileen returned the ring. Jack took off on a trip around the world to cure his depression, returned, apologized, got his ring back and fell in love again, this time with Ellen Tuck French, a distant Vanderbilt cousin. Their engagement, denied a week earlier, was announced on the last day of May. The wedding took place in Newport on the first day of July.

It was an affair that symbolized a different Newport. Simplicity rather than wealth and power was reflected in the decorations, the New York *Times* observed. The church was filled with five hundred people—half invited guests and half parishioners. In the street outside gathered perhaps a thousand others, mostly women of all ages and social status. Newspaper representation was heavy. The New York *Times* played the story on page 1 and gave it five full columns on an inside page, describing the bride as a "rather frightened little girl putting up a brave but somewhat wistful effort to appear at ease. . . ." Jack's mother was there, but her third husband, a young Italian prize fighter named Enzo Fiermonte whom she had just married, was not. Her second husband was, and one of their sons was an usher in the wedding. A gypsy orchestra played for three hundred guests at the reception, at which champagne, salad and sandwiches were served. At six o'clock the guests were told that Jack and his bride had slipped out the back, and the reception gradually broke up without the traditional throwing of rice. Jack and Ellen were upstairs where Ellen was getting some much-needed rest. They left at eight-thirty, drove to Providence and boarded Jack's private railroad car for the long, leisurely journey to Vancouver, British Columbia. With a quietly ironic touch, the *Times* included a short story about the sailing for Europe of Eileen Gillespie that same day.

Jack wanted to own one of the big cottages at Newport and in fact one of the biggest—O. H. P. Belmont's Marble House—was for sale at a fraction of the $2 million it had cost to build. Vincent was trustee for Jack's trust and took ten weeks to free up the money to buy Marble House, by which time someone else had put up the money and snatched the cottage away. Jack was forced to settle for Chetwode, a slightly less magnificent edifice bought in 1934 for $100,000 plus $50,000 for the furnishings.

Then, in a move that surprised a lot of people, Jack announced little more than half a year after his marriage that he was going to work. He discovered that a prep school dropout who had spent the last few years traveling first class about the world or sitting around New York was not a commodity heavily in demand in the job market. Vincent did get him a job with one of his companies at $25 a week, and Jack stuck with it for some eighteen months before finally quitting. He didn't think he was getting anywhere and although he never said so, probably resented his dependence on Vincent for upward mobility. Self-respect is not easily developed from the fulfilling of trivial tasks for $25 a week, especially if one's daily income is many times one's weekly salary. It was all faintly embarrassing, both intrinsically and in contrast with his father-in-law, whose brokerage business had failed and left him well connected but not well heeled. This irrepressible character had tried his

hand at driving a taxi back in the 1920s, without much success, and in 1938 had applied for welfare on the grounds he
was down to his last few dollars. He finally got another job
at a golf driving range, but he was never exactly a source of
pride to his son-in-law.

Tucky, as Ellen was called by her friends, produced a son
in 1935 who was named William specifically after his
great-grandfather. Jack was frequently told that he resembled his grandfather far more than his father, and certainly
there are several surface parallels—their appreciation of
feminine pulchritude, their dislike of high society coupled
with a love for a good time and their disinterest in gainful
employment. In 1943, Jack and Tucky gave up trying to
patch their tattering marriage and were divorced, Jack providing a handsome but undisclosed settlement and custody
of William being divided equally. By now the public had
classified Jack as the typical wealthy playboy, an object of
ridicule and snide asides. The image was one Jack never
shook, at least in part because his next marriage ended in
such a bizarre manner.

In 1946, Jack married Gertrude Gretsch, who provided
him with a daughter, Mary Jacqueline, who has probably
made all his troubles with her mother worth it to him. The
marriage was not eminently successful, and Jack was separated from his second wife when he tumbled hard for a
blue-eyed blonde named Dolores Fullman in 1954. He hus-
tled to get a divorce in Juárez, Mexico, which was quickly
granted although Gertrude had not consented to a Mexico
jurisdiction. The next move was a quick wedding to Dolores. As William Congreve once noted in his play, *The
Old Bachelor*, "Marry'd in haste, we may repent at leisure."
Jack's third trip to the altar was over in six weeks; his legal
battles were just beginning. In one year alone his legal fees
were considerably more than $100,000. What happened,

obviously enough, was that Gertrude contended she was still his wife. Dolores said she was. The courts couldn't make up their minds. After years of haggling, Gertrude finally helped out by getting her own divorce, legal in every state, but for years thereafter Jack was still married in some states and not in others. During the legal fray, Astor's net worth was figured at $4.75 million, based on cost rather than market value, and his pre-tax income was estimated at $250,000 annually.

One does not have to eat at the Automat with that sort of income, but for an Astor it is hardly astronomical. In 1948, Jack sold Chetwode for $70,000. It was too much to maintain. He once told an interviewer that he had been forced to run the place on a shoestring the last season he owned it with a mere four gardeners and six in inside staff. He was sorry to see the place go, he said, because he liked Newport and its people even if he did not particularly care for the summer resort life.

Today Jack is something of a recluse. He lives in Florida and has pretty much cut himself off from his friends as well as the public, according to his daughter. Winthrop Aldrich, attempting to pin down some points of historical interest at Rokeby a few years ago, wrote Jack asking if he knew anything about certain portraits that were supposed to have hung in Rokeby. Jack has developed the reputation of being a sharp collector of art with a good eye and good taste. Indeed, those who know him say that although he has allowed himself to grow fat and does not present a very pretty physical picture, Jack is a thoughtful, humorous and entertaining individual. At any rate, Wintie says he did not hear anything from Jack for almost three years. Then one day he received a telephone message to the effect that Jack Astor had called and that Mr. Astor knew nothing about whatever it was that Wintie wanted to know. In short, Jack is inaccessible.

The Astor presence is no longer felt in Newport except in the cottages that now welcome tourists even into the most private rooms. It would undoubtedly cause Caroline Astor great sadness to know that her cherished Beechwood can today be rented by anyone with a few hundred dollars for a party, a dance or a wedding reception. Beaulieu, the other great Astor mansion, is one of the few big cottages still in private hands and not open to the public.

Only around the Casino, where elegant tennis still is played before politely enthusiastic audiences, is an Astor aura retained, although most people would not recognize its Astorness. Here reigns Jimmy Van Alen, Caroline's great-grandson, and one of tennis' great and true amateurs. Tennis is not the exclusive game it was when Ava Willing Astor once tripped on a grandstand step, fell the length of the stairs, picked herself up and walked off as if nothing had happened—poise and courage personified, the dignity of the social elite preserved—but at the Casino one can still absorb the flavor of the old days. Van Alen is one of the main reasons for this; indeed, he is one of the main reasons for the continued existence of the Casino. His chief contribution to the game itself is the scoring modification known as the tie breaker, which he developed to prevent a set from dragging on interminably. Resisted at first, it is now generally accepted as an important innovation. Jimmy's brother William, who now lives in semi-retirement outside Philadelphia, had the coincidental distinction of being an architect in New York City at the same time as another New York architect named William Van Alen, who happened to design among other structures the Chrysler Building. The resulting confusion was occasionally humorous, infrequently disconcerting and never intolerable.

In August 1967, Jimmy Van Alen and his wife gave a dinner party before the annual Tennis Ball in honor of Jack's daughter, Mary Jacqueline (Jacquie or M.J.), who had made her debut on Long Island in June. It was a veritable family reunion. Jack arrived in the company of his first wife. His second wife and daughter were in the receiving line. His son was there. Jimmy was a jolly host, playing the guitar, offering to play the piano if the musicians would play in the right key and seeing to it that everyone got drinks. Jack was something less than loquacious but his attitude was markedly upbeat from atrabilious. To make Jack's evening complete, the former Eileen Gillespie, now married, was at the ball. Although Wintie Aldrich hints at a hidden desire to have a major family reunion someday at Rokeby, it is unlikely that so many Astors will gather under one roof in America again. Like Newport's cottages, Astor family tradition has been neglected if not abandoned by the younger generations. Oh, they express casual interest in family history on occasion, but in the main they lead their own lives. High society holds little attraction for most of them. Peace and quiet are worth almost any price.

It is perhaps a good thing that the vast Astor wealth is no longer concentrated in a few family hands. With the exception of Brooke, Vincent's widow, who controls income but not principal, the Astor fortune has been spread thin. Like so many of the fortunes whose owners lavished millions on Newport at the turn of the century, taxes, inflation and an increasing number of heirs have caused today's Astors to be merely rich. But they may take some consolation from Henry James, who held "the settled conviction that extreme wealth threatened its owner with psychological disarray."

In the last quarter of the nineteenth century, among the Astors and others, one could understand James's viewpoint.

PART V

CHAPTER 11

Willaim Waldorf Astor was "certainly something of an anachronism," a grandson, Michael Astor, has written. That may be as nice an evaluation as can be made of the man without forgoing all semblance of accuracy. William Waldorf was extravagantly wealthy; had he been otherwise, he simply would not have been tolerated. But bizarre behavior that results in institutionalization when exhibited by the average citizen becomes accepted eccentricity among the rich or famous, an expression of their independence and individuality.

Astor's move to England in 1890 after losing the Great Title Battle over who was to be called "Mrs. Astor," his wife or his Aunt Caroline, seems largely the act of a petulant, spoiled child. "America is not a fit place for a gentleman to live," said Astor, explaining his decision to take up residence on the other side of the Atlantic, where, according to Michael, lived "a leisured class of people whose lives were an extension of their tastes and inclinations. . . ." That was a concept to which William Waldorf could relate. In Astor's case, those proclivities seemed to run to spending his money lavishly on new homes, a vast country estate here, a castle there. The widely held assumption was —and is—that Astor was looking to buy a title. It did not come cheaply. Before he finally realized his desire, he had become an old man and spent several million dollars on Cliveden, the estate he bought from the Duke of Westminster, whose mansion had been designed by the architect for the Houses of Parliament, Sir Charles Barry; $10 million on the restoration of Hever Castle, once the home of Anne Boleyn; and a few more millions for several British newspapers and magazines to advance his causes before the public.

Although he was a man obsessed, says Michael, by convention and such relatively trivial things as punctuality, his manners, particularly as a host, were often outrageous enough to lose him friends, or at least guests. It is Michael's astute speculation that William Waldorf was a man who never found out what he wanted, it being a mistake to suppose that because someone demonstrates grim tenacity in acquiring something, he necessarily knows what he is after. William Waldorf was not a man who piled triumph upon triumph while in the United States. It is true that he enjoyed—if that is the word—a measure of success in England that had eluded him on the other side of the Atlantic, but that is perhaps because England was as much of an anachronism in her own way as he was in his. And somehow, success never seemed to equate with happiness.

The fiber of William Waldorf's being was not weak; it was twisted. He was a man of strong principle too easily warped because his wealth and his introspection insulated him from the standards, principles and customs of others. He was his own man, frequently a lonely and occasionally a preposterous proposition. His talents were misdirected, or rather, undirected, and there are indications that those talents were not inconsiderable. His novel, *Sforza*, for example, was published by Scribner's in 1889, and if it fell short of dramatic commercial or artistic success, it was a surprisingly well crafted effort with a plot and character development that hinted strongly at potential. The writing is, like most of his writing, fustian, but William Waldorf did, at least, have the good sense to write about a period and a class for which pomposity was not an inappropriate posture.

American newspaper treatment of this Astor had never been particularly flattering. His animus toward the U.S. press might even be said to have been inherited. He used to say that he had heard his father exclaim about news accounts of John Jacob that they were almost enough to make one emigrate. In 1892, William Waldorf, demonstrating a tenuous stability, allowed the news of his own demise to leak to the American papers, only one of which—James Gordon Bennett's—doubted the story sufficiently not to print it. For the most part, the notices, on page 1, were as disingenuous as the news itself, although W.W. could not have been ecstatic over the New York *Tribune*'s evaluation of the event. To wit: "The death of William Waldorf Astor, although not an event of great or lasting significance whether in the world of action or in the world of thought, will be generally deplored." Most of the commentary was more generous, not to say obsequious.

Testing the waters of public opinion with a premature death notice was but one of the strange behavioral quirks that colored William Waldorf's life, particularly once he moved to England. It is rather remarkable that a man who offended almost as many people as he amused (unintentionally on both counts) managed to become a baron and even a viscount. A couple of American publications may have found a key to the question. An 1893 issue of *Harper's Weekly* put it succinctly: "In England they take their millionaires more seriously than we do." Expressing a similar notion in a less magnanimous manner was a social columnist for the New York *Times* in that same year, remarking on the rumor that Astor was planning to bring some English acquaintances to America for the World's Fair. The fellow sniffed at the prospect "of an American millionaire who is spending much money in endeavoring to make himself and his wife personae gratissimae in English society."

In 1899, Astor became an English citizen. That same year Astor put out a genealogy that had the family descending from Jean Jacques d'Astorg, the son of a French count. This struck the New York *Sun* as unlikely enough to warrant some checking. The paper hired Lothrop Withington, calling him "one of the best known genealogists in Europe" while mispelling his name, and devoted more than four columns starting on page 1 to a dissection of the Astor genealogy. Astor's grasp of public relations was either tenuous or cavalier. Despite having bought in 1893 the *Pall Mall Gazette*, having soon thereafter started up the *Pall Mall Magazine* when the *Gazette* editor suggested that such a forum would be more appropriate than the *Gazette* for William Waldorf's literary efforts, and eventually having purchased the London *Observer* in 1910, Astor was always running afoul of public opinion and the media.

He didn't seem to care. The same year he became an English citizen he outraged a large segment of the American population by purchasing the flag of the U.S.S. *Chesapeake*, which had fought valiantly if futilely against the English in 1807, and presenting the flag to the British Royal United Service Museum. According to a New York

World story of June 29, 1898, Astor sold forty-one pieces of East Side New York land to Henry Morgenthau, leaving tenants, who believed the Astors would never sell and had made improvements on the land leased from Astor, in jeopardy of losing their life savings.

But perhaps his most bizarre behavior he displayed in his role as host. He entertained lavishly, to be sure, but his guests were subject to his whims, his obsession with schedules and, on occasion, simple rudeness. He often made it clear precisely at what time his guests were to depart, and sometimes even his own schedule didn't suit him, so that he would retire while a party was in full swing, leaving the guests to themselves. They may have been relieved. There is, for example, the oft-told tale of a lady weekend guest at Cliveden who dared to stroll in the garden during letter-writing time. A diffident servant approached her after no more than a moment or two and politely reminded her that it was letter-writing time. She explained that she had no letters to write. He explained that nonetheless guests were not supposed to stroll in the garden when they were supposed to be writing letters. She explained that she considered such constraints intolerable and would like her carriage called as she was going to leave. He explained that he could not call a carriage at an hour that was not appointed for the calling of carriages. She is alleged to have walked off the grounds carrying her own bag. At a concert he gave in his London town house, Astor spotted a gentleman he did not know. Approaching the hapless fellow at once, Astor asked him to leave after promising to make notice of the incident in his newspaper. The man, Captain Sir Berkeley Milne, had been dining with Lady Oxford, who had invited him to the concert, sure the host would not mind. Milne immediately sent Astor a written apology and explanation. Unaffected, Astor had his *Pall Mall Gazette* print a paragraph in which it was stated that the presence of Milne at Astor's concert "was uninvited." The incident raised a considerable stir, the Prince of Wales and Astor being among the few who remained unruffled, although the prince did invite Milne to the royal box at the theater. Finally, the exclusive membership of the Carlton Club demanded an apology from Astor, and, most likely because he was loath to lose his membership, Astor complied, printing what might more properly be characterized as an arrogant explanation than an abject apology.

Despite his earlier experiences in America with politics—or perhaps because of them—Astor was not particularly attracted to the common man. Before he took over Cliveden, the public had been allowed to use the grounds for boating parties on the Thames, which ran through the property, for picnics and for general sightseeing. Astor ended all that, going so far as to build a wall around the grounds and topping it with broken glass. Part of his aversion toward the public stemmed from what amounted to paranoia. When he first announced his decision to move from America to England, he gave as one reason having received kidnap threats directed at his children. In Britain the rumor was that he was deeply concerned about being assassinated. By his bed on a table he always kept two loaded revolvers. His London offices, on which he spent $1.5 million for refurbishing, were equipped with the latest in burglary prevention equipment, including a button Astor could press if startled by some unexpected noise or occurrence, a button that locked every door in the house, which contained not only Astor's offices but also an apartment. There was but a single door to the outside world. It had to be shared by servants and guests alike. This arrangement, some have said, required especially discreet servants.

Whatever social diversions William Waldorf may or

may not have pursued, there can be no question that his life was a lonely one. As a child, he had been delivered unto a governess whose frightening aspect he would never forget. He was not allowed much leeway as a boy, kept on a short rope and thin allowance and fed a strong diet of stern Protestant religion. In a letter he wrote years later William Waldorf says, "I was a mischievous little animal and everybody kept telling me I was so bad. The hellfire sermons of my childhood the like of which no congregation out of Scotland would listen to today frightened me silly and I knew those red hot things were being made ready for *me*." Probably the closest William Waldorf ever came to happiness was during the three years he spent as American minister to Rome in recognition of his political loyalties by President Chester A. Arthur.

The next six years were not a collection of halcyon days for Astor, whose disaffection with life in the United States was generally underestimated by the American people because of Astor's rather juvenile behavior in public as illustrated by his "unfit for a gentleman" remark. Speculating on Astor's expatriation several years after the fact, the prestigious *Harper's Weekly* wrote that if Astor had been born in London he might already be a peer. But starting as a middle-aged American, he couldn't expect so much, and he was not likely to swap allegiance just to make himself available for politics. A bad guess. The magazine then went on to ask "whether we ought not to make more effort to make our very rich fellow-citizens more useful and therefore more content at home." Astor's application for British citizenship half a dozen years after this article appeared was proof his unrest in America ran deep.

One insight into his feelings about the United States may be had from his biography of his great-grandfather, in which he commented on the staying power of family wealth, influence and tradition in America. He noted that the Society of the Cincinnati, founded by Washington and Lafayette to recognize such things, had died in six of the original thirteen states and contended that "not one ten-thousandth part" of the possessions of Revolutionary War families remained in the hands of their "lineal successors." The situation was one he clearly disapproved.

If William Waldorf accepted the style and tradition of life in England more readily than he did that in America, it is not clear that England promptly reciprocated. Both sides were inherently aloof to begin with, and the English, with few exceptions, are a restrained people at least some of whom must have been put off by the ostentation Astor brought along with his millions. Luckily for him, one of the above-mentioned exceptions was the then Prince of Wales, although even he is rumored to have been less taken with Astor's personality than with his wealth. Astor's character was of a nature that tended to isolate him from other people, his immediate family for the most part excepted.

In 1894 he was further isolated by the death three days before Christmas of his wife. A doctor had been in attendance full time during the final two weeks of her life, but her illness could not have been very prolonged because her death took her New York friends by surprise. She had always been a quiet, shy, domestically inclined lady with great compassion for the underprivileged, for whom she did much without receiving public notice. In the grand scheme of things it probably doesn't count for much but, in 1893 Mrs. Astor had hosted a fancy lace exhibit sponsored by the social lionesses of England and had then been presented to the diplomatic circle in Queen Victoria's drawing room, an honor accorded few American women. She had obviously helped the Astor quest for recognition and perhaps even title in their new homeland. Mrs. Astor's remains were returned to New York for burial in Trinity Cemetery. There, for a full year, her grave was covered daily by a fresh blanket of 3,500 to 4,000 lilies of the valley and as many more violets, a standing order from her bereaved husband.

His life continued but, unless one can accept the seeking of a title as a full-time, satisfying occupation, it is hard to know what exactly it was that William Waldorf did with his time beyond the spending of money. This he did often and lavishly. In an almost pitiable attempt to recapture a piece of the lost pleasure of Italy, he bought a $1 million villa in Sorrento the same year (1906) he presented Cliveden—from which, on a clear day, you could see if not forever at least seven counties—to his son Waldorf as a wedding present. He pursued his interest in fine wine and food with dedication, if not enthusiasm, but the solace of human companionship was elusive. His wife had given birth to five children, only three of whom lived to maturity. Waldorf, the eldest, developed early a liberal social and political bent his father was unable to fathom. Their relationship, especially in Astor's late years, was strained. John Jacob V, the youngest, was seldom in England once he grew up. Thus what filial devotion was accorded William Waldorf came for the most part from his daughter Pauline, who was most generous with her time for her father and spent hours reading to him. One can feel almost sympathetic toward this aloof, haughty old man upon reading of the birthday greeting he sent to a grandson in which he observed that he was alone drinking a glass of the finest brandy in his grandson's honor.

Private letters belonging to William Waldorf and first made public in a recent biography indicate that Astor was perhaps less lonely than has generally been thought. The letters reveal Astor in his last half dozen years as pursuing at least one romantic correspondence. However, in that the correspondence shows him capable of ardent emotions, he may require special pity, for there is nothing to show that such ardor was adequately reciprocated.

If the ultimate achievement of his goal gave him any extraordinary pleasure, its manifestations were few. The New Year's List of Honors in 1916 made Astor a baron. The same list presented novelist Henry James with the Order of Merit, an event generally given more coverage and comment than Astor's barony. The London *Daily Chronicle* did observe that the barony "will excite the most interest" among the appointments in the list. But the periodical *New Witness* voiced a different view: "It is a bad precedent at a time like this [mid-World War I] to create any more peers who are not of British birth. . . . The only effect of the elevation will be to evoke a certain amount of renewed anger in America against the Astor family." Actually, the World War and the quarter century that had passed since Astor's abandoning of America had pretty well dissipated American hostility toward him.

At his son's home, in Cliveden, was where the hostility lay. Son Waldorf was not at all enchanted by his father's barony, and after a discussion with his son on the matter, William Waldorf vowed never again to speak to him. William Waldorf, says Grandson Michael, was without the human touch. While Waldorf may have felt a twinge of remorse, one imagines he survived his father's threat experiencing a minimum of trauma.

The following year William Waldorf was made a viscount. Another Astor barony was bestowed in 1956 upon W.W.'s younger son, John.

Meanwhile, William Waldorf's self-imposed isolation continued to grow more complete. On October 18, 1919, he retired to the bathroom after dinner and did not re-appear. Eventually an alarmed servant broke in and found Astor dead. The newspapers reported he had died in bed. Unlike the last time his death had been reported in the papers, this time the story was at least partially right: he was dead.

In his last years William Waldorf's public appearances were few and far between. He visited the House of Lords just twice, to receive his two titles. His redesigning of the Astor crest to include the falcon that also sat on the shield of the Middle Ages Astorga who Astor liked to think was an ancestor inspired an American cousin to compose an ir-reverent sonnet suggesting that a butcher's cleaver might have been more appropriate. At the time of his death, the London *Times* quoted a friend of Astor's: "In himself and in the lonely life he led amid the environment he had acquired or created—surroundings partly noble and mag-nificent, partly fantastic and baroque—Lord Astor was an extraordinary and singular personality. In the end he seemed almost inaccessible—an imprisoned soul immersed within walls of his own making, high walls with few win-dows and doors, though with much space within." What filled that space will never be known. As he wished, he was cremated, his ashes placed in Cliveden chapel.

Astor's will disposed of three major trusts and that prop-erty he had not already given or bequeathed. The younger son received more than the elder as the result of a late codi-cil to the will, but despite some rumors to the contrary, John and Waldorf were treated more or less equally, al-though the father clearly preferred his younger son. The main trust, worth $50.2 million if Astor's New York real es-tate holdings were properly valued, was divided equally be-tween the sons. Waldorf already had Cliveden; John had Hever Castle. Two other trusts with a combined value of

$25 million were divided so that John received half and Waldorf's children upon reaching their majority divided the other half. This disparity was undoubtedly the final result of the quarrel Waldorf had with his father over the latter's titles. Waldorf had been elected to the House of Commons in 1910 and wanted to stay there. His inherited title, hard as he would try to relinquish it, would force him to move over—he would never have considered it moving up—to the House of Lords, a fact on which turns much Astor, not to mention English, history, as well as the next chapter.

It was nearly fifty years after William Waldorf's death that the public learned of his extraordinary collection of letters and documents relating to American history, as well as British politics and letters. Charles Dickens, Dr. Samuel Johnson, Benjamin Disraeli and many American Presidents were represented in the collection. There were also letters from Major John André, whom the British sent to negotiate with Benedict Arnold for the betrayal of West Point in 1780, who was captured dressed in civilian clothes just before he could make good his escape and who was executed as a spy. Perhaps the pièce de résistance of the collection was a letter from George Washington to the father of Major General John Armstrong, in turn the father of William B. Astor's bride, in 1788 discussing the ratification chances of the Constitution and expressing his reluctance to come out of retirement if asked to do so as the new nation's first President.

William Waldorf had collected as he had lived—exercising discrimination and keeping his own counsel, seeking neither advice nor approval from others.

CHAPTER 12

Whatever American roots the English Astors possessed were quickly cut. Although Waldorf, his brother John and his sister Pauline were born in the United States, they were brought up British—Eton, Oxford, public service for Waldorf, foreign service for John. His son Michael says Waldorf went to an English boarding school at age nine, probably a couple of years younger than he actually was but a year older than Michael himself was when he was first sent away. At any rate, Waldorf appears to have adapted readily. His career at Eton was distinguished; he carried away many honors and could hardly have helped provoking some jealousy among his English classmates at this upstart American. He was Captain of Boats, treasurer of the Eton Society, captain of his house, editor of the *Eton Chronicle* and winner of the Prince Consort's French prize. He was, says Michael, serious, conscientious and modest. He grew a mustache and, one suspects, an accent.

At Oxford the zeal with which he pursued excellence flagged somewhat, and he wound up taking a fourth-class degree as he substituted fencing, polo and fox hunting for scholarship. It was during these schooldays that Waldorf developed a heart condition—Michael says he strained it rowing—that, coupled apparently with a mild case of tuberculosis at age twenty-six, caused his doctors to prohibit strenuous exercise. Delicate health never prevented Waldorf from leading an active life, but it did periodically confine him to his bed for long months at a time. His tuberculosis, if indeed that was what it was, must have struck his father as bitterly ironic, especially after William Waldorf's younger sister, Gwendolyn, died from the disease in 1902. Years before that, William Waldorf had fallen madly in love but had acceded to his parents' wishes and abandoned this love because it was understood that tuberculosis ran in the woman's family. At least one family member has contended that William Waldorf never got over the incident. Son Waldorf's delicate health may have contributed to what became a life spent in the shadow of his feisty, indomitable, occasionally outrageous wife, although many would argue that robust health wouldn't have helped. Her husband, whoever he was to be, was destined to play the supporting role in Nancy Langhorne's life drama.

More has been written about this English Astor, who was neither English nor an Astor, than about any other member of the family. The force of her personality captured the imaginations and hearts of such diverse characters as Lawrence of Arabia, George Bernard Shaw and Philip Kerr, eventually Lord Lothian. Her effect on events was substantially less than her effect on people. The best thing about her may well have been Waldorf. The two of them could not have been less alike, but their relationship perhaps defined, or at least personified, symbiosis and synergism. More simply, they were good for one another.

When Nancy Langhorne first appeared cantering across the English countryside, she was recovering from a first marriage whose disastrous outcome would have cured the impulsive streak in a less willful woman. The year was 1903. While Waldorf's father was naturally disconcerted by the prospect of his eldest marrying an American divorcee rather than an English or at least a European noblewoman, in most respects Nancy was as good for Waldorf as he was for her. If he helped her forget her first marriage, she helped him forget—or at least defuse—his attraction to the future Queen Marie of Rumania, who although married, had shown an interest in this rich commoner. Romance is probably too strong a word to describe the relationship but, unrestrained, it might have become embarrassing. Nancy saw to it that restraint (and then some) was exercised. In 1906, after some scrambling to find a cleric willing to marry a divorcee, Nancy and Waldorf, who fate had decreed would share the same birth date, May 19, 1879, were married. Neither William Waldorf, nor Nancy's father, Chiswell Dabney Langhorne, was able to attend the ceremony, a fact that hindsight would have seen as a bad omen had history treated the pair with less kindness. But although it was sometimes said that Nancy was incapable of romantic love and Waldorf was at times painfully shy, their life together was full and fascinating if not always happy. Nancy might be accused of having used Waldorf, perhaps, but it was not a use about which Waldorf ever much complained.

Nancy's contribution was the revitalization of the English Astors, or, as her son Michael put it: "When she came to Cliveden and when she came to know my grandfather, she saw that his family had reached an impasse. Its members were aloof and desperately shy. Like a bundle of heavy logs that had become jammed in a river they needed some propellant to set them moving with the current." In this respect, Nancy was dynamite.

She was the youngest of five Langhorne sisters, the eldest of whom married Charles Dana Gibson and became the original "Gibson girl." Their father was a self-made man who acquired a fortune by deciding that you didn't have to know anything about building a railroad to get the contract for doing so and then proved the point, promoting a contract for himself and hiring someone else to do the actual work. He was not untypical of the new, post-Reconstruction breed of Southern gentleman—rough around the edges, thick-skinned, softhearted and accustomed to having his own way, not because he had earned it but because he knew how to demand it. He would have made a good politician, and he would have given up everything for his daughters. Like her older sisters before her, Nancy as a teenager enjoyed the attention of the best sorts of beaux from her home state of Virginia to Newport and Boston. She was not beautiful—at least compared with her eldest sister—but she was vivacious, trim and smart. One imagines that many a person lost his breath trying to keep up with her.

In 1897 she married Robert Gould Shaw II, whom she had met through her passion for riding, which he shared. Shaw's father has been identified in two earlier Astor biographies—by Lucy Kavaler and by Harvey O'Connor—as the famous white Boston abolitionist who died in South Carolina in 1863 at the head of a regiment of black troops. There are two problems with this: the chronology doesn't fit and Mr. Shaw, Nancy's father-in-law, was very much alive during Nancy's courtship, marriage, separation and divorce. The abolitionist was Nancy's husband's great uncle. At any rate, the Shaws were a proper, wealthy Boston family. The son played for the Harvard polo team. Nancy was young, to be sure, and there were rumors that Shaw was inclined to drink too much, but "Chillie," as Nancy's father was called, liked the young man. The couple were married at Mirador, the Langhorne estate near Charlottesville, Virginia, and went off to honeymoon at Hot Springs, where the happy twosome remained together for less than twenty-four hours. Nancy's memories, recorded in 1951, of those days are hazy and nightmarish. What is clear is that despite her father's strong efforts to keep the marriage from foundering, despite several attempts over the next few years at reconciliation, the Shaws' match was not one made for durability, although it did produce a son, born in 1898.

Divorce was another matter. Nancy was always a woman of strong religious convictions. Divorce was anathema to her. It is quite likely she would have been content to live out her life separated from Shaw but undivorced, but Shaw forced her to take action. He apparently told a girl friend he was divorced and went through some form of wedding ceremony with her. His parents then asked Nancy to institute divorce proceedings to avoid the public nastiness that was bound to arise if and when this other woman found out that Shaw retained certain legal obligations toward Nancy. In 1903 the divorce decree was issued, and Nancy fled to England to recuperate. It was only a matter of days, if not hours, before Nancy made her first riposte of so many recorded for posterity. Asked by an English lady in a light conversational tone if she were in England to capture "one of our husbands," Nancy replied: "If you only knew how hard a time I've had getting rid of the first one, you wouldn't ask that." Where this woman was three years later, on the occasion of Nancy's marriage to Waldorf, has not been preserved. Wherever she was, she surely smiled to herself.

If William Waldorf was truly disappointed in his son's choice of a wife, he managed admirable restraint. As wedding presents, the groom received Cliveden and the bride a $75,000 tiara that included the famous Sancy diamond as its focal point. The first thing Nancy did was a massive redecoration job at Cliveden, removing the rather ornate, heavy-handed touch of its previous inhabitant and enlivening the place in keeping with its new mistress. The prim English may have been a bit hesitant about this brash bird suddenly nesting in their midst, but it was not long before Cliveden became the place to be when you were socializing, regardless of whether your vocation was politics, letters, science or simply enjoyment of hereditary privileges. It helped, of course, that King Edward VII found Nancy entertaining. The king was secure enough to laugh when Nancy declined an invitation to play bridge with him by saying, "Oh, but I wouldn't know a king from a knave!" If some self-appointed members of his entourage cringed, that was their problem, not Nancy's.

Under William Waldorf, with his affinity for solitude, Cliveden never reached its potential either as a home or as a place to entertain. Under Nancy's steady, firm hand, Cliveden recaptured its lost glory and then some. The task was not an easy one, and Nancy was not an easy taskmaster. Operating Cliveden at capacity was no less demanding a job than running a sizable hotel. The guest wing had room for forty visitors. Rosina Harrison, Nancy's personal maid for thirty-five years, listed the inside servants' roster in her autobiography. At the top was the butler, Edwin Lee, considered by many as the best in the business in his day. Then: the steward/butler, the valet, the underbutler, three footmen, two odd men, the hallboy, the house carpenter, the chef, three kitchenmaids, a scullery maid, a daily, the housekeeper, two stillroom maids, four housemaids, two more dailies, four laundry maids, two ladies' maids, a telephonist and a night watchman. That adds up to thirty-four

people. The outside staff, according to Rose, was much
larger. Throw in a guest list that frequently mixed Liberals
and Conservatives, Laborites and Tories, coarse businessmen and subtle intellectuals, and one can easily understand the fullness of Nancy's life, even before she became
embroiled in politics herself. Nancy kept everyone on his
toes. She was unpredictable. Just because something had always been done a certain way did not mean that it would
continue to be done that way if Nancy felt an improvement could be made. Form and tradition, so highly prized
among the English, mattered rather little to Nancy, but because she was not imperious in the exercise of her will, she
usually got her way without ruffling too many feathers.
One could even change her mind on occasion. Lee did it
once by pointing out that, despite Nancy's desire to have
the dining-room table seat more people, it would not do to
crowd each place setting into eighteen inches. His mistress
was about to argue the point when Lee added that at
Buckingham Palace thirty inches was considered an absolute minimum. Nancy capitulated.

Her father-in-law visited Cliveden only once after he
gave it as a wedding present to his son, vowing never to set
foot inside again. He broke the vow in 1907 upon the birth
of his first grandson. For one of the few times in her life,
Nancy cowered—one might even say retreated—falling back
to her bedroom after leaving instructions that she was not
to be troubled. William Waldorf was a perfect gentleman
and doting grandfather despite Nancy's worry that he
might be furious upon finding his old home in its redone
and unrecognizable state. He visited Nancy in her bedroom
and was sweetness personified. They didn't see much of
each other, but the evidence indicates that the old man's
affection for his daughter-in-law grew with the years and
mellowed his feelings toward his eldest son. His main busi-

ness interest in his latter days was journalism, and in 1910 he decided that he had to have J. L. Garvin, then editor of the prestigious Sunday paper, the *Observer*, as editor for his *Pall Mall Gazette*, which had fallen on hard times since Astor had fired Harry Cust in 1896. Cust had been a superb editor but had refused to alter his position on a given issue if that position happened to give offense to the magazine's owner—and his boss. Waldorf was sent to find out what it would take to acquire Mr. Garvin's services. It was simple, actually: Astor could have Mr. Garvin by buying the *Observer*. The arrangement suited the old man, who four years later gave the paper to Waldorf.

In 1910, Waldorf was elected to Parliament from the district of Plymouth, beginning an association that would flourish during the next thirty-five years. And on April 15, 1912, an era ended—the era to which Nancy's Cliveden was England's principal monument. In his distinguished biography of Edith Wharton, R. W. B. Lewis described a visit to Cliveden by Mrs. Wharton and her friend Henry James in July of 1912. Also at Cliveden were Colonel John Jacob Astor IV's widow, Madeleine, and his son Vincent. In retrospect, says Lewis, it seems clear that the sinking of the *Titanic* marked the end of an unquestioning faith in science and technology as well as the end of a general veneration of the very rich. With the sinking of the *Titanic*, certainly with World War I, life lost its simplicity, its innocence. Waldorf and Nancy's son Michael put it another way, recalling that the grand approach to living as manifested at Cliveden survived only symbolically World War I and failed to survive at all World War II.

The major turning point in the lives of Nancy and Waldorf was probably October 18, 1919. With the death of his father, Waldorf was forced to resign his seat in the House of Commons and accept one in the House of Lords. Poor

William Waldorf was barely cold before the rumors began
flying that Nancy might make a fine substitute for her husband. For one thing, she could afford it. The Plymouth
Conservative Association saw the light and extended
Nancy an invitation to run. One suspects she would have
settled for an excuse to run. And once she started, she
proved virtually unstoppable for a quarter century. The
timing could hardly have been more propitious. The end of
World War I had left England sufficiently shaken so that
accepting new notions and new faces was now possible.
Nancy, after four sons and a daughter, must certainly have
considered her childbearing duties to Waldorf to have
been fulfilled. From 1907 to 1916, according to Michael,
she had suffered periodically from nervous exhaustion,
spending several weeks at a time in bed, but a suggestion
from a sister in 1914 that she study Christian Science had
imbued her life with new vigor. Devoutly religious from
the age of fifteen, she became almost fanatical about Christian Science and its restorative powers virtually overnight.
Waldorf, even with his more intellectual approach to med-
icine as a science, could withstand the relentless onslaught
of his wife only so long, adopting Christian Science at
about the same time he adopted abstinence from alcohol,
another of his wife's quixotic crusades. From the day
Nancy accepted the offer to run for her husband's Commons seat, the public image of this imagination-stirring
couple shifted, the spotlight swinging from husband to
wife. Waldorf's political ambitions, which soared when in
1916 he was appointed parliamentary secretary to the
Prime Minister, Lloyd George, had collapsed several
months earlier when Lloyd George, after winning the 1918
election, had failed to bring in new blood, Astor's as well as
others', in forming the new government. From 1919 on,
Waldorf appeared content to remain in the wings, stage-

managing his wife's suddenly star-quality career. Nancy swamped her opposition, getting more votes than the Liberal and Labor candidates combined. She ought, she said, to feel sorry for her two opponents, but the only person she felt sorry for actually was "the poor old viscount here." Her pity was wasted, if there was more to it than rhetoric, for Waldorf's heart was surely swelling with love and pride. He wasn't, of course, enchanted with his new position in the House of Lords—even attempting legislation to allow a peer to resign his title—but he would not have countenanced a single cloud enshadowing Nancy's sunny triumph. Although she was not the first woman ever elected to the House of Commons, she did become the first woman ever to serve.

Nancy was not, and never became, a consummate parliamentarian. What she was was a good campaigner and a good pioneer, two things that also made her an instant celebrity. During World War I, Cliveden life had been subdued. After the British had declined the Astors' offer of Cliveden for use as a hospital, the Canadians had accepted. The tennis court building had been turned into a 200-bed hospital and, things being relatively quiet in the main house, Nancy had turned her attention upon the patients, nursing, cajoling and sometimes prodding them back to health. With the end of the war, Cliveden was revitalized, the party begun again. Nancy stood at the center, basking in the company of the great and near great but reminding them of their human frailties on occasion. Women weren't looking for superiority over men, she once said. They had always had that; what they wanted now was equality with men. Someone has compared Nancy to a cross between Joan of Arc and Gracie Fields, although Joan of Arc and Phyllis Diller is perhaps more appropriate. Subtlety was never a device with which Nancy felt comfortable; sometimes she could muster a reserve of restraint, but she seemed most happy, or at least very much at home, out among her constituents trading jests and jabs. The record of these exchanges is exhausting. The wit is more caustic than clever, surviving less on its own merits than on the gumption, vitality and refreshing unorthodoxy of the woman delivering it. Indeed the most memorable exchanges occurred not between Nancy and her constituents but between Nancy and Winston Churchill, and inevitably Sir Winston had the last word. Nancy would deliver the opening insult as a hammer blow; Sir Winston would respond with a rapier. In the most frequently quoted of such exchanges, Nancy told Churchill that, were he her husband, she'd poison his coffee, and Churchill replied that, were Nancy his wife, he'd drink it.

Nancy valued a sense of humor almost above all else, however, and if she and Churchill never became the best of friends, they did maintain a civil, even respectful relationship. Her son Michael says, "Humor was the standard by which she judged the intelligentsia." Also irreverence. It is hard to imagine two more dissimilar individuals than Nancy and George Bernard Shaw; yet they became the closest of friends. Nancy's biographer and relative by marriage Elizabeth Langhorne says Shaw first became intrigued by Lady Astor upon hearing she had exclaimed, "Rats!" during a debate at the House of Commons. His sentiments exactly, virtually regardless of the debate subject. Receiving an invitation to Cliveden in 1927, Shaw readily accepted. Their friendship was immediate. They delighted one another with their witty verbal fencing, and both enjoyed reducing the world's complex troubles to simple, common-sense aphorisms. Nancy's emotional, intuitive approach complemented Shaw's intellectual one. And not least of all, Shaw liked pretty women. In 1927, Nancy was nearly fifty but looked thirty. Her biographer, Christopher Sykes, recalls that his first impression of Nancy came about this time and was one of "dazzling beauty." For her part, Nancy must have been thoroughly enchanted with this wonderfully bizarre, radical even, self-contained wit and intellect. Nancy always possessed a highly developed sense of theater, another bond between the two.

In March of 1931, Nancy and Waldorf celebrated their twenty-fifth wedding anniversary quietly at Cliveden. Waldorf was not inactive apart from his wife. He was always prominent in civic and charitable affairs and was chairman of the influential Institute of International Affairs. His son Michael says he detected in his father a sense of obligation to England, to a life of public service, evolving from his father's conviction that William Waldorf had been rather negligent in this respect. This obligation was a difficult one for Waldorf because he had inherited his father's stuffy shyness and lack of human touch. But he tried. Says Michael, "The measure of his success in life, in my opinion, cannot be judged only by the 'good' and constructive things he did, of which his record is modestly impressive, so much as in the quality of his struggle to think, and where necessary to act, independently of inherited belief, which was not easy for him. . . ." Waldorf's pleasure came from his horses—his racing stable, one of England's finest, produced five second-place finishers in the Derby— and from fishing at his place on Jura in the Hebrides. He was also a first-rate agent for his wife, a role some have assumed he must have resented but that indications are he thrived on, delighting in the love and admiration and attention she attracted wherever she went, loving her completely and selflessly, and accepting his position as policy maker and rescuer of Nancy when she waded in somewhere over her head. He had no interest in the arts, neither smoked nor drank and, although he belonged to several, seldom darkened the doors of London clubs. In many ways Waldorf was too good to be true. What is more, his virtues complemented Nancy's. They both appeared to thrive during the 1920s.

Toward the end of that decade their Christian Science belief was put to its most severe test when their daughter Wissie, by then a popular debutante, injured her spine in a riding accident. Nancy's unwillingness to call in a surgeon was met with such stiff opposition from friends and family that she agreed to a compromise, inviting a surgeon who had once operated on her successfully to take a look at Wissie. He, an abdominal specialist, launched such a furious tirade at Nancy that she agreed to the bringing in of an orthopedic specialist, rationalizing the step by telling herself it would make no difference what he did anyway. The man was able to effect a complete, if slow and painful, recovery for Wissie, whose gratitude undoubtedly made up for whatever indifference her parents may have displayed toward the doctor and his ministrations.

The economic crisis that rocked the world in the wake of the stock market crash in the fall of 1929 in America appears to have affected the political life style of the Astors more than the social. Unemployment, bread lines and human suffering permeated nearly every stratum of the world's society, but not the topmost. This is not to say that the Astors were unaware of or indifferent to the misery in the world, but only that its direct effect on them was minimal, a matter for concerned discussion, surely, but on an abstract, somewhat removed level. It is interesting that despite her well-known and genuine concern for the welfare of the average person, Nancy—and therefore Waldorf—was unusually quiet in her public posture during the early years of what became known as the Great Depression. By her own admission, Nancy relied on her intuition to tell her the right side of an issue. The intellectual intricacies of economics she did not grasp, nor did she have the patience or the will to learn them. Her intuition offered no solutions, and intellects more vast and better trained than hers failed of solutions as miserably as had her intuition. Although it was not always the case, in this instance at least, Nancy showed the good judgment to remain silent on matters about which her opinion was not highly valued. Temporarily, her issues—women's rights, drinking, public health—and she along with them lost their glitter, their glamor, shoved from the limelight to the back row by the cataclysmic grimness of the Depression. Nancy was not long out of the limelight, although this time she had to share it.

Her friend Shaw had become something of a hero in Russia. He was forever referring to himself as a communist, and the Russians apparently assumed that his definition would not radically differ from their own. Shaw was invited to visit Russia in the summer of 1931. His wife was not well enough to make such a trip, and he said he would accept only if he was allowed to bring some friends. The Russians agreed, and Waldorf, Nancy, their son David, Philip Lothian and two or three others prepared to join Shaw on his trip. Philip Kerr, 11th Marquess of Lothian, was a Christian Scientist, a brilliant student of politics who would become England's ambassador to the United States during the early phases of World War II, and a devoted friend to Nancy and Waldorf. It has often been said he was in love with Nancy. For her, the relationship was purely platonic but very strong. Discreetly, she referred to him as Waldorf's friend. It was a congenial group that headed for Moscow, but Nancy and Waldorf traveled with a heavy burden of sorrow and concern.

Just days before they were scheduled to leave England,

Bobbie Shaw, Nancy's son by her first marriage, had been arrested for homosexual activity. The denouement had been brewing for some time, for Shaw's deviant proclivities were accompanied by an uncontrolled tendency toward self-destruction. British authorities attempted to look the other way, but Bobbie would neither desist nor leave the country. His arrest was the first indication his mother or stepfather had about his preferences and must have come as a profound shock to them both. Not unnaturally, one of their first concerns was about publicity. They managed that matter well enough so that no report was published in any newspaper, but the price exacted by the situation—the trip to Russia had been heavily publicized—was that Nancy and Waldorf were required to behave as if nothing had happened. They were inside Russia for only nine days, one of them being George Bernard Shaw's seventy-fifth birthday. Shaw was the main actor in the drama; Nancy was relegated to a supporting role, which she probably preferred, given her circumstances at the time.

Upon his return, Shaw told the press that were he a younger man he would emigrate to Russia immediately and recommended that course for thinking young men. Nancy and Waldorf ruffled no feathers, giving bland responses to the questions of newsmen whom they could not avoid. Even when Winston Churchill published a devastating attack on Shaw and his pro-Russian views and mistakenly attached similar sentiments to Nancy, whom he also excoriated, Nancy remained silent. Indeed, relatively speaking, she remained quiet for the next four years. At least part of the reason she appeared subdued must have been her grief over her son Bobbie, whose condition continued to deteriorate after he was released from jail, having served a four-month sentence. He lost his popularity with the social set when he lost his discretion. He was isolated,

and though he made repeated efforts to regain the main-
stream, his abandonment by all but a handful of friends
and family was complete. Soon he was dealing with this situation by attempting to drown its manifestations in liquor,
an attempt that must especially have upset his mother. For
more than thirty years thereafter, Bobbie Shaw dwelt in
the background of the Astors' life, a periodic reminder of
the impermanence of worldly comfort, joy or happiness.
Only two months before Nancy died in May of 1964, Bobbie made his final appearance in her life. He attempted
and, almost ineluctably, failed to commit suicide. Nancy
was told he had had a stroke.

As the 1930s unfolded, the fearful story of Hitler and
Nazi Germany was told. It is surely easier to predict the
ending in retrospect than it was as the drama was being
played out. One has only to look at the great divergence of
opinion on the subject of Russia's intentions today to understand that Hitler and his objectives were not always obvious. The role that Waldorf and Nancy played in determining England's posture toward Hitler, especially during
the early years of his rise to power, has received extravagant
attention. Its importance has undoubtedly been exaggerated. The fact is that Nancy was a fascinating personality,
publicly and privately, but she was not someone whose advice would have been much sought or much heeded in
matters of international diplomacy. The conjuring of conspiracy inspired by Claud Cockburn's reporting of "the
Cliveden set," starting in November 1937, is a sleight-of-
hand feat, a manipulation of the facts. To the extent that
some reports go so far as to question the Astors' loyalty to
England, they become absurd. Both Nancy and Waldorf,
whose lead Nancy was undoubtedly following in the matter, hoped for peace, perhaps even after peace had become
a hopelessly lost cause. They wanted to believe the Ger-

man assurances that each act of aggression would be the last; they wanted to believe their friends, the British leaders who continued to believe the Germans when such belief required an Olympian leap of faith, and they were slow to see the inexorability of Hitler's ambition. But they were not alone, by any means, and their position was not one of leadership. They were, it is true, host and hostess at gatherings where crucial decisions were discussed, if not made. But their contribution to these events appears to have been more or less limited to providing hospitality and privacy, and a measure of public support for positions reached for the most part without the benefit of their wisdom.

The most curious aspect of the whole "Cliveden set" affair is that its start—Cockburn's story in his own paper about a mission by Lord Halifax to Hitler behind Foreign Secretary Anthony Eden's back having been hatched at a weekend party given by the Astors—flies squarely in the face of the facts, none of which was particularly obscure. Just for example, Cockburn originally reported that Halifax was a guest at Cliveden that weekend. The fact was that he was not, that actually the Anthony Edens were featured that weekend. But what caught the public fancy was not the story Cockburn told in its particulars but the catchy tag he gave it—"the Cliveden set." The times were emotional. If something went wrong somewhere, more often than not the cause was either complex or arcane. It was easier to blame "them" or, in this case, "the Cliveden set." In this scenario, it wasn't that England and her leaders didn't know what was going on; it wasn't that they lacked the courage to act. It was that the government was being subverted—there were two Foreign Offices acting in opposition. Of course there were denials. Who would dare admit the truth?

As Christopher Sykes points out in his biography of Nancy, the truth is that the Astors were involved in but one or two actual incidents that might be construed as evidence of complicity in extragovernmental efforts to negotiate with the Germans. In no case does an incident not have a reasonable alternate explanation. It is true that a couple of the Astors' good friends engaged in some extracurricular activity that lacked discretion, and it is also true that Nancy on occasion allowed her tongue to outrun her good sense in making statements that could be interpreted as pro-German, if not pro-Nazi. But the sum of the evidence reveals nothing sinister. Naïve undoubtedly, but not sinister. Philip Lothian, about whom Nancy once said, "I've never known Philip wrong in twenty years on foreign politics and never right on home politics," was perhaps the strongest advocate of the appeasement policy for which Neville Chamberlain has taken so much abuse from history, urging appeasement all the way up to March 1939. War is, after all, a terrifying prospect for most rational men. Lothian was not alone in wanting to believe Nazi assurances long after the grounds for such belief had been washed away. Until the move into Poland, however, there was just enough of a trace of right—from a German nationalist point of view at least—in what Hitler said he was doing, if not in what he actually did, to allow the grasping at straws. Nancy was not pro-Nazi, or even particularly pro-German. War, however, was a no-win proposition in her view, and if Hitler's actions prior to invading Poland had been upsetting—the sorts of behavior Nancy could not have condoned in Britain—they were not sufficiently outrageous to overcome Nancy's abhorrence of war.

Sykes is most likely correct in his explanation for the longevity of "the Cliveden set" myth, although he offers that explanation rather tentatively. Neville Chamberlain was a

popular man in England. As the dreamlike quality of his
appeasement policy became clear, many people divided
their time between being awake to reality and asleep
dreaming of peace, wanting to have their cake and eat it
too. When appeasement became impossible with the invasion of Poland British self-esteem required some minor re-
visions to history that would show England the victim of a
wicked plot. There was enough inaccurate reporting in the
newspapers—documents of historical record—along with
some accurate record of Nancy's indiscretions (of speech
only) to allow the building or solidifying of the myth.
Nancy's American heritage—as well as Waldorf's—no
doubt did not hamper the mythmakers. Things could be
believed of a foreigner that would not be believed of a loyal
British subject. Finally, neither Nancy nor Waldorf did
much, either at the time or later, to refute or dispel the
myth, perhaps because they saw it as so outrageous a
fabrication as to be humorous rather than threatening. This
is not to say that the tales of "the Cliveden set" did not gall
the Astors, but only that they perhaps felt that to make a
fuss over the allegations would be to give them a credibility
and importance they wouldn't otherwise have and didn't
deserve.

At any rate, when the Astors dropped their approval of
appeasement, they dropped it completely. Their contributions to the war effort and the British spirit, although in
some places the subject of considerable hyperbole, are nowhere denied. Both at Cliveden, where once again the Canadians set up a hospital, and at Plymouth, the city Nancy
represented in the House of Commons, the Astors behaved
with courage, showing their feelings most clearly in the
codicils they wrote to their wills expressing the wish to be
buried in a common grave with the other casualties if they
died in an air raid on Plymouth. The Astors had become

deeply attached to Plymouth. Besides being the district that elected Nancy to the House of Commons seven straight times between 1919 and 1945, Plymouth had also made the Astors Lord Mayor and Lady Mayoress in 1939. From the beginning of the Battle of Britain, Nancy and Waldorf had watched Plymouth being reduced to rubble and had vowed to rebuild it. The spirit of the Plymouth people needed no rebuilding, but nonetheless Nancy made sure it did not flag. She and Waldorf were constantly out among the people in the aftermath of an air raid and frequently during one. Nancy decided dancing would help and saw to it that a band played every evening on the Hoe, a harbor embankment park.

Noel Coward is quoted in a biography by Cole Lesley after a visit to Nancy at Plymouth in this period: "Lady Astor very breezy, noisy and au fond incredibly kind, banging people on the back and making jokes. The people themselves stoic, sometimes resentful of her but generally affectionately tolerant. The whole city a pitiful sight, houses that have held sailor families since the time of Drake spread across the road in rubble and twisted wood. . . . Watched the people of Plymouth dancing on the Hoe. A large dance floor, white coated band, several hundred girls gaily dressed, dancing very well with sailors, soldiers, marines, etc., in the strong evening sunlight. A sight so touching, not that it was consciously brave but because it was so ordinary and unexhibitionist. The English do not always take their pleasures sadly, at least not when they are surrounded by death and destruction."

Waldorf echoed these sentiments about the English people in a letter he wrote a cousin back in the United States, Margaret Aldrich, on June 17, 1940, the day after France had asked to be released from its obligations under an Anglo-French agreement barring a separate peace and the very day on which France asked for armistice terms from Germany. He was, he said: ". . . mentally shattered by the announcement that France had let us down and had run out on us. . . . This is a magnificent people here—both in adversity and in success they are staunch and cheerful."

Plymouth became even more special for Nancy when it became home for the 29th Division, U. S. Army, a force that featured men with Southern accents. In July 1943, General C. H. Gerhard was sent to Plymouth to take command of the division, arriving with three orders. One of them—it may even have been the first—was to get along with Nancy. When General Gerhard opened their first conversation with "My mother was Richmond," he was an instant hit. She enjoyed telling his soldiers, "When you behave yourselves here, say that you are from Virginia, but when you get drunk and disorderly, tell people that you come from New York."

In a way, Nancy thrived on the war. She once said, "Only I and Mr. Churchill enjoy the war, but only I admit it." She was neither insensitive nor ghoulish, but she was always at her best ministering to the sufferers. She seemed capable of losing herself in alleviating the misery of others. Her ability to cajole, caress or badger with effect was legendary. At Cliveden during the first war she had come across several Canadians badly wounded and prepared to give up the ghost. "Well," she said, "if I were faced with having to return to Canada if I lived, I probably would just as soon die." The thrust was accurate. Their will to live rekindled in their desire to defend Canada, the soldiers soon recovered, doubtless unaware of the psychological magic show they'd been a part of. Her barbed sense of humor was honed by crisis, and no one escaped. Rose Harrison, her maid, remembers a time during World War II when Waldorf's valet brought back a maternity smock after Rose had ripped her regular one. Whether it was all that was available or whether the valet was having his own little joke Rose was never sure, but when she put on the new smock Nancy looked at her and said, "I didn't know you were in that sort of trouble." Rose of course protested vigorously, but Nancy was unswayed. "No use blaming that on enemy action," she pronounced solemnly.

For all her wealth, fame and good works, Nancy found out she was not above the law. She was hauled into court and fined £50 at one point after a censor had read her letter to a friend in the United States asking for nylons and other items unattainable in wartime England. The news prompted one of her sons to remark that it was probably a good thing she was caught, that she was working too hard and could use a year in the pokey.

If the war years appeared to feature Nancy, Waldorf was not inactive, although his health was not as good during this period, and he did spend much time bedridden. The hectic pace Nancy set between London, Cliveden and Plymouth would have tested someone in robust health. Nonetheless, Waldorf directed the show in which Nancy starred. He also wrote the script, although no one could prevent Nancy from ad-libbing with a certain unpredictable regularity. From a different viewpoint, Nancy could have been seen as the field representative, assessing the wants and needs and reporting back to Waldorf, who took appropriate action. The point is simply that it is too easy to forget Waldorf when in Nancy's consuming presence, but Waldorf ought not to be underestimated. In his quiet way, Waldorf pulled the strings.

With the end of the war, many things ended. The most traumatic for Nancy and Waldorf was his decision that she should not stand for re-election to the House of Commons. Waldorf, his health tenuous, saw the end of the war as a time to step aside for new blood. He and Nancy were both of retirement age. He knew he could no longer be of much help to her, who had never contested an election on her own, and he feared that if she won she would become an anachronism in Parliament, a relic who might leave herself open to the humiliation of being laughed at or, worse, ignored. Nancy fought this decision, lost and never forgave Waldorf, even after his death. The decision opened a gap between them that neither knew how to close. Rose sensed that her mistress attempted to avoid Waldorf once the decision became final.

Waldorf also trimmed the household budget after the war by selling the great house on St. James's Square and replacing it with a smaller establishment at 35 Hill Street, where the Astors had to make do with a reduced staff consisting only of a butler, a footman, a housekeeper, a housemaid, a chef, a kitchenmaid, a chauffeur, an odd man, Rose and a flock of dailies. The pace of life slowed, the decibel level dropped. Nancy's immediate reaction was restlessness, the dread of growing old. In her eightieth year, she had mellowed: "Years ago I thought that old age would be dreadful because I should not be able to do the things I want to do. Now I find there is nothing I want to do after all."

The danger in chronicling Waldorf and Nancy's life together is that one will get carried away with their public lives, especially during the early years, when in fact a look at their domestic existence may actually be more revealing, even though the picture is sometimes blurred by contradictory reports. The availability of alcohol at the home of the teetotaling Astors, for example, has been the subject of some disagreement. The New York *Times* claimed liquor was not served at Cliveden but was smuggled in by guests and Astor children, one exception being a granddaughter's coming-out party where champagne and beer were provided. However, Christopher Sykes quotes Edwin Lee, the Astor butler, as saying that drinks were always served at the Astors' at lunch and dinner, and Rose Harrison in her autobiography recalls Lady Astor ordering Lee to use Cliveden's best claret for a claret cup, saying, "You'll order no more until that's used up." Lee, Rose says, considered the order "a bloody sacrilege."

The stories about Lee are as legendary as those about Lady Astor. Cleveland Amory says Lee was known in the back halls of Cliveden as "Lord Lee." He knew his place, but he was not above reminding Lady Astor of hers if she strayed. Amory tells the story of how Nancy insisted on approving the hiring of a new footman and during an interview told a prospect that he would have, of course, to clean windows. He asked her pardon and said he would only perform a footman's duties, whereupon Nancy refused to hire him. When Lee explained the propriety of the would-be footman's position, Nancy apologized, asking Lee to call the fellow back. Lee said he could not. "You have created a situation," he told his mistress, "from which there is no retreat." According to Rose, Lee would occasionally, although always with respect and discretion, provide a commentary on Nancy. "She is not a lady as you would understand a lady, Miss Harrison," Lee once said, a remark interpreted by Rose to mean that Nancy was not a conformist. On another occasion he told Rose: "Lady Astor is not a religious woman; she's all the time looking for a light she can never find." Lee was unflappable, a quality Nancy tested to its limits on more than one occasion. If Rose is to be believed, the supreme test may well have come on an evening when, minutes before the expected arrival of members of the royal family, Nancy clambered atop the dining-room table in her stocking feet, knocking over glasses and silverware, spilling water, tugging at the floral arrangement and yelling disparaging words to anyone within hearing.

Accepting that there was no such thing as an average or normal day for the Astors or for Cliveden, it is still possible to construct what might be called a composite day. For Waldorf the day began with coffee at six-thirty in the morning. Nancy's schedule, according to Rose, began with breakfast at eight-thirty, then a cold bath followed by the daily Christian Science lesson. After that Nancy attended to the day's mail and phone calls before dressing for the day's exercise—golf, tennis, squash, swimming, skating or skiing were all activities in which she indulged on occasion. She then returned to her rooms for a warm bath after which she was off to the House of Commons, a friend's house or a shop or two. Lunch on the late side, a change of clothes for the afternoon and another change before dinner, making all told five dressing sessions a day. It may be that Rose is exaggerating in a search for sympathy, but clearly Nancy's maid had her hands full, starting early each morning with the cleaning of Nancy's shoes and the ironing of their laces. Nancy was also, Rose says, a contrary creature, who would ask for one dress, look at it scornfully and claim she had asked for a different one, and then put on the first while Rose fetched the second. Rose quotes Nancy as telling her once, "Rose, it's my ambition to break your spirit," but it is obvious from Rose's book that Rose was devoted to her mistress, who would take a mile if given an inch but who would admit the error of her ways and apologize if stood up to. Rose remembers Lady Astor asking her if she would like a chocolate and, when Rose said yes, Nancy would take a bite of one and give the remainder to Rose, saying it was a kind she didn't like. Rose would throw it away, and the whole scene would be repeated. The impression one is left with is that Nancy enjoyed jabbing away at Rose but only to the extent that Rose proved a worthy opponent, capable of absorbing the punishment without visible effect and of dishing out an occasional saucy return. Rose, who first went to Cliveden as maid to Nancy's daughter, watched while Nancy trampled her way through four maids in a matter of a few short months before usurping Rose.

Nancy seems always to have been on stage. Family evenings at home almost always involved charades or mimicry, with Nancy and her sons Bobbie Shaw and Jakie creating the laughter while David shared in the fun and Bill and Michael represented the quiet side of the family on the sidelines. Michael has written that visitors imposed "a modicum of restraint" but that "when we were just the family all sense of personal privacy evaporated." Rose says Nancy could cry on command and dominated virtually every gathering of which she was a part, being cowed by only three people—Queen Mary and two of her (Nancy's) older sisters. She was on time only for trains, royalty and the seating of the House of Commons. Perhaps because she was nearly always running late, Nancy had a habit of running red lights. She was stopped frequently but never prosecuted, says Rose.

Nancy was, Michael says, congenitally incapable of recognizing any limits to what she could do. Or spend. In the lower dining room of the London house hung two portraits —one of John Jacob Astor, the other of Nancy. She used to tell her guests they pictured the man who made the millions and the woman who was spending them. For all her fame and fortune, looks and success, Nancy was a cantankerous sort. The word among the servants at Cliveden, Rose wrote, was, "Satisfy Lady Astor." Pleasing her, the implication was clear, could not be done. Rose says in her book that the other Astors used to tell her she made all their lives easier by keeping Nancy happy, relatively.

Michael places the religious habits acquired by his parents as roughly coinciding with—although in no way but circumstantially connected to—his birth in 1916. Actually, Nancy was conspicuously religious long before then. She did, however, change allegiance about then, becoming a Christian Scientist. She went to church twice a week and spent several hours a day reading religious material. For his part, Waldorf reserved time in the mornings and the evenings for his own reading and prayer.

In many respects Waldorf's personality was antipodal to Nancy's. Rose compared the two by saying that Waldorf was "the epitome of an English gentleman," easy, unassuming and showing his love for Nancy in everything he did, while Nancy "wasn't equipped to show love." The Cliveden gardener put it another way, noting that if Waldorf wanted something, he asked if it was possible; Nancy demanded it. The fishing trips to the Astor lodge on Jura that were such a joy to Waldorf frustrated and bored Nancy, who once threw four golf balls at the Jura house while putting on the lawn outside. Two of them hit—and shattered—windows.

Waldorf's mastery of interpersonal relationships was always somewhat suspect. The best of intentions did not always provoke the most appropriate of actions, but if his notions of propriety ever conflicted with those of fairness, the latter won out. He once gave a butler he fired £1,000, explaining that the man had to be fired because he had been caught dipping into the sauce, but that he received the £1,000 because when sober he was an excellent servant.

If Michael is right, Waldorf was not a very happy man. In *Tribal Feeling*, Michael writes poignantly, "What I was not able to say to him was that I wished to heavens he would not be so unselfish, and that he would try kicking over the traces and find some way of having a good time." Perhaps Michael in his youth mistook exuberance for happiness. Certainly exuberance was missing from Waldorf's life, except as he partook vicariously of his wife's. The evidence points to his having found peace, at least, in the year before his death. Confined to a wheelchair because of his heart condition, he exuded benevolence. The benevolence had always been there, latent behind his cool, stern exterior, but now, in 1952, at the age of seventy-three, he apparently had decided that the family no longer required his tight discipline, his rigid leadership. And so he gave his love, which was probably the real side of him anyway. Quietly, as he had lived, he died on September 30, 1952. The New York *Times* noticed his passing the next day on page 33. His last words to his eldest son were, "Look after Mother," repeated with urgency.

The indomitable Nancy lived on, remaining mostly in London with her two small dogs and Rose, who cared for the dogs and listened to her mistress complain that she took better care of the dogs than of her mistress. One of Nancy's inscrutable quirks was a profound fear of cats, a fear that long ago had resulted in a standing order to the Cliveden gamekeepers to shoot cats on sight. In 1958, as she neared eighty, Nancy sold the home on Hill Street and leased a residence at 100 Eaton Square. That year she was honored by the residents of Plymouth and honored Rose by, for the first time, giving her a key to the front door. Her memory was failing, and as the months dragged into years, senility enveloped her relentlessly despite occasional flashes of her old acid wit. In 1963 her son Bill, the third viscount, was involved in the tawdry and sensational Profumo affair, receiving considerably more publicity than his very minor role as the unknowing host to some of the major figures warranted. It taxed the imagination and resources of her staff, but Nancy was kept in the dark. Radio stations would be switched just before news broadcasts, or Nancy would be called away before she could listen by a fake telephone call. Then one morning the old lady slipped one over on everyone, getting up early and collecting the morning papers before anyone else rose. She read all about the scandal and, rising to the occasion, told her son David that she must be driven down to Cliveden so that the public could see the family solidarity and son Bill could have the support he must surely need. David agreed. On the way, Nancy asked several questions, and it became clear she had forgotten why she was going to Cliveden, turning the trip into a pleasant but trivial visit rather than the visitation of an angel of mercy.

In April 1964, Nancy suffered a crippling stroke. On the second of May—just seventeen days before her eighty-fifth birthday—Nancy whispered, "Waldorf," and died. The New York *Times* acknowledged the event the following day at the bottom of page 1, giving it the same play as Northern Dancer's winning of the Kentucky Derby. She died at Grimsthorpe Castle, the home of her daughter Wissie, now Lady Ancaster, wife of the Earl of Ancaster. The London *Times* said, "Her worst fault was a habit of interruption, which, however tempered with wit, was apt to cause annoyance." The New York *Times* chose to remember her comparison of England and the United States: "England is older and wiser than America. America is very young, very large, very rich and very bumptious and I don't blame her. So when you come across a 100 percent American, don't be frightened of him, pity him and put him in his place." The London *Times* noted that she had publicly acknowledged her debt to Rachel McMillan,

Arthur Balfour, Philip Lothian and Henry James. An odd collection, that. Rachel McMillan died in 1917, some nine years before Nancy met Rachel's sister Margaret. The McMillans were involved in some pioneering public health work. Margaret and Nancy became close friends, despite Nancy's normal scorn for mystical beliefs such as Margaret's conviction that her sister's spirit vitally influenced her work. Balfour, a Conservative, was a former Prime Minister and good friend who died in 1930. Lothian was perhaps Nancy's closest friend, male or female. And Henry James was an early and admired acquaintance whose contact with Nancy was, however, intermittent.

It was James who capsulized Nancy with subtle but pinpoint accuracy when he affectionately called her "a reclaimed barbarian."

CHAPTER 13

Perhaps the most interesting Astor of the twentieth century lived a remarkably quiet life off stage, content to allow the footlights to shine on his sister-in-law, Nancy, despite his own record of accomplishment, which in some ways she could not begin to match. This man was born John Jacob Astor V in 1886 in the United States and died Baron Astor of Hever, exiled in the south of France, in 1971. If Jack Armstrong, the All-American Boy, had an English inspiration, it might well have been this Astor, or perhaps Yale's Frank Merriwell would have been a more appropriate offspring.

J.J., as he was sometimes called en famille, was a splendid athlete as a young man. He loved games—cricket, squash, racquets, polo, golf, to name a few. In the 1908 Olympics he won a gold medal in racquets doubles competition and a bronze medal in singles, but his winning of the Parliament squash championship in 1926 and again in 1927 may have been even more dramatic triumphs, for he won playing on but one leg. John, you see, was also a war hero—not just an unfortunate victim but a genuine hero. After joining the 1st Life Guards in 1906 and serving as A.D.C. to the Viceroy of India starting in 1911, John went to France in 1914 with the Household Cavalry. He was wounded but stayed at the front, refusing two staff appointments. Finally he was given a battery command in the fall of 1917. Two months before the Armistice, John was wounded again, in fourteen places. His right leg had to be amputated, and he was retired as a major. During World War II he was made an honorary colonel and commanded the City Press Battalion of the Home Guard. His tenacity as an athlete permitted his playing sports well into his seventh decade despite the fact that the loss of his leg meant constant discomfort and not infrequent pain. Astor was the rugged outdoor type, enjoying shooting parties at Hever Castle, which he had been given by his father before the latter's death, tree-felling and working his dogs. But he was not just muscle and bone. He liked good conversation as much as a good game and played the organ and painted. "He was a man," said the London *Times*, control of which he had purchased for $7 million in 1922, "who, once he had decided to interest himself in anything, was prepared to give it unlimited attention." The article was written after Astor's financial interest in the *Times* had dropped from 90 to 15 percent. One assumes his editorial influence fell accordingly.

Bowing to what was rapidly becoming an inviolate family tradition, John essayed Parliament in 1921, was defeated in a close election and tried again in 1922. He won and remained as the Conservative representative from Dover until the end of the Second World War. Ironically, for a man whose public shyness was so pronounced he would on occasion be reduced to whispering, John spent much of his adult life in public service, managing to do so with relatively little recognition. From his position at the *Times,* he went on to become chairman of the Commonwealth Press Union and the Press Council. He was a substantial benefactor of the Middlesex Hospital, to which, for example, he gave £300,000 in 1948 to build a nurses' residence and £450,000 between 1955 and 1957 to rebuild the medical school. He was chairman of the governing body of the hospital, starting in 1938, and of the medical school, starting in 1945, until 1962 when he was forced to give up his residency in England and go into exile in the south of France because of new tax laws that would have left his heirs with but a small part of his fortune upon his death had he remained a resident of Great Britain. The Royal College of Music and St. Bride's Church also reaped the benefits of his generosity. In his obituary, the *Times* said, "No man can have done good with a greater absence of fuss."

While John and his brother Waldorf were close and saw one another often in London, their respective wives found little to relish in each other's company and family visits were few and far between. John did not mingle much with Nancy at Parliament although their terms largely coincided. He could be seen at times blushing with embarrassment at his rash relative's disruptive outbursts. John did not altogether escape "the Cliveden set" furor because the *Times,* over which John exercised no editorial control under his contract with editor Geoffrey Dawson, supported appeasement and, being Astor-owned, tended to be included in the amorphous collection of institutions, people and ideas dubbed "the Cliveden set." John must not have been too badly damaged by this association, as he served from 1937 through 1939 as a member of the General Advisory Council for the British Broadcasting Co.

Perhaps John's most embarrassing public moment took

place in 1924 when he came home from a trip abroad and dashed down to Parliament—he had just been re-elected without opposition—to cast his vote on a tariff matter. He had not been sworn in. It is considered bad form to vote in the House of Commons without having been duly sworn. John's election was voided, and he had to stand for re-election all over again. His constituents were apparently untroubled by John's lapse and in due time he was once again properly installed in his seat in Parliament. The incident must have been doubly painful for this man who could not bear publicity of any kind, not to mention adverse publicity. It is rather ironic that so shy a person as John was immensely popular with the public. Luckily for him, it was not the popularity bobby soxers bestowed on Frank Sinatra or groupies gave to Mick Jagger but more the restrained, respectful attention reserved for the admired. John personified the perfect English gentleman—sportsman, war hero, public servant, quiet club member, lord of a distinctive but unostentatious manor. Lord, at least, in all but title, and that little oversight was rectified in 1956 when the list of New Year's Honors included John as Baron Astor of Hever.

In a long life of doing the right thing, John never made a happier decision than the one leading to his marriage in 1916 to Lady Violet Mary Elliot Mercer-Nairne, daughter of the 4th Earl of Minto, who had been Governor General of Canada and Viceroy of India. Lady Violet's first husband was killed early in World War I, and John began seeing her while recuperating from a shrapnel wound. One thing led, rapidly and with the impatient prodding of John's delighted father, to another. The marriage was long, happy and fruitful, Lady Violet bearing J.J. three sons. She was by all accounts appropriately named Violet, being, like her husband, generally reticent and reserved by nature, although not lacking in verve.

All England was touched by the sad spectacle of Lord and Lady Astor in 1962 pulling up stakes and roots to move to France for the sake of their children's inheritance. Both were in their seventies and enjoyed great popularity. Many still remembered the great parties J.J. used to throw before World War II for the entire staff of the *Times*, family and friends, a group that could reach 3,000. Whether you ran a linotype machine or a government, the atmosphere was warm and festive. The Astors weren't the sort of people you forced into exile in their old age. Well, at least they had each other. Just after the New Year of 1965, on January 3, Lady Violet died following a short illness. J.J. struggled on alone for six and a half years, dying in the south of France in July 1971. The Astors had had good lives and were not bitter about having to move away from England. In fact J.J. had set up a charitable trust aimed at the medical and education fields with the money he saved by moving and the proceeds from a sale of many of the Astors' non-portable possessions.

The story persists that William Waldorf was so enchanted by the prospect of his younger son's marriage to Lady Violet that he offered her $4 million and $30,000 a year for life if she would agree to a wedding within six months. She did, but if she received the money from William Waldorf it did not show up in her estate after she died. The New York *Times* reported her estate as $340,800.

The standard method for keeping the English Astors of today straight is to distinguish between Cliveden Astors, the descendants of Waldorf and Nancy, and Hever Astors, the heirs of J.J. and Lady Violet. Waldorf and J.J. had a sister, Pauline, who married a fellow named Spender-Clay and had two daughters. Since the Astor name was lost upon marriage, keeping these folks in the right place presents no difficulty. J.J.'s and Lady Violet's three sons are named Gavin, the eldest and the present Lord Astor of Hever; Hugh Waldorf; and John. The three sons have thirteen children of their own—five each for Gavin and Hugh and three for John, who is, incidentally, without the Jacob for a middle name. The eldest in this generation is Gavin's son John Jacob VIII, born in 1946. The eighth namesake of the original John Jacob was, of course, educated at Eton. At twenty, he was commissioned in the Life Guards, serving for five years in Hong Kong, Malaya, Northern Ireland and London before becoming a private citizen and joining Savills, surveyors and property agents. Johnnie has since started his own real estate business and gained some notoriety by impressing Queen Elizabeth with his playing of the bagpipes at his father's sixtieth birthday party in 1978, a dinner at which the guests of honor were the Queen and Prince Philip.

The contrast between Johnnie and his father, Gavin, is prototypical of the changing life styles among the Hever Astors of their respective generations. It is closely paralleled within the Cliveden branch, too. Through World War II, Gavin's life was patterned after his father's—Eton, Oxford's New College, military service during a war. Gavin was taken a prisoner of war in Italy nine months before the war ended. As his father gradually withdrew from an active role at the *Times*, Gavin took over, even following his father as chairman of the Council of the Commonwealth Press Union. Like his father, he has held a number of largely honorary or ceremonial positions. But in 1967 an event took place that symbolizes the changing status of the Astor family (again, there is a near parallel on the Cliveden side)—the *Times* and the *Sunday Times* were merged.

Gavin, who had acquired 100 percent control of the *Times* four years earlier, became honorary life president, but the equity of the new enterprise was divided 15 percent to the Astors and 85 percent to the Thomson Organization. Gavin and his brothers and the children of Nancy and Waldorf represent a transitional generation. Their parents could do more or less whatever they wanted, depending only on how firmly tied to tradition and traditional expectations they were. Money was—in a way that few families have ever experienced—truly no object. The children have had to exercise some economies, or at least curtail the more outlandish extravagances. *Their* children are going to work. One need not yet offer condolences. The Astors are largely self-employed if they wish to be—employers rather than employees—and if money is now an object in their lives, its lack is not a major obstacle. They still enjoy most of the comforts of wealth and station. Fewer servants, smaller manors, but servants and manor houses. Hever Castle is now run as a commercial venture, open to the public most of the time despite the fact that Gavin and his family continue to live there.

Gavin and his wife Irene's three daughters provide a compact guide to the range of opportunities beyond self-employment Astors are now availing themselves of. The eldest, Bridget, born in 1948, is a professional photographer. Louise, the next child, is a registered nurse and a master of foxhounds. The youngest, Sarah, is married to the younger son of the 6th Baron Roxborough. It was she who made something of a name for herself in 1970 by riding her pony from Land's End to John o'Groats to help raise money for the World Wildlife Fund, causing more than one wag to raise a rhetorical eyebrow in recognition of the irony implicit in such an act when performed by a direct descendant of the original John Jacob Astor, who did

so much toward decimating the fur-bearing animal population of North America. Such recognition is more a clever
historical note than an accurate contrast, however, the
truth being that old John Jacob probably had great respect
for and understanding of wildlife and would have been just
as concerned about irreversible damage to it as Sarah. His
life, after all, depended on it.

Gavin farms about 3,500 acres and has several dairy
herds. Besides Hever, he has a substantial place in Aber-
deenshire, Scotland, whereon royalty is not an infrequent
guest. Shooting is Gavin's recreation. John, the youngest
brother, is, like Gavin, a farmer now with about 1,000 acres
in England. Honoring an Astor tradition, John served as a
member of the House of Commons for ten years, until
1974. If ingenuity is a genetic characteristic, John displays
his in the vineyard, an experiment he began in 1971. He
now corks a few thousand bottles a year of white and rosé
wine, whose market price is justified by its quality, which is
modest. The middle brother, Hugh, is the nearest thing to
an adventurer the Astor line has produced (excepting those
irrepressible Chanler boys) since the original John Jacob.
Hugh's business interests are ordinary and clearly influenced by older brother Gavin, to whom he has always
been close. At play, Hugh is primarily a coverer of long distances. He flies his own plane and once competed in an air
race from London to Australia, managing to finish, which
was more than many of his fellow competitors did. He also
enjoys ocean racing, at which he has had several significant
successes over relatively short distances, like Oslo to Ost-
end.

But ocean racing and piloting your own plane all across
the globe are the kinds of activity that belong to an era
whose final chapter is now being written. No one recog-
nizes this fact any more clearly than the younger Astors,

one of whom was quoted by Alan L. Otten in a 1979 *Wall Street Journal* article as saying that the family fortune was "petering out at exactly the right time" to keep the Astors alive and on their toes. The speaker is a Cliveden Astor—a grandson of Nancy and Waldorf, Michael's eldest, David, who was thirty-five at the time of the story and who listed his occupations as farmer, rare bookstore proprietor and lobbyist for the English National Theater. He can count an interior decorator, a teacher and an engineer among his working relatives. "There's a lot of us around and we have to start working," David told Otten. "And it's about time we did." David has a brother, two sisters and fourteen first cousins in his generation of the Cliveden branch, making thirty-one English Astors in that generation, up from eight the generation before. Add taxation to the equation and it begins to become clear why a vast fortune of yesterday divided by its heirs may equal something almost paltry, from the viewpoint of the noble rich, today. Even without the help of mismanagement, frivolity or carelessness.

The eldest child of Nancy and Waldorf was, naturally, William Waldorf Astor, named for his grandfather, who had chosen in naming Waldorf to drop the William from his own name. He was, of course, from an early age destined to be the third viscount, and he grew up appropriately—reserved, obedient, "a traditional eldest son," as his brother Michael has put it. Bill, as he was called in the family, grew up in the shadow of his mother. As cox of the Eton crew Bill won his race the first day of a particular meet but lost on the second day. His mother explained to him why. For her, the facts were simple: Bill had attended Bible studies the first day and had skipped them the second. And Nancy was not the sort to tolerate being humored about her beliefs. There was nothing humorous about them. Bill was born in 1907 and by the early 1930s

was doing considerable traveling, first for the Institute of
Public Relations in the Far East, then as private secretary
to Lord Lytton on the League of Nations Commission of
Inquiry to Manchuria. He held a variety of public service
posts until his father died in 1952 and he became the third
viscount. In 1935 he was elected to Parliament, the first
M.P. in British history to sit in the House of Commons
with his mother. After service in the Mideast during
World War II, Bill returned to lose his House of Commons seat in 1945. He lost another election in a different
district in 1950, won in that new district in 1951, but had
to resign in 1952 when he moved to the House of Lords.
Bill's chief charitable interests were hospitals and aid to
refugees. His sport was horse racing and breeding, where he
was quite successful, although not a serious rival to his father. One claim to fame Bill and his family would undoubtedly have been happy to relinquish involved Bill in
the scandalous Profumo affair, in which Russian spies, call
girls and British statesmen were discovered in various compromising positions. Some of the fun and games took place
at Cliveden, because Bill knew Dr. Stephen Ward, more
socially than professionally, and rented him a cottage on
the estate. Ward and Bill saw art in a pretty face, a well-
turned ankle, and Bill probably enjoyed having the gaggle
of girls with which Ward was usually surrounded loll deco-
ratively around his swimming pool. Bill also, of course,
knew Jack Profumo, then Britain's War Minister, because
Viscount Astor knew such people. But Bill could in no way
be linked to the relationship that developed between one
of Ward's lovelies, Christine Keeler, and Profumo. Still, it
all stirred up quite a fuss in the newspapers, and for a few
days Cliveden was under siege, with reporters hovering
overhead in helicopters and crawling about behind every
bush. This was even better than the old "Cliveden set,"

which was arguably too cerebral to appeal to a broad range of readers. But put sex, wealth, nobility, top government officials and espionage together and you really had a story. The trial started in July of 1963. It proved too much for Ward, who was found guilty and sentenced himself, committing suicide. Bill survived the ignominy of it all but died three years later while on holiday in Nassau, a victim of cancer. He was fifty-eight.

The next of Waldorf and Nancy's children was Nancy Phyllis Louise, Wissie, whom younger brother Michael has described as "older but lovely." Rose Harrison, who was Phyllis' maid before being appropriated by Nancy, says Phyllis was more like her father than her mother and was not dependent on Nancy. "She got interference, of course," Rose wrote. "None of the children could avoid that, nor indeed could any of the staff." Having been rebuffed, one infers, in the past, Wissie was not inclined to ask her mother for the loan of any jewelry, furs or other accouterments, but Rose was able to prevail on Nancy, thereby surprising Wissie on occasion by presenting her with a fur coat or a piece of jewelry on loan from her mother, if Rose's version of the situation is to be believed. Wissie's wedding to Willoughby de Eresby, heir to the Earl of Ancaster, was advertised as a simple affair, which says more about the normal state of lavishness at Cliveden than it does about the wedding, for which a special train was hired to bring five hundred guests down from London to Cliveden for the ceremony and celebration. Nancy decreed that there should be no canopy outside the church, telling the workmen, "We will let the sun get at them. Happy the birds on whom the sun shines." Nancy did not let go easily. Rose remembered a vociferous exchange between Wissie and her mother after the marriage about a dress Wissie was wearing. Nancy insisted that Wissie change it; Wissie refused. Rose arbitrated. Wissie may be the last of the English Astors to recognize roots in America. In the late 1930s she applied for membership in the Colonial Dames of America, filling out a form in which she spelled Cliveden "Clivedon" and called her father the first viscount in the family (he was No. 2).

Nancy and Waldorf's next two children are David and Michael, very unlike in many ways but sharing a conviction that the traditional values and trappings with which they were surrounded growing up are not all life has to offer. Both might be described as rebels, but unlike their counterparts in the wealthy families of the United States, David and Michael have not forsworn the system or trod the radical path. They simply have carved out some space for themselves, changing a few rules or ignoring them, but not insisting that those rules are inherently evil and need to be changed for everyone. Neither Michael nor David abjures his heritage or his inheritance, as some Rockefellers, du Ponts and others are inclined to do. David is the humanitarian, the liberal, the champion of the underprivileged. Michael is the artist, turning inward for solutions.

David is best known as the former editor of the *Observer*, one of the United Kingdom's most prestigious newspapers. His younger brother Michael contends David was alone among his parents' "Cliveden set" in suspecting the true aims and motivation of Germany, Hitler, Russia and Stalin in the mid-thirties. Sadly, no one asked him his opinion. Although his political opinions were anathema to most of the family, David ran the *Observer* with an élan no one questioned. Under him, the *Observer* began publishing writers like Arthur Koestler, George Orwell and Cyril Connolly, whose style and ratiocination were impeccable even if one cringed at their conclusions. With David calling the shots, the *Observer* became the champion of decolonization, fought racism, traditionalism and classism and prepared Great Britain for the cultural revolution of the 1960s. It then began to lose some of its appeal, says Godfrey Hodgson, writing in the Christmas, 1976, issue of the *Nation,* because it became increasingly shrill in its deploring of the revolution's manifestations. David would no doubt argue that "manifestations" is the wrong word, that the *Observer* denounced "the excesses." At any rate, the *Observer* was further plagued with financial troubles, problems far more important than the disenchantment of some readers. The *Observer,* one of Britain's most influential Sunday papers, was not part of a vast commercial empire able to absorb relatively small losses to preserve a worthwhile British institution. The red ink was on the ledgers for nearly a decade before David finally succumbed to the pressure to sell. Rupert Murdoch seemed for a while the leading prospective buyer, a prospect David rationalized by saying it was "better to have an efficient Visigoth than nothing at all." Then along came Robert O. Anderson and the oil money of Atlantic Richfield. Hodgson speculated in his article that Anderson appealed to Astor because he could afford to leave the *Observer* alone whereas Murdoch would have made some changes. If that is true, it would appear Astor has made a wise choice. He is a member of the new Anderson board of directors for the *Observer,* able to keep an eye on, if not control of, his old paper, and Anthony Holden, the paper's chief correspondent in the United States, says he has received no interference at all from the new owners, even when he has been stridently critical of U.S. oil companies. David is yet another Astor in whom the oxymoronic characteristic of shyness combined with politeness tends to dominate his public image, making him seem very modest. In writing about the viability of yet another Astor biography in the

summer of 1979, David said: "The real trouble is that few
members of my family either in the past or at present have
played a conspicuous role in business or in politics. . . . It
is true that the family name has a certain resonance, particularly in the last century. But that was simply due to the
family's exceptional wealth, rather than because they were
engaging in interesting activities." The point David misses,
even if you concede the ones he makes, is that the activities
of the rich are intrinsically intriguing. As Louis Auchincloss writes in his introduction to Dixon Wecter's *The
Saga of American Society:*

"One should be able to learn at least something of the
aspirations of an era by a study of its fashionable set, for
what those people are up to may to some extent represent
what the masses would like to be up to." Further along in
the same paragraph, Auchincloss adds, "There have even
been times, wandering through European palaces crammed
with the portraits and collections of the rich and mighty,
that I have wondered if anything at all survives of history
but the toys of the ruling class." Astor tales have an even
broader appeal, one inherent in all stories about the super-
rich. For every person interested in the historical or socio-
logical revelations to be had in a study of wealth, there
must be at least one hundred people salivating at the prospect of an enrichment of the gossip store. When someone
has eggs and bacon for breakfast, that is never news, but if
the right person eats them, that becomes gossip.

Among the English Astors, Michael, Nancy and Waldorf's third son, is easily the most accessible, if for no other
reason than that he has written a solid autobiography. He
also has been working on a sequel. It is from Michael that
one gets the clearest picture of the life at Cliveden for a
growing boy. Like his brothers, Michael was sent away to
school at an early age, in his case, eight. Despite the com-

forting presence of David at the same school, Michael was
not happy, concealing his misery by day but suffering
nightmares for several years. About the time he left the
Sussex school for Eton, he says, was when he realized his
mother was famous. Life at home during these years is
described by Michael in a matter-of-fact tone as servants, a host of them, performing. Cliveden's atmosphere
was a combination of Christian Science, Puritanism and
social gaiety. Life was often fun but usually formal. Michael writes of taking a cardboard shield and a wooden
dagger to riding one morning and having the groom
confiscate them until the ride was over. He and his siblings
were made to toe the mark by the threat of hiring a French
governess "or much worse"—a trip to France. They seldom
measured up, and trips or governesses were regular results.
The most fun places for a kid at Cliveden were the kitchen
and the carpenter's shop. Michael remembers being un-
impressed as a child by Lloyd George or Lord Balfour.

At Eton, Michael accumulated an impressive record,
winning colors for football and cricket, being captain of his
house and getting elected to the Eton Society. He went on,
of course, to Oxford, struggling with his identity. "Who
am I beyond my heritage?" He began to look at art as a
way to find himself. At Oxford he might have been described as "left wing," an appellation his family would not
have relished, but Michael says the term at Oxford meant
more about one's romantic, exploratory tendencies than
one's political leanings. Like his sister with her riding accident, Michael, too, almost became a victim of his
mother's Christian Science beliefs but managed, he says, to
return from death's door and recover from a combination
of pneumonia and pleurisy although Nancy compromised
her beliefs only to allow a doctor to look at Michael from
a distance. This period was not an easy one in the relation-

ships between Michael and his mother and father. Nancy suffocated him, he writes, with religious appeals and pleas for his affection while his father handed out unsolicited advice on punctuality, drink, smoking, Michael's career and his language. At twenty-one, Michael finished at Oxford and moved out of Cliveden, never to live there again. Nancy considered the move traitorous. "My roots were still family roots," Michael recalls, "and as they became severed I came to live uneasily outside of the stream of life. . . ." He was plagued by doubts about religion and self, went off to America and returned to enlist in the Army, recognizing earlier than most the inevitability of war. After seeing some action—and being bothered far more by the stench of war than by its sight—Michael was able near the end of the war to resume his study of art. He wondered whether the truth of one's own vision was worth working on. With the war winding down, Michael was trying to decide whether to study art in Paris or London or to seek a seat in Parliament.

To his surprise he was offered a "safe" seat. He took it, wondering if he was behaving like a coward. He managed to lose because he froze while making his first big public speech. But he got a second chance in a district far different from the first, where the constituency had been generally compatible, and this time prevailed. Michael saw the House of Parliament as having its own personality, which no individual had ever successfully challenged. Naturally, he didn't try. Once, running for re-election, he was asked by his father to allow his mother to give a campaign speech on his behalf. Waldorf asked the same of Michael's brothers, Bill and Jakie, who were also running. They could not but agree. Nancy and Michael discussed what she would say, and she began pulling his leg. She'd tell them her son was an artist, she told Michael, a Lothario who didn't care about politics. Or perhaps she'd tell them how privileged they ought to feel that they could vote for her son and listen to his mother. Seven decades hadn't dimmed her bright sense of humor, a fact Michael surely appreciated. He did not stand for re-election in 1951, deciding that he wanted to initiate ideas, not just transform them into law. Michael might be accused of dabbling today. He farms, plays tennis, travels, paints, writes and entertains Oxford professors. In short, he does more or less as he pleases. In 1954 he wrote an article for *Vogue* in which he argued that, despite their lower living standard, the English were happier than the Americans, in part because the British accepted things while Americans were restless. The English way of life, its form of expression, he wrote, is more individual, more understated than its American counterpart. True enough—for Michael, at any rate.

The youngest of Waldorf and Nancy's chilrden is Jakie, a carefree, humorous roller-with-the-punches. Waking up after an auto accident in 1939, Jakie startled the concerned assembly by asking, "I've lost my memory; has anyone got it?" Jakie inherited half of his father's horses—the other half went to Bill—and until 1975 was among England's top breeders and racers. He still is an avid horse enthusiast, but he has sold the breeding operation. In the summer of 1978, Jakie was knighted for his work as chairman of the Agricultural Research Council.

The grandchildren of Waldorf and J.J., the active Astors today, must live within certain financial constraints about which their grandparents never had to worry. In London, pieds-à-terre have replaced mansions. In the country, homes are large but no longer manorial. Cliveden is today rented by the National Trust to Stanford University as an overseas campus. The current viscount, William Waldorf III, the wealthiest Astor in his generation, has a modest apartment with no servants in London and a moderate manse in the nearby country whose staff consists of a nurse for the viscount's young son, a cleaning woman and a combination gardener and handy man. "There's no question that my children are not going to be able to sit around and live off their inheritances," he told the *Wall Street Journal* in 1979. The viscount, not yet thirty, works, running large farms in Scotland and England and two manufacturing companies. "If I stopped now, I would definitely have to cut down the way I live," he says.

While the English Astors do not equivocate about their nationality—they are British, despite their American heritage—they maintain close, or at least regular and friendly, ties with the few remaining American members of the family and continue to have some business interests in the United States. In the 1976 Christmas issue of *Forbes* magazine a story on who owns New York estimated that at the peak period during the 1920s the Astor family owned $450 million worth of Manhattan real estate that produced $30 million a year in income. The story went on to say that, since 1962, the British Astors had disposed of control positions in some $500 million worth of Manhattan properties, bringing Astor holdings down to four properties worth $6 million. Gavin Astor says the story is not accurate but declines to elaborate. During the early 1960s, First National City Bank bought 535 acres on Flanders Bay in Southampton, Long Island, acting on behalf of the British Astors. The bank has since brought suit against the New York State Environmental Conservation Department because new tidal wetlands regulations have allegedly decreased the value of the land.

What the future holds for the British Astors should make a particularly poignant story. It can be argued that, as they go, so will go the British monarchy, at least to the extent that it depends upon the survival of nobility. The Astor chance for survival in anything resembling the present style and form is as good as, perhaps better than, that of most noble English families outside the royal one. The Empire is gone. Is the monarchy next?

PART VI

PART VI

CHAPTER 14

Ava Alice Muriel Astor, the first American Astor born in the twentieth century, may have been a little mad toward the end of her life. Certainly she believed some bizarre things and entertained some strange people. But it is perhaps safer to describe Alice as the only truly tragic figure in the Astor family. Born in 1902, she grew up having everything. She was beautiful in a haunting fashion, bright over a broad spectrum of knowledge and, of course, rich. And there is every indication she overcame the one great void of her childhood, the lack of a father combined with a mother who gave her everything she could have possibly wanted except unselfish love. Alice spent her entire adult life seeking inner calm, a relief from the restlessness, the vague dissatisfaction that dogged her footsteps. She never found it.

When her parents—Ava Willing and Colonel John Jacob Astor—separated in 1909, Alice remained with her mother while her brother Vincent, eleven years her elder, stayed with their father. At one point during the summer of 1909 the little Alice attempted to forge a reconciliation between her parents, helping to bring them together for a meeting at Ava's brother's house in Newport, but the meeting broke up with Ava in tears and the colonel immersed in melancholy. Alice grew up rootless, whisked back and forth across the Atlantic at the whim of her mother, who seemed unable to make up her mind between England and New York. Increasingly, she grew to resemble her mother. Not quite the absolute beauty her mother was, Alice made up for this with an intellect that shone and a charm that dazzled. She was, unlike her acid-tongued mother or sometimes atrabilious brother, nice to everyone, regardless of how she felt about him. Ineluctably, given her upbringing and background, she was strong-willed and frequently ruled by whimsy. It was a matter of self-defense as much as anything. To be less than willful in the presence of Ava was to risk complete domination. Her daughter learned early to survive in a test of wills.

There is some confusion among surviving relatives as to when Alice first began believing she was the reincarnation of an Egyptian princess and a disciple of Ikhnaton, upon whose death this princess had been forced by her father to abandon her newly found religion of light and hope and return to the old Egyptian beliefs in the mystery of death and darkness. King Tutankhamen was Ikhnaton's son-in-law. Ikhnaton was the husband of Nefretete and the man who changed the Egyptian religion from polytheism to a monotheism based on the sun. Realists will continue to believe that Alice was among the first four people to enter King Tut's tomb when it was found in 1922—thereby defying the putative curse surrounding it—because of her friendship with the Earl of Carnarvon, not because of her earlier associations. At any rate, in she went, eventually coming out with a priceless necklace from the tomb, a necklace many people, including her first husband, Serge Obolensky, found disturbing, even numinous.

Alice's mother, by now remarried to Lord Ribblesdale, had high hopes for her daughter, raven-haired, dark-eyed, long-legged and generally most desirable. Perhaps the one social virtue Alice lacked was humor. She was essentially a serious woman. In her own right, she had a trust of $5 million left her by her father in his will. The package added up, in Ava's eyes, to something any of the world's most eligible bachelors ought to be delighted to make an offer on. Ava, however, failed to recognize how strong was the will she had built in her daughter. Alice met Serge Obolensky for the first time at a party at Lord Curzon's home when Serge bumped into her while dancing. The meeting was memorable only because the next encounter was. This was on the golf course in 1922. Serge had Baba Curzon as a partner while Alice played with Boy Browning, who later married Daphne du Maurier. Serge remembered Alice as being the best player of the four. Afterward Serge and Alice went waltzing together and started something. They saw a lot of each other from then on. Alice told Serge about her conviction that she had been an Egyptian princess in an earlier life, said Serge in his autobiography. (Another autobiographical book by another relative suggests her belief came much later, spurred by mystical friends and acquaintances.) Serge appears to have been a little nervous about this side of Alice, but his love for her more than offset any reservations he might have had.

Alice and Serge were soon engaged, an event upon which Ava did not look favorably. Ava quickly paraded a group of England's most eligible bachelors before her daughter and finding her unmoved, sent her flitting about Europe to meet and be wooed by young male wealth and aristocracy. Serge lost no ground with Alice during all of this. Indeed,

it is likely that had Alice found the perfect match somewhere she would never have recognized it, so determined
was she not to be the victim of her mother's will. Ava was
not through trying, however, and in the spring of 1923
towed her reluctant daughter to America. Alice told Serge
not to fret. She would be twenty-one in July and free to
make her own moves. Ava was not immediately taken with
Serge despite his Russian royal credentials going back
more than eleven hundred years to the Grand Duke of
Novgorod and Kiev for two simple reasons. The lesser of
them was that he was already married, an obstacle that
could be easily enough overcome. More important in Ava's
eyes was the fact that Serge was, if not impoverished,
hardly rolling in money.

But Ava turned out to be a gracious loser eventually, and
on July 24, 1924, shortly after Serge's divorce was official,
Alice and he were married . . . and married . . . and married. There was first a civil ceremony, then an Episcopal one
and finally a Russian Orthodox service. Ava was the perfect
hostess at the wedding breakfast. The message of the three
weddings might then have been interpreted two ways—
either Alice and Serge were the most firmly married couple
around or the repeated ceremonies were an omen of things
to come. In retrospect, the latter interpretation clearly
holds.

The year between Alice's having turned twenty-one and
their marriage had not been an easy one for Alice and
Serge. Alice bought a Rolls-Royce, and Serge became close
friends with the chauffeur. Alice and Serge were often seen
in public at major social affairs, where Serge's exuberance
and charm could not but make him a standout. The English Astors had recently purchased the London *Times* and
so Astors were big news as well. Privacy was at a premium.
Somehow they managed, and on June 23, Serge's divorce

became final. On American Independence Day, July 4, Alice and Serge were engaged, a date dictated no doubt by Serge's sense of irony and humor, a sense that helped him get along with his famous cousin-in-law, Nancy Astor. When they first saw each other after Nancy's trip to Russia in 1931, deposed Russian Prince Serge recalled Nancy's opening thrust at him: "What a wonderful job they've done over there in such a short time!"

After honeymooning in Deauville, the couple went to Canada where Serge was convinced he could make a go of it as a grain farmer. He says he and his bride had agreed before the wedding on the desirability of spending part of each year away from the crowds of social people with whom they were so often surrounded. But the solitude depressed Alice, and the couple went to visit Vincent at Ferncliff in Rhinebeck before returning to England. They, or rather Alice, bought a handsome home in Regent's Park and staffed it with a chef and his wife, a maid, the chauffeur and his wife and a butler/valet. The people from whom Alice purchased the house quickly offered to buy it back at a premium, and Serge's generous bride suggested they accept the offer and that Serge keep the profit as a present. This Serge's pride would not permit, and they kept the house, moving in in the spring of 1925, shortly before their son Ivan was born. Alice was always trying to shower lavish presents upon her husband, who finally convinced her to start a foundation for Russian émigrés instead.

The first half dozen years of their marriage were, from all accounts, a constant dash to remain a step ahead of boredom. Serge described these years. In midsummer, he wrote, they went to the United States, visiting Newport and then Rhinebeck in the fall. Back to London for Christmas, then off in January for skiing at St. Moritz. Next on the annual itinerary was a stop in Paris followed by a trip to the south of France for the spring. The start of the new season found the peripatetic couple back in London again. "I remember things like a ghastly rough crossing on the *Majestic* or the explosion of an oil heater in Helen [Mrs. Vincent] Astor's house as being among the foremost of our trials of the time," Serge wrote. Eventually, they built their own home in Rhinebeck on about a hundred acres of land given them by Vincent. They moved into it, having invited guests for the weekend, without having worried about such details as linen, kitchen utensils or the like. Unperturbed, Alice managed to find someone to send up the appropriate items at a modest surcharge. Price was in those days hardly an object. For Alice, neither was time. She was always late. She tried setting all the clocks in the house ahead by forty minutes, but she knew they weren't right and paid no attention to them. One of her troubles was that she could never decide what to wear and was constantly changing from one outfit to the next after agonizing moments in front of a mirror. She would even, on occasion, show up late at parties in England at which members of the royal family were guests, a definite breach of British protocol. One might think that with nothing else to do, Alice could arrange to get places on time, but the fact was that with nothing much to do, the time to do it in became insignificant. "Alice and I had no difficulties in those early days aside from the problem of being late for dinner," was how Serge put it.

Their existence was not particularly conducive to the solidifying of a happy marriage. In its essence, it consisted of one indulgence followed by another. Consideration and responsibility were not likely to thrive in such an atmosphere, and a spoiled child was virtually sure to remain a spoiled child. Alice found herself losing the race with boredom. She asked for a divorce. It was not a readily granted request. Serge loved Alice and would love her all her life, never giving up hope that someday she would return to him. Vincent was furious at the prospect, being happily married to Helen Dinsmore Huntington and determined to prove that permanent bliss was an achievable marital state. The couple separated, Serge going to New York where Vincent gave him a job and generally looked after and sympathized with him. Before very long Alice followed, bringing along more than two dozen trunkloads of paraphernalia in her wake. Vincent and Alice were not getting along particularly at this point, but in the past they had managed despite Vincent's disapproval of his sister's spendthrift ways. For her part, Alice would not be reasoned with, having grown up learning to war with her mother. She was so irrepressible that many found it easy to believe the rumor that she bought a New York taxi for her own use, finding it more fun than a limousine. Alice's arrival in New York did not, as Serge had hoped, signal a reconciliation. She continued to demand a divorce, while Serge and Vincent continued attempts to persuade her of the folly of her ways.

Although Serge says tardiness was their only problem early on, he later conceded that the trouble began in the summer of 1926, just two years after their marriage, when Alice invited a male friend of hers along on a trip she and Serge took to Holland. Serge agreed to have the fellow along, but he was seething inside. The following year Alice became jealous of the nurse who was taking care of their son Ivan, and Serge came to the woman's defense. They had quite a battle although Serge recalled being very much in love with her at the time. When friends invited them to the Riviera, she said she didn't want to go but he went anyway. Eventually she joined the group in Cannes, and they went on to Venice, where Elsa Maxwell was engaged in lavish entertainments. Back in London, Alice made it clear to Serge how much she resented his having gone off to the Riviera without her.

For several years relations between Alice and Serge fluctuated, although they never rose so high as to feed rumors of reconciliation. They did rise enough so that when Alice finally decided in 1932 to establish residence in Nevada and get herself a divorce, she was pregnant. Vincent showed where his feelings in the matter lay by having his own lawyer represent Serge in the proceedings. Custody of Ivan and his education were the main points of contention. Serge believed Ivan belonged in the United States; Alice thought England would be better. Serge won, getting custody of Ivan, while Alice received custody of Sylvia, their daughter born while Alice was living in Nevada. Serge was never bitter about the turn of events, and Ivan, then seven, would spend his next summers in England with his mother, who used the time in an attempt to rectify the shortcomings of his American education through the good offices of a tutor. Ivan has said that in retrospect at least, he learned a lot that has proved useful in those summers. But his main sentiment, remembering those days, is the wistful conviction that his mother and father should have reconciled because despite their differences, they remained in love with each other.

Not long after her divorce Alice remarried. Her new husband was Raimund von Hofmannsthal, son of the poet and librettist for Richard Strauss, Hugo von Hofmannsthal. The marriage was almost a clandestine affair as the couple wanted to avoid publicity and slip off to Austria, Raimund's native country, before the news was leaked. Fate decreed otherwise. Only hours before their ship was to sail, Alice learned that Ivan was very sick. Legally, the problem was Serge's, but Alice could not leave her son until he was well again. By that time the newspapers had had their field day. Raimund was a bon vivant and a writer, the first of many writers Alice would eventually befriend and assist. But helping worthy artists get started and being married to them are not the same thing. After a daughter, Romana, was born, Alice divorced Raimund and began looking around again for those elusive creatures, love and happiness.

During World War II, Alice met her third husband, allegedly while helping to man a gun, a sight at least one relative considered ludicrous to contemplate. He was Philip Harding, an English newspaperman, then with an anti-aircraft battery. Another daughter, Emily, came from this union before it, too, was dissolved after the war upon Alice's return to the United States. Meanwhile, Alice and Serge were seeing each other periodically, and Serge, who became something of a hero during the war, dined occasionally with Alice in London. Once, during an air raid, Alice refused to go to the shelter and the best Serge could manage by way of protecting her was to coax her into sitting under rather than at the dining-room table while the bombs fell. Another time a nearby bomb killed Serge's friend, the chauffeur, and his wife, Alice's secretary.

New hope that she might remarry him flooded Serge's breast when Alice divorced Harding, and he was deeply disappointed when she went instead for husband No. 4, David Pleydell-Bouverie, an architect and cousin of Lord Radnor. This marriage was blessed with no more staying power than any of the others. It was Alice's last trip to the altar. "I knew she was unhappy," Serge wrote in his autobiography about this period, leaving the reader to infer with whom the cure could have lain.

From husbands Alice turned to artists for company. Her

first major venture in the arts patronage field had occurred some years before in England, where she was a substantial supporter of the Sadler's Wells Ballet. She tried to talk promoter Sol Hurok into taking the Sadler's Wells company to the United States for a tour, but Hurok was highly skeptical about the financial viability of such an enterprise. The project made the leap from dream to reality when Alice offered to underwrite the trip and guarantee it against loss. She didn't bother to deal for a percentage of the profits, should there be any, an oversight that in a lady of lesser means might have been tragic, so grand was the success of the tour. Alice had enough money.

After the war and back in New York, Alice gave the same support to the New York City Ballet that she had lavished upon Sadler's Wells. Around her grew a fascinating circle of friends that included Tennessee Williams, Aldous Huxley, Gore Vidal and Dame Edith Sitwell. As she grew older, the artistic gave way to the arcane among her interests. Huxley was among those who honed Alice's attraction to—later obsession with—things mystical. Alice developed an almost dual personality. She was a good homemaker and mother. Her houses were warm and inviting. Her kitchen was excellent, and she was a charming hostess. Yet she seemed to fall in over her head as she grew more and more absorbed in the world of mysticism and extrasensory perception. Much of her mystic devotion was focused on Egypt, but one of the tragic aspects of these years for Alice was that she was unable to discriminate among scholarship, legitimacy and quackery. It was not so much that she went in for some exotic gimmicks like the copper hat with the horn poking out the top, which her son tried on one day, claiming his perceptions became clearer—these things had arguable, and in some cases even demonstrable, value. It was Alice's soft heart. No one

could ever get anywhere telling Alice what to do, but beg-
ging her was another matter altogether. Her former butler,
Stanley Martin, says Alice was surrounded in her later years
by sexually ambiguous groupies and gave away an awful lot
of money. In many instances, the recipients of her largesse
were pure and simple frauds or impostors who told unlikely
tales of mystical experiences or pretended to have extraordinary powers of some kind.

Alice started to learn Sanskrit as her fascination with
Egypt took a tighter hold on her. She had a recurring
dream in which an elaborate mummy's case would appear
in the corner of her bedroom and the lid would rise to reveal the body of a woman dressed in rags but wearing jewelry that signified high birth. The woman looked just like
Alice. She would attempt to rise from the case, and at that
moment a hand would appear from the darkness and push
her back inside. It was a haunting vision.

In the summer of 1956, Alice was fifty-four. She had
aged well, friends said, and while those who knew her well
worried about the influences of mysticism on her psyche,
most agreed she seemed in good spirits. Her former butler
remembers it was a Wednesday night and she had driven
into New York from Rhinebeck to have dinner with her
lawyer. Martin says her maid found her early the next
morning in her bathroom. She was dead.

As it had much of her life, mystery surrounded her
death, or perhaps it would be more accurate to say that
rumor loaned her death an aura of mystery. There were
those who said it was suicide, a notion still not completely
laid to rest. Martin recalls hearing she had taken a couple
of pills or something and had apparently hit her head on a
doorknob in the bathroom. But the final word should probably go to Brooke Astor, the widow of Alice's brother Vincent, who has written that Vincent ordered an autopsy

after two men visited him and said they could suppress an autopsy report that would show Alice had committed suicide. Vincent apparently wanted the truth, for himself and for her children, and, according to Brooke, the truth was that the autopsy showed Alice had died of a heart attack. Her system contained a trace of one drink and a mild sedative. The suicide rumor—probably based on nothing more substantial than the fact that she appeared in good health just before her death and had long been so fascinated by ancient Egypt and its cultural absorption with the mysteries of death—refused to die, and even today people who should know—or perhaps should know better—continue to hint at the possibility.

Alice's death marked the beginning of the end for an Astor era. The glitter days were coming to a close. Within less than three years her mother, Lady Ribblesdale, and her brother Vincent would follow and write finis to the times when the Astor name was automatically synonymous with wealth and social prominence in America. It was Vincent who sealed the family fate.

CHAPTER 15

Ironically, William Vincent Astor, who wound up with most of the money, led a rather spartan childhood compared with his half brother, John Jacob VI, upon whom was lavished extravagance after extravagance. William Vincent's youth was not a joyous occasion. He was born in November 1891 and was an only child for eleven years. His father was a strict disciplinarian and would react to his son's transgressions either by taking a strap to his backside or by sending him to his room with only a glass of milk for supper. Such treatment may not have provoked an enthusiastic response from the boy, but it was greatly to be preferred to the scorn bordering on loathing heaped upon the child by his mother. Part of the problem was that if Ava was a swan, her son was an ugly duckling. He was a gangly, awkward boy, forever banging into things or knocking something over, and his mother, perhaps embarrassed, seldom hesitated to humiliate him in front of whoever was presently paying her homage. It was not a happy home in which William Vincent spent his early years.

As time passed, it became increasingly clear that while she may have had good use for his money, Ava had little or no use for John Jacob Astor IV. Their quarreling grew increasingly strident, and as father and mother began to put distance between themselves, father and son became very close. Before that, Vincent had spent most of his time in the charge of nannies and tutors. From the age of eight until he went away to school at twelve, Vincent was tutored each morning from nine-thirty to noon. In the winters he would be subjected to another hour after lunch, but in the summers he was free to play. He would roller-skate or ride a bicycle. At Ferncliff he had a pony. After an early supper he would read in bed—Rudyard Kipling and Robert Louis Stevenson in particular. He was never a very robust boy. When he was twelve he was operated on for a throat ailment and also had his appendix removed. During the winters his father would take him to St. Moritz, hoping to protect the frail lad from tuberculosis.

In the fall of his twelfth year William Vincent went off to Westminster, a boys' boarding school, where he managed to make himself rather unpopular by going about bragging to anyone who would listen about who and what he was. A sinus problem kept him out of school the next year. He then spent the next five years at St. George's, where he made do with an allowance of fifty cents a week. This less than handsome sum would, his father threatened, be cut to thirty-five cents if his marks or his behavior fell below the acceptable point. To help insure that his marks, at least, did not, a young newspaper type who was to make a name for himself not quite as familiar as Vincent's was hired as a tutor. His name was H. V. Kaltenborn. Astor's name by now was Vincent. He had decided to drop the William and add, he thought, distinction. For his fifteenth birthday his father gave him permission to drive about the

property at Ferncliff, a present that might at first appear
niggardly but which in actual practice was a princely gift
indeed. Vincent loved speed and was not afraid to tax his
ability, the car's capacity and the road's efficacy to their
limits and beyond. During the summers, it was said, nothing at roadside was safe. Trees, fences and the occasional
other automobile all fell victim to Vincent's Juan Fangio
delusions.

As the years passed, Ferncliff was not the only place
where discretion in the presence of an Astor auto became
the better part of valor. In Newport shortly after the divorce of his parents, Vincent was rushing over to see his
mother before he and his father departed on a cruise up to
Bar Harbor, Maine, aboard the colonel's yacht, *Noma*. He
was in a bit of a hurry and was what today would be called
tailgating the car in front of him. Turn signals had not yet
been invented, and when the first car made a turn into a
driveway, Vincent was caught unawares. He rammed the
vehicle square amidships, almost turning it over with the
force of the impact. Within the car were the Duke Franz
Josef of Bavaria, U. S. Representative and Mrs. Nicholas
Longworth and Mrs. Robert Goelet. No one was hurt, and
Vincent, after making sure everyone was all right and
promising to pay for any damage, hurried on his way.

If Vincent liked anything more than cars, it was the sea,
a love that manifested itself early and stayed with him all
his life. Upon graduating from St. George's, Vincent expressed a strong desire to go to Annapolis and the Naval
Academy, but his father would have none of it, insisting
that he behave like everyone else and go to Harvard. By
now he was more or less full grown. He stood six-four and
weighed about a hundred and fifty, with narrow shoulders
and chest. He had thick lips and a large head, matched at
the other extremity by large feet. He walked with his toes

pointing out, giving him, especially when he put on white tie and tails, the appearance of a penguin, which bird became a favorite emblem of his. He was not very athletic, although he played on the St. George's tennis team and was an undistinguished oarsman at Harvard. Being outdoors made him happy. A story, probably apocryphal, contends that Vincent's first romantic interest was a gardener's daughter when he was six. He was shy and given to writing poetry to admired females, whose responses are largely unrecorded.

Vincent was essentially miserable at Harvard. His wardrobe received more attention than he did, with rumors flying that he had brought up to a hundred suits with him. The fact was he had three suits and a dinner jacket. His allowance was $2,000 a year and was supposed to pay his tailor as well as other expenses. He actually wound up borrowing $40 to buy a one-cylinder motorcycle on which to get around. Over Christmas vacation that first—and as it turned out only—year, Vincent went to see *The Quaker Girl* on Broadway. A massive infatuation with the show's star, Ina Claire, set in. Overcoming his shyness, Vincent asked her out. He being who he was, she accepted, more than once, although dignity and her image required her to dismiss the whole thing by telling reporters that of course he was only a boy and could not be taken very seriously. Vincent's father and new stepmother were away on a prolonged honeymoon, and Vincent had taken one of his father's cars and stripped it down to make it a racer for his first date with Ina. The potential consequences of his father's discovery of this deed may never have occurred to Vincent. At any rate, on April 14 any discussion of what those consequences might have been became academic, as for the next week or so Vincent went through the most traumatic experience of his life.

At first not overly concerned, Vincent became almost physically sick with worry while camped out at the offices of the White Star Line, owner of the *Titanic*, aboard which his father perished. The news that provoked this reaction was the number of survivors. Vincent left the White Star office and spent the night at his father's office. In the morning he went home for breakfast, his first food in twenty-four hours, but was soon back at his father's office. At his suggestion, the office contributed $10,000 to a fund for needy survivors. At about five in the afternoon the complete list of survivors was released, and Vincent collapsed upon learning his father's name was not on it. He went home, but was back at the office the next day. For a week, until his father's body was found, Vincent continued to hope, buoyed by the tales of his father's heroism in the last moments of the *Titanic* and by the knowledge that his father was a strong swimmer with a sound constitution. For many, many years afterward, Vincent carried the gold pocket watch found on his father's body.

Luckily, Vincent had little time for contemplating the dirty trick played on him by fate. Almost overnight he had become America's most eligible bachelor, at least if money were the sole criterion. He had an estimated income of $10,000 a day from an estate valued at about $78 million, the most reliable estimate among a wide variety. He was the first Astor to inherit the fortune unencumbered by such things as generation-skipping trusts. It was all his and he was not yet twenty-one. He decided he could learn more in the office than in the classroom. His distaste for Harvard was acute anyway and long-lived: More than forty years later he refused even to see Harvard president James Bryant Conant when Conant came down to New York on a fund-raising mission.

Perhaps the most impressive thing about this shy, awkward and fabulously wealthy youth was his genuine desire to help ameliorate the human condition. In February of 1913 he talked well past midnight with the governor of New York about how he might serve humanity. One result of that conversation was the starting of a major experiment in agriculture and farming on Vincent's Rhinebeck estate, Ferncliff.

If Vincent took pride in Ferncliff's apple orchard, the largest in New York State, or his distribution of tested oat seeds, such things were hardly enough to keep him fully occupied. He undertook myriad good deeds, some better and more efficacious than others. His efforts ranged all the way from taking mothers and children from the slums on boat rides to having a playground built on Astor land in Harlem valued at $1 million. He established a home for underprivileged children who were hard to manage and raised the salaries of the people who worked for him at Ferncliff. When the Rhinebeck fire department made him head of a committee to rasie money for motorized equipment, he bought the vehicles himself and threw in a playing field and grandstand for the village baseball team. He became director of the Public Schools Athletic League and went to all the big events, pontificating that games were not just sport but "a means of moral, physical and social uplift." He added that it was "better to have dead grass in Central Park than sick children in tenements."

Occasionally Vincent's efforts would go off the deep end and fall into the bizarre. In 1913, for example, he hired a team of private investigators to go around ringing doorbells in the tenements he owned on the West Side because he had heard rumors that some of them were being used as brothels. Not surprisingly, the sleuths uncovered a bare minimum of salacious activity and managed to make a number of tenants irritable about the invasion of their pri-

vacy. The tenements were a source of particular embarrassment to Vincent, who quickly made up his mind to try
to improve the situation. His forebears had built an occasional hotel, but for the most part they had left the improvement of their land to others. Vincent decided to do it
himself and hired architects to make studies of the areas
where he owned property to determine what sorts of buildings were needed. He chose to invest $3 million a year in
this project, which figured to increase the value of the
property and develop good will, an item of no small importance to Vincent.

The toll all these efforts took on Vincent was substantial
and taken quickly. He collapsed from exhaustion early in
1914. His congenitally fragile health was unable to withstand the demands made on it by Vincent's frantic schedule, which included a full social life as well as all his business and philanthropic activities. The American public
seemed to like Vincent without any effort on his part. It
was as if he were America's answer to England's Prince of
Wales. On occasion he found himself mobbed by women.
Although he sometimes managed to get away—perhaps on
the speedboat he purchased on his twenty-first birthday
along with a $6,000 racing car capable of 100 miles an hour
—the pace was a hectic one. It did leave enough time for
falling in love.

In the fall of 1913, Vincent became engaged to Helen
Dinsmore Huntington, whom he had known more or less
all his life. Both the Dinsmores and the Hungtingtons had
riverfront estates not far from Ferncliff. People said she
was a dead ringer for Ina Claire. Her family was wealthy
and well connected. She was, not unlike Vincent, almost
aloof in her cool beauty and perfect poise, but those who
knew her said her exterior manner concealed a wealth of
warmth and thoughtfulness. She could trace her descent

from Samuel Huntington, a signer of the Declaration of Independence. The couple were married in 1914 while Vincent was still suffering the effects of his collapse and the
discomfort of minor injuries sustained in a motorcycle accident. The wedding was therefore small and mainly family
but did involve all the appropriate accouterments—white
orchids, a hidden orchestra, champagne and the like. Helen
and Vincent slipped away early and boarded the *Noma* for
a honeymoon cruise on the Chesapeake. It was one of the
few occasions when Helen accompanied Vincent on a
yachting trip.

Back in New York, the newlyweds held a series of dinners for experts on and leading citizens concerned about
the plight of the immigrant, unable through ignorance to
take full advantage of U.S. citizenship. The result of these
dinners was the setting up of several centers to help immigrants learn about the meaning of U.S. citizenship. Another and rather innovative Astor project of this period was
the building of an ornate public market on Broadway at
Ninetieth Street. Vincent even imported tile artisans during the construction. The market opened and was an immediate hit. For the first few months shoppers flocked to this
unusual bazaar, attracted not only by the structure but also
by the good prices and fresh produce. But it was not long, a
matter of months, before the merchants fell victim to their
greed, deciding that people would come to such a won-
drous place even if they had to pay a premium, rather than
receive a discount. The merchants were wrong. The cus-
tomers left, and Vincent was required to sell the market at
a loss. It wasn't the money lost that bothered him but the
failure of the concept. Vincent was not above pursuing
the usual avenues of noblesse oblige as well as being a
pathfinder. In 1915 he bought 1,000 Christmas turkeys and
had them distributed to the poor, earning for himself the

scorn of Union Square orators who called him a pater-
nalistic plutocrat.

Two years earlier he had received a letter from a young
socialist author named Upton Sinclair, who had apparently
seen a newspaper article about Vincent's Ferncliff estate
and its extravagant appurtenances. Sinclair warned Astor
that the poor, realizing the rent they struggled so hard to
pay each month was going to finance such luxury, would
be deeply bitter. Sinclair predicted a cataclysmic uprising
in the near future. Vincent was obviously upset by the letter, and after consulting friends and associates as diverse as
labor pioneer Samuel Gompers and tycoon Ogden Mills,
he wrote back. He was, he wrote, cognizant of the wrongs
and hardships within the system, but he was also convinced
that these would be rectified without resorting to an overthrow of that system. Vincent denied the likelihood of a
cataclysmic event on the horizon, giving Sinclair the opportunity, which he did not avail himself of, to say I told
you so when the First World War broke out less than eight
months later. If this exchange effected no direct results,
it did help to keep Vincent determined to work for the
betterment of mankind and the alleviation of human suffering, naïvely broad and idealistic goals, perhaps, but
maybe not when you are among the richest men in the
world.

Astor continued to dabble in reform. He put up some
money for a bank that was supposed to put a halt to usury.
Astor and some friends subscribed for $2 million in pre-
ferred stock and found themselves with a position equal to
the bank's promoters, who had put up only $600,000. Astor
and his friends got out. Another project involved supporting a group who were investigating the nation's food and
drug laws. At the time the Supreme Court was considering a case in which the use of nitrogen oxide as a

bleaching agent for flour was being questioned. The impact of Astor and his group on the matter was less than dramatic.

By the fall of 1915, Vincent's time and energies were increasingly being taken up with the war. He was generous in the amount he took when J. P. Morgan underwrote the first Allied war loan. Less than a month later Vincent and Helen helped found the National Americanization Committee and provided it with headquarters in an Astor building. In their mansion at 840 Fifth Avenue, first built as a double home for Vincent's grandmother and his father, the Astors promoted Allied causes and American patriotism with elaborate parties. Vincent could even be found on occasion guarding the entrance to the Brooklyn Bridge against sabotage. As United States entry into the war became more likely, Vincent became more actively patriotic. In February of 1917, shortly after the break in diplomatic relations with Germany, Vincent undertook the organizing of his fellow yacht owners, setting the good example by proffering the *Noma* to the government. In this effort Vincent first got to know Franklin Delano Roosevelt, who was then Assistant Secretary of the Navy and who would become, despite his strong political differences with Vincent, a close friend.

In April, America entered the war, and Vincent immediately subscribed to $2 million worth of the Liberty Loan. He also offered Ferncliff as a hospital, following his cousin Waldorf's lead in England. But the action was on the other side of the Atlantic, and in June he and Helen headed over. Helen did YMCA canteen work in Bordeaux. Vincent was a naval port officer for a while and then spent six months laying cable off the coast of France while rising to senior lieutenant and executive officer aboard the *Aphrodite*. He may also have seen some action while on sub-chasing duty, but the record is a little murky. When the war ended, he returned with Helen to New York and echoed the sentiments expressed by his father upon his return from Cuba, when he said he had "thoroughly enjoyed every minute of the service that I have been able to render my country."

While the sea in general and the U. S. Navy in particular always held a special meaning for Vincent, thus making ships his favorite toys, anything mechanical that moved people from one place to another, preferably at high speed, fascinated Vincent. His love for automobiles was already matured as was his love for ships when the airplane struck his fancy. Just before the war he had been offered the position of commander of the Portuguese Air Force by that country's former king, Manuel, contingent upon the success of Manuel's efforts to overthrow the republic and restore the monarchy. He declined, of course, and the republic endured. Not long afterward, Vincent was made head of a naval militia air battalion, which needed a plane, appointed Vincent armaments chairman, and soon enough had its plane with his compliments. He learned to fly and bought a hydroplane with which he practiced take-offs and landings on the Hudson River. While Vincent enjoyed direct participation in the thrills of high speed, some thrills were vicarious. In 1916, for example, he put up a $10,000 prize for which young pilots raced around a 250-mile course at Sheepshead Bay on Long Island. Probably the No. 1 trophy in American yachting was the Astor Cup. And it wouldn't be many years before Astor had a lingering and intense affair with miniature railroads.

Starting in 1919, Vincent went on a selling spree. He sold his old yacht. He almost sold it to a man from Chicago, who offered $250,000—Vincent was asking $200,000—if Vincent would pay $5,000 for a pet orangu-

tan, Frieda, to whom the Chicagoan was very attached but
for whom life in Chicago was a trial. This was Vincent's
kind of deal and he accepted. The man eventually backed
out of buying the yacht, but Vincent took and kept Frieda
anyway, finding her amusing enough for four years and
then giving her to the Bronx Zoo. Astor also began a decade of heavy real estate selling. By the fall of 1927 he had
successfully disposed of about $40 million worth. The big-
gest single transaction brought him more than $7.5 million
for his half of the old Waldorf-Astoria, which would soon
be sold again and torn down to make room for the Empire
State Building. Also sold were the Longacre Building in
Times Square for $2.4 million, the site of the Paramount
Building for $3.8 million and the Schermerhorn Building
for $1.5 million. The St. Regis Hotel was sold to the Duke
family, who had made a fortune in tobacco in North Carolina. The Knickerbocker Hotel was converted into an office
building, Vincent taking space himself. In 1926, Vincent
sold the family home at 840 Fifth Avenue for $3.5 million
and Richard Morris Hunt's great spectacle was razed and
replaced by a synagogue.

But all was not divestiture. In 1926, Astor took about
300 acres in the Port Washington, Long Island, area and
developed them into a fancy subdivision with tennis
courts, bridle paths and even a casino. The Depression
made a failure of this ambitious project, but others were
more successful. He invested $200,000 in the first version
of the motion picture *Ben Hur* and was rewarded with a
profit of $371,000. This he used along with the money
from the sale of his old yacht and an additional $500,000
or so to build a new *Nourmahal,* of which he took possession in 1928. She was built in Germany and became Astor's
pride and joy, perhaps even his first love. She was 264 feet
long, could cruise at sixteen knots and had a range of 20,000

miles without refueling. There were eleven staterooms, each with its own bath, a sun deck for games, a pine-paneled library, a huge lounge with an open fireplace and a dining room that ran the width of the ship. The ship required a crew of forty-two and an annual bill for maintenance of her readiness to answer Vincent's sudden whims of $125,000. Next to the *Nourmahal*, Astor's new six-story Georgian town house on East Eightieth Street, now the home of the New York Junior League, was a modest structure at best, with a price tag of only $250,000. Vincent was not the least sentimental about his grandmother's house and its contents, but he did insist on preserving his father's bedroom and bath and having them reproduced in his new home. The vast marble bathtub caused considerable consternation years later when the house was being renovated for the Junior League. It had been installed during construction and was too big to be removed through any of the doors or windows. Workers finally were forced to break it up into irreparable pieces before hauling it away.

Right after the war, when Vincent was only twenty-eight, he was sitting on the boards of directors of some rather substantial companies, including Western Union, Illinois Central and Great Northern railroads and American Express. His favorite, however, was a relatively small firm, the Roosevelt Steamship Co., which was eventually merged into International Mercantile Marine. Ships were special.

In 1927, Vincent bought some land on Eighty-sixth Street between what were then known as Avenues A and B and today are York and East End avenues. Not long afterward the area became one of the city's most fashionable. In a sense the purchase closed an Astor property circle, for the land Vincent bought was part of the original John Jacob Astor's Hell Gate estate, which John Jacob had left to his favorite grandson, Charles Astor Bristed. Bristed had turned around and sold the land to a nunnery. Vincent reclaimed part of it.

At home, domestic tranquillity, if not bliss, reigned. Vincent and Helen learned early to respect each other's pleasures and not to spoil them. She had a place in Paris where Vincent seldom ventured. He had his *Nourmahal*. She had her arts and music—an almost consuming passion in which Vincent, who was virtually tone deaf, had no interest—and he had his model trains and miniature railroad at Rhinebeck, where he could actually play engineer and drive his train along three quarters of a mile of track, pulling up to twenty-seven guests along behind. He did not particularly like her friends and would excuse himself from her dinner parties. He didn't have many friends for her to worry about. On the surface, it didn't seem to be much of a marriage. The rumormongers whispered incessantly of impending divorce. But despite their many differences, Helen and Vincent had a deep and abiding affection for each other. Furthermore, Vincent had not yet become reconciled to the concept of divorce. It was anathema to him.

The stock market crash and the ensuing Great Depression affected the lives of the Astors only in minor ways, unless one credits the Depression with bringing Franklin Roosevelt, Vincent's increasingly close friend, to the White House. Ever since Roosevelt had been stricken with infantile paralysis in 1921, he had come over to Ferncliff periodically from his estate at Hyde Park nearby to use Vincent's swimming pool for therapy and rehabilitation. Just before his inauguration in 1933, Roosevelt spent some ten days aboard the *Nourmahal*, and Astor was in one of the cars behind the President-elect when Giuseppe Zangara, who didn't like any Presidents, shot at Roosevelt and killed the mayor of Chicago. Only moments before the incident, Astor had been speculating to Roosevelt adviser Raymond

Moley about how easy it would be for someone to take a shot at the President. What Roosevelt saw as his duty as President strained his friendship with Astor considerably, but even after he told Vincent that if Vincent could afford to keep his yacht prepared to sail at a moment's notice then maybe it was time to "soak the rich," the two remained friends.

If Astor was perhaps developing a persecution complex during these years, he had some reason. The public no longer gave the very rich its uncritical, full devotion. Roosevelt was applauded for his "soak the rich" remarks. Then Vincent came under attack from Senator Gerald Nye and his committee looking into profiteering during World War I. It was true that Vincent had done some proselytizing for the war but, far from profiting by it, he had taken something of a financial shellacking from it. For one thing, the expense of the war effort resulted in an escalation of the graduated income tax that continued on into the 1930s, so that his income after taxes shrank from 63 percent to 21 percent of his pre-tax income. Still, Vincent remained firmly loyal to the United States, perhaps carrying his patriotism a bit far when he told the New York *Times* at the close of 1932, "During the present depression in the States, I feel that I should spend my money in my own country, so I will open my Florida home this winter. Later, however, when the States recover, I plan to enjoy the winters in my Bermuda home."

Whether or not the effort was conscious, Vincent seemed more than once eager to follow the lead of his British cousins. There was his offering of Ferncliff as a hospital during World War I. And in 1933, Vincent determined to ape his cousins again by buying a major news medium. His unlikely partners in this venture were Averell Harriman and Harriman's sister, Mrs. Mary Rumsey. Harriman and

Astor didn't much like each other, and Vincent was not an easy man to get along with if he didn't like you. Nonetheless, the Harrimans had lined up Raymond Moley, Roosevelt confidant and Assistant Secretary of State, to agree to edit whatever publication they came up with, and Moley and Astor had become very good friends. In fact, over the next few years Moley became the only person to whom Vincent found it possible to be civil early in the morning. Astor was generally a man to be avoided before breakfast, a period during which the world and everyone in it took on a black hue.

The Harriman-Astor combine first took an interest in the Washington *Post* but failed to outbid Eugene Meyer for the property. Nothing else around and even marginally available seemed prestigious or influential enough, so the group decided to start its own publication, a news magazine to compete with the decade-old *Time* and the new *News-Week*. The Harrimans, brother and sister, put up $125,000 each, matched by Vincent's $250,000. Roosevelt became the first subscriber and the first issue of *Today* appeared in October of 1933. Vincent became the dominant owner when Mrs. Rumsey was killed a year later in a fall from a horse and he bought her interest.

Moley soon became disenchanted with the Roosevelt administration and left its employ. The magazine began printing none too subtle attacks upon the President, which undoubtedly created a strain in the relationship between Astor and Roosevelt. But, again like his English cousins, Vincent exercised no control over the editorial content of the magazine. As Moley once pointed out, Vincent may have disagreed with Roosevelt on most issues, but he still voted for him four times. Moley admitted to having voted against Roosevelt three times, and it was his view that prevailed at the magazine. Roosevelt and Astor remained friends until Roosevelt's death.

The magazine was not a healthy child and struggled to stay alive. In 1937 it outlasted rival *News-Week*, which was merged into its operation. The new publication was called *Newsweek*. Malcolm Muir, president of McGraw-Hill, was enticed away to run the magazine while Moley became contributing editor. Luckily for all involved, Vincent could be rather tenacious when he chose. *Newsweek* swam in a pool of red ink for some nine years before it was able to clamber up onto the safe dry land of profitability. It has been estimated that during that time Vincent pumped $5 million into the magazine to keep it afloat. As he grew older, this sort of expenditure became very much a rarity. A former business associate remembers that among his most difficult tasks was convincing Astor of the good financial sense made by the spending of some of Vincent's money.

Besides his magazine, Vincent kept busy during the 1930s administering his real estate holdings. Two deals in particular required attention. In 1934, the first year of Fiorello LaGuardia's eleven-year reign as mayor of New York, Astor's tenement holdings once again came under public scrutiny in a series of articles in the New York *Evening Post* prompted in part by a new rash of tenement fires. Astor was a man with thin skin. He had been trying to do the right thing for more than twenty years now. The tenements haunted him. Finally he told the commissioner of New York's Housing Authority he could have the large majority of Astor's remaining tenement holdings for whatever he thought was a fair price to pay. The commissioner was no Santa Claus, writing Astor a check for $189,281, an amount less than half the assessed valuation. That was okay with Vincent. He was delighted to have the tarnish removed from his image. In any case, Astor did not view the gesture as philanthropic, considering the property to be in decline. The one substantial benefit to New York deriving from Astor's action was to allow the Housing Authority to get on with some projects that had been held up by the high demands of other slum lords. By 1938, Astor had fewer than a dozen tenements left among his real estate holdings and those were boarded up and vacant.

In 1935, Astor got the St. Regis back. Why the Duke family defaulted on the mortgage, allowing Astor to acquire a property valued at $10 million for $5 million at the foreclosure auction, remains something of a mystery. Astor paid the Dukes an additional $300,000 for the furnishings and equipment. The best guess seems to be that when Benjamin N. Duke died with the hotel in his estate, his executors deemed it best to unencumber the estate of this holding. Astor was delighted to have the hotel back, even though occupancy was low. He decided that a hotel operated and equipped like one in which he himself would enjoy staying would be a viable proposition and proceeded to turn the St. Regis into just such a place. He hired Serge Obolensky, by then divorced from Vincent's sister, to act as promoter, consultant and trouble-shooter. Serge says the reason was that he "had lived much of my life in the best hotels of Europe." That may have been part of the reason why Serge was such a success at his job, but the reason Vincent hired him had more to do with the simple fact that he liked Serge. Thanks to an ingenious device Vincent himself helped develop using ice and huge fans, the St. Regis became the first centrally air-conditioned hotel in the world. Vincent had the hotel redecorated, calling on Helen to help. Serge saw to the adding of a wine cellar, some good music and improved cuisine, devoting virtually all his time to the hotel until 1939. Vincent would even poll his friends as to the precise thickness of an ideal lamb chop or the most desirable mustard for corned beef. Until Vincent died, every egg consumed at the hotel came from the huge chicken barn at Ferncliff. It was not long before the St. Regis was flourishing. So determined was Vincent to make the St. Regis his idea of the very best that he sent some members of the hotel management team to study the operating methods of Europe's great hotels, like Claridge's in London and the Ritz in Paris. One thing the St. Regis learned was that the great hotels get to know their guests, learning their names, their likes and their dislikes. The St. Regis established a card file on its guests, frequently astonishing return guests pleasantly by "remembering" them so well.

In a sense, the St. Regis was a sort of landlocked yacht for Vincent. The staff catered to his every whim, often anticipating him. The guests could just as easily have been his guests for the most part. It has been said, although with more hyperbole than truth, that Vincent kept the St. Regis even though it was a money loser simply because he liked to have lunch there. The hotel wasn't a money loser in those days, and Vincent was capable of eating elsewhere, but in the sentiment reflected the story has a ring of rightness. Nonetheless, even the St. Regis could never replace the sea and the *Nourmahal* in Vincent's affections. For a few months each year he would escape aboard the *Nourmahal*, cruising to different exotic corners of the world. He made several trips to the Galápagos Islands off the west coast of South America, taking with him the nation's leading scientists in such fields as ornithology, botany and marine biology. They would collect rare specimens, like the fish Vincent presented to the Bermuda aquarium or the cactus planted in Panama.

Once Vincent even tried to transplant lobsters from the

waters off Newport to Bermuda waters, installing special tanks aboard the *Nourmahal* for the purpose. The heat got to the lobsters before they got to Bermuda. Not a one made it to Vincent's island retreat alive. On another trip Vincent, with Obolensky and Minnie Cushing (who would become Vincent's second wife) as guests, went searching for pirate treasure on an island off Costa Rica. They arrived to find others already engaged in the search, and the story is that tempers overheated to such a degree that the Costa Rican government was forced to send troops in, if not to prevent a bloodletting, then at least to insure Costa Rica its share of the treasure. Despite Vincent's strong conviction, no one found a thing.

As the United States moved ever closer to World War II and Vincent began the rationalization process that would allow him to divorce Helen and marry Minnie, he appeared to the public as a complex, even contradictory man—at times a little boy, at times a sullen giant, at times a thoughtful and gentle man, at times a bright conversationalist. People said he was the most wonderful man they knew; other people said no bigger jerk walked the face of the earth. Actually, Vincent Astor was simply a private, and rather spoiled, individual with few remarkable abilities and a large ego that was more or less inevitable, as a former adviser notes, given the fact that he was surrounded, because of his wealth and position, from an early age by sycophants. He tended to belittle the capacities of Presidents, statesmen and other leaders of his time, his judgment being not so much absolute as comparative. He could have done the job just as well if not perhaps a little better, seemed to be his attitude.

Beneath an often gruff, even surly exterior beat a heart that was in the right place. Serge Obolensky told the story of a friend of Vincent's who was well up in years—in his nineties—and who moved in with Vincent in 1931, having nowhere else to go. The man brought all his furniture with him, which caused a considerable clutter at 130 East Eightieth. Vincent finally talked the man into auctioning the furniture, but the fellow went to the auction and re-purchased it all. Vincent agreed to pay for transporting the furniture to and from the auction place and the auction fee because his friend could not afford it. Vincent defied Astor tradition by donating generously to charity. His friends said that the amount given publicly was but the tip of an anonymous iceberg.

Vincent's day usually began at seven in the morning. He had breakfast in his room, for which those living under the same roof were grateful as his company in the early morning was not something to which anyone looked forward. He would reach his office normally by nine. In the afternoon he would attend directors' meetings after lunch and a nap, from which he often awoke in a bad mood. He belonged to some thirty-eight clubs, including the exclusive Creek Club on Long Island, which he helped to found, but frequented only the Brook Club. During the day he would smoke two and a half packs of cigarettes, switching to a corncob pipe after dinner. Dinner usually was served at seven-twenty in the evening, shortly after "Amos 'n' Andy," a radio show for which he had been known to cancel or change appointments. An acquaintance has told the story of calling the Astor residence just after seven and being told that Mr. Astor was out but would be back by seven-twenty. When this happened several more times, the man asked Vincent about it and was told that Vincent wasn't really out, just glued to his radio. Bedtime was generally 11 P.M., but Astor would occasionally stay up late drinking, talking about the sea and ships or playing chess. He talked with a voice that was not easy to understand be-

cause he spoke rapidly and rather indistinctly. His move-
ments were those of a clumsy non-athlete, abrupt and
jerky, and he wouldn't dance because he knew he wasn't
good at it. If a question caught him unprepared with an
answer, he had a habit of cupping his right ear in a stall for
time. While he was not, by most accounts, a man's man,
he sometimes attended the major heavyweight fights and
enjoyed the camaraderie of drinking, singing, telling tall
tales and thumping the table. On Sundays he would go to
church. He liked church. As he saw Him, God was merci-
ful, not wrathful.

Vincent was used to having things done for him. Although he scorned formal society, some of its privileges
and customs were necessary for him. His valet, for example, was indispensable. One day the valet was sick and unable to work. It took Vincent all morning to get dressed. He
had no reason to know where his clothes were kept and
simply couldn't find socks, shirts, collars, ties or even the
dark business suits he always wore. Another time he went
away for the weekend without the valet and came down to
breakfast the first morning wearing socks but no shoes. He
explained defensively that he had misplaced the ones he
had been wearing and was unable to remove the shoe trees
from the others. His hosts' reaction to this news has unfortunately gone unrecorded.

No one enjoyed a good—or even, for that matter, a bad—
practical joke more than Vincent Astor. His mirth would
spill over uncontainable at the sight of a rubber hot dog, a
fake snake or any such dime-store novelty. He was trans-
ported by the antics of a waiter hired especially to insult
the guests and spill drinks and food. But he could also
develop some rather elaborate schemes, money being no
particular object. One of his favorites was the fake stock report, which he found to be especially effective with guests

aboard the *Nourmahal,* where he was able to control the lines of communication. On one occasion Vincent came close to carrying the joke too far. Having carefully prepared for the event by surreptitiously obtaining a list of the man's stockholdings, Vincent contrived to receive a wireless report on a guest's stocks some three days out of New York on a *Nourmahal* cruise. The poor man's fortune was disintegrating before his eyes. For the next several days the news grew only worse, as Vincent piled financial disaster upon market calamity. Finally Vincent realized the man had had enough and that the joke was on its way to becoming a serious incident. The fellow was so relieved he forgot to get angry with his host.

The stock hoax vied with the old scandal-sheet gambit for first place on Vincent's list of favorite tricks. The latter would begin with Vincent composing a gossip column replete with innuendo linking a guest to some shocking public scandal or private affair. Astor would then have his story printed and placed in a newspaper, the rest of which was real. This personalized paper would be placed on the guest's breakfast tray while Vincent began chuckling in anticipation of the reaction it would provoke. It was Astor's experience that such a ploy was more rewarding when the victim was a woman, but he did not discriminate by sex in the playing of these jokes. Once, when he heard a potential victim was tuned in to the possibility of her role, he had a stack of phony papers made up and distributed throughout the neighborhood, even coaxing the man at the local newsstand to display some of the doctored papers.

During the late 1930s, Mary Benedict Cushing—one of her sisters married first Franklin Roosevelt's eldest son, James, then John Hay Whitney; another married William S. Paley—was an increasingly frequent guest aboard the *Nourmahal.* His relationship with Minnie, as she was called, caused Vincent great stress as time went by and he realized how much he cared for her. He also cared deeply for Helen, despite their independence of each other, and wanted very much to avoid any action that might hurt her. Furthermore, his feelings on the subject of divorce were widely known; the line between flexibility and hypocritical inconstancy was at best thin. Finally he did ask his wife for a divorce, and she went quietly and graciously to Wyoming, established residence and sued for divorce on the grounds of "mental cruelty," a term that sounds far more harsh than it is.

Minnie and Vincent were married in September 1940. It was a small wedding, graced by the presence of Vincent's mother, Lady Ribblesdale. Out of sentiment more than necessity, Minnie wore the same dress her sister had worn at her wedding a year earlier. The couple went off on the *Nourmahal* soon after the ceremony, no doubt giggling to themselves over the fact that the crew was as yet unaware of their marriage.

With the coming of World War II—which Vincent had perhaps anticipated when he had had gun emplacements installed aboard the *Nourmahal* during its construction— Vincent eagerly sought active duty, although he was nearly fifty. He gave the *Nourmahal* to the government and, for some reason, never tried to get it back after the war, thus allowing an era to slip away unnoticed at the time. He was given convoy duty, carrying war matériel to Europe and bringing wounded soldiers back. Minnie worked with the Navy Relief Society and was particularly effective organizing parties for sailors enjoying leave in New York.

After the war Vincent sealed the fate of the American branch of the Astor family, insuring that he would be the last of the wildly wealthy family in the United States, or at least the last to hold a lion's share of the original fortune.

In 1948 he founded the Vincent Astor Foundation, to which he would leave half his estate outright, causing his half brother, John Jacob VI, who had long felt his $3 million share of the Astor wealth inadequate, to remark a little petulantly, "Not the way my great-great-grandfather would have wanted it." In the beginning the foundation, sweepingly dedicated to "the alleviation of human misery," contributed mainly to the children's home Vincent had started some years before in Rhinebeck. The home hadn't been doing very well, and Vincent thought that perhaps the Catholics would handle it better than those he had placed in charge. Legend has it that he let it be known at the Brook Club one day that he would like to meet Cardinal Spellman, and good connections being what they are, a luncheon was arranged for the following day. At any rate, Spellman agreed to take over administration of the home, and he and Astor became good friends. It may have been part of the agreement that Astor's foundation would contribute in an important way to the support of the home. In later years the foundation limited its beneficiaries to New York institutions and people.

Vincent's second marriage was, according to some of his friends, sustained more by his love than Minnie's. She was fourteen years younger than he and a gay, blithe spirit who must have felt weighed down by Vincent's more somber, serious ways. The practical joking seems to have gone with the *Nourmahal*, part of a lost time. In 1953, Minnie left him and married an artist, James Whitney Fosburgh, as soon as the divorce became final. The blow to Vincent was softened considerably when he met Brooke Russell Kuser Marshall shortly after her second husband died. Actually, Brooke and Vincent had known each other on a casual basis for years and had many mutual acquaintances. The warming of their friendship took place while Vincent and

Minnie were still ostensibly together, or at least attempting
to keep up appearances. According to Brooke Astor, in her
memoir *Footprints*, Vincent told her that Minnie had
been after him to grant her a divorce but that he had so far
refused. Now that Brooke had come into his life, he went
on, he would grant Minnie a divorce if Brooke would
marry him. Vincent was tenacious as a bulldog, refusing to
take maybe for an answer and pleading his case at every opportunity. He finally wore Brooke down and on October 8,
1953, they were married in Maine at the home of Liz and
Joe Pulitzer, who, along with a lawyer, a minister and
Brooke's son, were the only witnesses to the marriage.

Vincent was sixty-one and behaving like a boy again.
While there will always be a few envious or mean individuals contending that Brooke married Vincent for his
money, most of the people who knew the couple at all well
consider Brooke to be, as Vincent's business manager,
Allan W. Betts, put it, "the best thing that ever happened
to Vincent, although I'm not sure he was bright enough to
realize it." That is an observation not meant to be snide or
smart. The fact is that Vincent—because his thinking and
feeling were socially liberated and because, unlike his forebears, he felt obligated by his wealth and concerned by the
plight of the less privileged—has been treated as an innova-
tor and something of an intellect when he was not much of
either. In most ways, Vincent was an ordinary man with an
extraordinary fortune.

Like many wealthy men, Vincent's attitude toward
money was complex and occasionally contradictory. For an
Astor, he was a most generous contributor to charity, but
in his personal life, especially in his later years, he seemed
overly concerned by the possibility that someone would try
to take advantage of him. He very much resented being
asked about his income, which was $813,000 after or $1.5

million before taxes in 1924 and went up from there. He
did not believe in the ostentatious social affairs on which
his grandmother had thrived, considering them dull and
the cause of civil unrest and wishing the rich would exercise more discretion. He also believed that public service,
not money or breeding, should be the measure of social
standing. He was a hedonist to the extent that he enjoyed
the good life, good food and good wine. A waiter at New
York's "21" club recalls Vincent's coming into the place
and asking for a bottle of 1947 Dom Perignon, a 1947 La
Tâche (Romanée-Conti), fresh cucumbers and fresh fruit
and then commanding the waiter to make sangría, an order
akin to asking for the best chateaubriand in the house and
commanding that it be chopped up for hamburger.

For a man who would make sangría out of the best
champagne and burgundy, Vincent could be remarkably
stingy. Someone once gave him a donkey and he had a
shed built for it at Ferncliff. The man who did the job put
a corrugated aluminum roof on, believing, no doubt, that
Astor would want the best, there being no other instructions. Vincent saw the roof and hit it. He phoned New
York immediately to inquire as to its cost and the
difference between the fancy roof and a regular one. It was
a matter of several hundred dollars. The man had been
with Vincent for many years; Vincent fired him on the
spot. The man who served as Vincent's accountant and
business manager for years was also summarily dismissed
when Vincent discovered that the man had set up a net-
work of "spies" within Vincent's various households so
that the man could better anticipate Vincent's needs and
whims. The butler for Vincent's sister and later his first
wife remembers Vincent as giving $10 to the servants at
Christmas.

Vincent did not treat himself all that much better, relatively speaking. Betts says Astor was always reminiscing about the *Nourmahal* and the good old, forever gone days. One day Betts showed him a picture of a yacht about a hundred feet long and needing a crew of twelve to operate her. It was, Betts knew, a ship Vincent could afford, but he was unwilling to spend the money. Or perhaps, subconsciously, he was even a little afraid to. In 1938, just a couple of years before he gave up the *Nourmahal*, the ship was caught off Long Island in a severe hurricane. A piano was hurled through the side of the ship by the force of the storm, and the *Nourmahal* nearly foundered. It was, if you thought about it enough, almost too much like the *Titanic*'s and his father's fate.

During the 1950s, Vincent seemed to become obsessed with the dangers of capital exposure. He was almost psychotic in his fear of the risk involved in spending money, investing capital in a project, a deal or a stock and having catastrophe strike. He was not impressed by the advantages in capital gains or accelerated depreciation, even back in those days when the top tax bracket was 91 percent on income and 25 percent on capital gains. When Betts went to work for Astor in 1954, Vincent's estate was worth about $90 million. Considering inflation, it should have been worth more nearly $250 million, properly managed. Of that $90 million, about $50 million was spread through some 3,200 different tax-exempt bonds, in no one of which was more than $25,000 invested. Vincent apparently figured he was limiting his exposure. The remaining $40 million was in bits and pieces of largely run-down real estate. Betts, who had been hired at the suggestion of Hoyt Ammidon to manage investments while Ammidon specialized in estates and trusts for Astor, found it very difficult to persuade Vincent that stocks, with their potential for capital gains, were a much better inflation hedge than tax exempts. "Vincent's idea of fighting inflation," Betts recalled, "was to make sure he had twice as much income as he needed to live on so that if prices doubled he would still have enough. You never could convince him to live off his capital gains."

And in the 1950s capital gains were not difficult to come by if you had some capital to start with. Betts did finally convince Astor to put $1 million a quarter into a stock investment program, but Astor always worried about it. "He had a real thing about stocks," Betts said. "He was scared to death of them." He would periodically ask Betts for a comparison of his stockholdings performance with that of his Phoenix real estate. The stocks were doing better. In fact, they were outperforming the Dow Jones Industrial Averages by some 40 to 50 percent at the time, but Vincent would always manage to find a stock that was down and complain. At the time of his death, although the stock investment program had been in operation barely four years, his stockholdings had a $19 million gain on paper.

If Vincent worried about his stockholdings, he agonized over real estate. He was urged to sell the St. Regis and buy another hotel to take advantage of the laws concerning accelerated depreciation. He demurred, not because he liked to have lunch at the St. Regis but simply because he didn't want to spend the money to buy the other hotel. He would have been smart to pour money into the St. Regis so that if and when he sold it the dollars coming out would be capital gains, but Vincent wouldn't even have the St. Regis sandblasted after Betts had found him a remarkable bargain for the job.

The St. Regis was a minor consideration, however, compared with Astor Plaza and another, smaller project in Cleveland. These were the two major real estate investments he made with the proceeds from the sale of the

many bits and pieces of land he held in his portfolio in
1954. Astor Plaza involved the Manhattan block between
Fifty-third and Fifty-fourth streets, Park and Lexington avenues and began with plans for a 46-story luxury office
building at a cost of about $75 million. Vincent had some
trouble obtaining the financing for the project. His English
cousins, who owned the land, refused to mortgage it, not
out of any animosity toward Vincent or distaste for his
project but simply as a matter of good business practice.
The plan was modified to make the building more utili-
tarian, but financing the project remained difficult and
Vincent was running scared, which didn't make the financing any easier. Citibank took the project over in March of
1958. "Our biggest mistake," says Betts, "was not realizing the projects were bigger than the man." Had Vincent
hung onto the project for just five years or so, he would
have realized a profit of $12 million, according to Betts,
but all he could see was his exposure. Betts says the decision was finally made to get out of both the Astor Plaza
and the Cleveland projects when Brooke called the office
and said, in effect, that she didn't know whether or not
they were good investments but she did know that if Vincent didn't get out of them they would kill him. Betts says
the estate lost $3 million on Astor Plaza, considerably less
on the Cleveland deal.

Vincent did not always have as good a reason as his life
for selling things. In the post-*Nourmahal* days he bought a
Grumman Goose amphibious airplane to use commuting
between New York and Rhinebeck. He sold it because he
had to have it cleaned every time he landed in the Hudson
River. He sold his house in Bermuda after a bizarre falling
out with some officials there. Bermuda was losing its cedar
trees to a bug that had infested them. Vincent, it seems,
found a bug that ate the bug that ate the cedar trees and

provided Bermuda with swarms of the good bug, but a hurricane came along and blew all the good bugs out to sea. Vincent thought it was the government's turn to replenish the supply of good bugs. The government disagreed. Vincent left.

After 1954, Vincent's health, never robust, began to deteriorate. What enjoyment he had found in life began to fade, and he became irritable and difficult. The doctors allowed him one martini a day, a restriction Vincent mocked by having his in the largest glass he could find. He would take a nap promptly after lunch, disappearing no matter at what stage a party might be in at home. At work, Betts remembers, Vincent would sometimes wake up grumpy and call him up ranting about some figures or something. "Usually, he had misunderstood something," Betts said. Vincent was fascinated by figures in those years. He would ask to see the drink price list for the St. Regis and several other hotels and could spend the whole day mulling the advisability of raising the price a nickel here, lowering it a dime there.

Although every indication is that Vincent was devoted to both his second and his third wives, he remained throughout his life very close to Helen, who had become Mrs. Lytle Hull and who was mistress of a splendid estate on the Hudson not far from Ferncliff. He was, recalls a cousin, frequently late to lunch at Ferncliff because he was down at Helen's place finding out who was there and what was going on. Vincent left Helen $25,000 to give to a charity of her choice in his will as a token of his esteem and devotion. The same cousin says that Helen was more than once consulted by Vincent's other wives in their efforts to better understand the man they married.

The last six months of Vincent's life, good spells were followed seriatim by bad ones. In the fall of 1958 he went to London to meet Brooke, who had gone to Europe for the coronation of the Pope. They went to Cliveden for a weekend with Vincent's British cousins and both caught colds. A doctor said Vincent, who had by now given up smoking, had a spot on his lung and ought to have a thorough checkup when he got back to New York. According to *Footprints*, Vincent's trouble was finally diagnosed as cardiovascular. The prescribed treatment was a better climate, the avoidance of stress and no smoking ever. Stress had not lately been an easy thing to avoid, what with the unexpected death of Alice and all the worry over Astor Plaza. But these things were behind him now and perhaps his condition could be improved, or at least stabilized. As January of 1959 ended, Vincent showed marked recovery. He was anticipating a trip to his Phoenix, Arizona, home with relish. He and Brooke were scheduled to leave on February 4.

On the third, Vincent was virtually his old self. He and his wife lunched at the St. Regis at their favorite corner table. That evening they were to have dinner at the Malcolm Muirs'. The editor of *Newsweek* had had a recording of *Newsweek* made for blind people that he wanted the Astors to hear. Vincent begged off, citing the early hour of their departure the next day, but urged his wife to go and report back. It was only moments after she had returned just before 11 P.M. that Vincent died.

There were nearly $130 million in Vincent's estate, almost $100 million in securities. He was the first principal Astor inheritor to leave the bulk of his fortune in a commodity other than land. He was the first principal Astor inheritor to die an also-ran in the race to be wealthiest American; his forebears weren't always first, but they were always close. Finally, he was the first principal Astor inheritor to leave the bulk of his fortune to a charitable founda-

tion. What John Jacob Astor I had started in the United
States, Vincent Astor essentially finished. But his tragedy
was really a personal one. He was never all that comfortable with his wealth. It is very revealing that he cherished
his title as commander in the U. S. Naval Reserve as much
as he cherished anything. He had all his mail addressed
that way and made no secret of his fondness for his days in
the Navy. Indeed, he told his third wife that those days in
the Navy during World War II were the happiest time of
his life.

There is no cliché more tired than the one about money
being unable to buy happiness, but there is also, perhaps,
no more fitting epitaph for William Vincent Astor.

CHAPTER 16

The Astor name has not lost all its glitter today, but the luster is now more an indirect glow, a product of memory and a lady, Brooke, who is an Astor only by a marriage of less than five and a half years. There are four adults in the American family today with the name Astor—Brooke; Jack, Vincent's half brother; and Jack's two children, William Backhouse and Mary Jacqueline. Brooke alone can be considered any sort of public figure. It is a rare issue of W that does not carry her picture, which may grate in a way on this lively lady. She would like, one suspects, to be known primarily as president of the Vincent Astor Foundation. She is acknowledged in some circles as an involved and dedicated philanthropist. But the general public knows her —if it knows her at all—socially, as one of those people who get their names in the gossip columns in boldface type.

Around New York City, Brooke still carries some clout. The foundation's work has been limited to the city, and in several important areas it has made significant contributions. In 1977, for example, the foundation made grants amounting to $9.7 million, including a $5 million grant over five years to the New York Public Library, an old Astor favorite. The foundation also gave $1 million to endow a chair of medicine at the Memorial Sloan-Kettering Cancer Center, $100,000 to New York's public television station, on whose board Brooke sits, and $5,000 for the general support of the Pierpont Morgan Library, to list a sampling. At the end of 1977 the foundation showed net assets of $52 million, down from $67 million a year earlier. The 1978 annual report shows much the same sort of funding, noting with pride that the foundation was able to act within a week to provide the funds, along with Warner Communications, that allowed the New York Landmarks Conservancy to buy the block in lower Manhattan that includes Fraunces Tavern and is the only complete block of nineteenth-century brick buildings in that entire section of Manhattan. Although the foundation's net assets continued to decline—to $47.8 million at the end of 1978—as the foundation continued a policy of making grants in excess of its income, the year was one in which the foundation received as well as gave: Mary Cushing Astor Fosburgh, Vincent's second wife, died and the foundation received $890,000 from her estate.

One of the foundation's first major items of business upon the death of its founder was the sale of *Newsweek,* by then a substantial property. The foundation believed it was inappropriate for it to own an influential molder of opinions, and therefore wrote some half dozen publishers informing them that if they were interested they could look at the figures on *Newsweek* for the last ten years and make a single bid for the magazine. The highest offer would prevail. *Newsweek*'s books were to be made available for a month before the bidding deadline. Less than a week before the deadline Averell Harriman, whose sister and he

had been the original partners with Vincent, called the
foundation offices and requested that Philip Graham be
given a chance to submit a bid. Graham had married the
boss's daughter at the Washington *Post* and become one
of the nation's premier editors. Allan Betts, who was execu-
tor for Vincent's estate, didn't think Graham had enough
time to put together a sane proposition, but Graham said
he could do it and was given the chance to prove it. "He
was the most dynamic man I ever met," Betts recalled.
"He set up a direct telephone line from his suite in the
Carlyle to my office. At one meeting with his lawyers and
ourselves, he told the lawyer to shut up, that he'd do the
talking."

When the bids were opened, Graham had bid $50 a
share for the *Newsweek* stock and so had Doubleday & Co.
The foundation was carrying the magazine on its books at
$4.00 a share, according to Betts, who said Malcolm
Muir, the editor brought in when *Today* and *News-Week*
merged, had 40,000 shares for which he had paid ten cents
each. Muir was not happy, apparently, with the sale of the
magazine, maintaining that he had been promised the
magazine by Vincent. The claim could not be substan-
tiated, Betts said, and the two bids—Doubleday's and Graham's—were taken to *Newsweek*, where the magazine's ex-
ecutives, minus the Muirs (father and son), chose the
Graham bid because of the better deal for the Muirs, who
would receive generous employment contracts, and also because they believed that the Washington *Post* affiliation
would be more helpful to a news publication than would
affiliation with a book publisher. *Newsweek*'s employees,
afraid of what a sale to the highest bidder might foist upon
them in the way of new ownership, attempted to raise a
bid of their own, but they were unable to match the
nearly $9 million that Graham laid out.

The foundation also sold the St. Regis, a transaction that took many of the hotel employees by surprise when they failed to distinguish between Vincent Astor's and his foundation's priorities. In all, the foundation wound up with upwards of $75 million and a president who was determined to be an active and humanitarian boss. To be sure, the foundation has not ignored bricks and mortar over the years, but the projects in which Brooke Astor, foundation president, seems to take most pride and pleasure are those designed to impact upon people. "I'd hate to be thought of as a grim-faced public institution," she once told *Vogue* magazine, which reported that she greeted the children at the Boys Brotherhood Republic on the Lower East Side by name and that they returned the compliment.

When Brooke took over as president of the foundation, she was not short of people giving her advice, most of it unsolicited. The advice she wound up heeding was some she asked for, from John D. Rockefeller III. Rockefeller told her to immerse herself in the foundation's projects as well as its finances, to control the giving as well as the money. She has said more than once that she is proud of the fact that the foundation never gives to anything she hasn't personally looked over. Neighborhood projects— parks, redevelopment work, and people-to-people programs —receive a lot of attention from Brooke and the foundation, although the foundation's more glamorous undertakings, involving Rockefeller University or the Metropolitan Museum of Art or the Bronx Zoo, receive most of the publicity.

If Brooke is something of a name-dropper—her recent autobiographical book is filled with the names of the famous—it is simply because she has parlayed her innate wit and charm and Vincent's fortune into a close association with the important people of today. She appears to be genuinely stimulated by them and their ideas, not just their positions. While she can be strong to the point of contumaciousness, she abhors controversy and would go to great lengths, short of compromising principle, to avoid it. She is, in short, a stately and appropriate symbol of Astorness. But she is a symbol, not the real thing.

The closest to the real thing in the United States is Jack Astor, Vincent's half brother, whom, according to Brooke's account, she has never met. Jack lives in Miami now and, according to his daughter, has pretty much cut himself off even from his friends. His son by his first wife, Ellen Tuck French, has been quoted as saying he would become the next Astor millionaire—by making the money himself. But William Backhouse Astor, as his father named him, now lives a quiet, bucolic existence in Vermont, dabbles a little in local politics and seems only to want to be left alone. His half sister, Mary Jacqueline Astor, whose mother was Jack's second wife, Gertrude Gretsch, says her half brother may have once made the "next millionaire" remark back when he was eighteen—he was forty-five in 1980—but "everyone says things like that when he's eighteen."

Jacquie Astor, although she is more of an Astor than Brooke, is somewhat overshadowed by Brooke's public image, which is okay with her. She is, like her father and brother, no publicity hound. She is a striking blonde, rather animated and very poised. New York is home, but Jacquie is comfortable more or less anywhere in the world. Especially in Europe, where she says she spent three months every summer for about eighteen years with her father. In recent years she has made about three trips abroad a year, an indication that, while she may not be in a league with past Astors, she can play the moneyed game in just about any park she chooses.

It is perhaps old-fashioned, but the first question that

comes to mind in Jacquie's presence is why she has never been married. She is on the high side of thirty—certainly old enough. She is pretty, bright, unaffected, possessed of a ready laugh and otherwise supremely qualified—enough to make wedding bells virtually unavoidable. She admits that she almost took the plunge in 1978 with a fellow from Houston but finally made the tough-minded decision that her love would wilt in the Houston humidity. Asked where she expects to be ten years from now, she says she has no plans but wouldn't be surprised if she were married and mothering three kids. "Isn't that what everyone wants eventually?" she asks.

Meanwhile, Jacquie works at Sotheby Parke Bernet in the Manhattan real estate department and likes it. She has a lot of free time, she says, and doesn't sell that much because there just isn't that much to sell. But when she does sell, it is a major transaction, and in the interim, as she points out, she gets to inspect all the great New York apartments and town houses and meet a host of interesting people. Before Sotheby Parke Bernet, she was in the production and marketing end of the television film business and left simply because she wanted to try something different.

Yet another indication that Jacquie's views of money are not tinted by past or prospective penury pops up when she talks briefly about her Uncle Vincent, who she remembers left her and her half brother $50,000 "or, I don't really remember, something small." She is obviously very fond and slightly protective of her father, aware apparently of a past public image that was not very flattering. "He's a nice man," she says. "Whenever we see each other, we always stay up until six in the morning. He has lots of good stories." Some of them, not unnaturally, involve his half brother Vincent, who, he has alleged, never consummated his union with Brooke. Jacquie says she used to dismiss this notion but that he insisted and told her part of his suit to break Vincent's will was based on that contention. About the suit, without implying any validity to her father's contentions, she says, "I don't know why he didn't win."

That he did not, settling eventually for $200,000, has not made her at all bitter, she says believably. Her so far suppressed desire is one day to be a part of the Vincent Astor Foundation. She says neither her father nor her brother has any particular interest, but as one of the last Astors and living in New York, she is very much interested. For the present, she is not too optimistic about the chances of having her desire fulfilled because, for some reason she cannot fathom, Brooke has chosen to avoid contact. At a funeral once, Jacquie says she turned around to say hello to Brooke and Brooke got up and left before any words were exchanged. She says that when mutual acquaintances bring up her name during conversations with Brooke, Brooke says quickly how nice Jacquie is and changes the subject. Given Brooke's aversion to controversy, she may only wish to avoid an unpleasant scene, but Jacquie doesn't want to fight any more than Brooke does.

Jacquie admits that her interest in the Astors blossomed late. It was 1978, in fact, when she first got to know the English branch of the family reasonably well. Past trips across the Atlantic had usually taken her to the Continent. She is fluent in French and working on a similar degree of proficiency in Italian. But after spending some time with her English cousins—in particular Gavin's son John—she has developed a curiosity about her heritage. It seems an appropriate development for the youngest adult American Astor.

Besides Jack Astor and his two children and the descendants of the Chanlers, not too much remains of the Astor
family in America. The Astor connection has grown tenuous as it has been passed down on the female side, thereby
losing not only the Astor name but the major parts of the
fortune as well. Still, the impression that there is next to
nothing left is a misleading one. There is, for example, a
thriving clan of Van Alens who claim Caroline Astor's eldest daughter, Emily, as a forebear in the direct line. True,
that was three and four generations back, but it has not
been forgotten. Actually, one must retreat yet another generation to find the last Astor in the Chanler line and the
same is true for the surviving Careys, who must return to
the original John Jacob's granddaughter, Mary Alida, to
find their Astor connection. One member of that family
has achieved a certain prominence on his own, as mayor of
Rye, New York, and as a senior partner in the New York
law firm of Coudert et Frères. The Drayton family traces
its Astor connection to another of Caroline Astor's daughters, Charlotte Augusta. Its most prominent members
today are probably Christopher H. Phillips, who followed
his distinguished father in a career with the State Department, and William Astor Drayton, perhaps the hardest-
working member of the family in his job as assistant administrator for planning and management at the Environmental Protection Agency. Carrie Astor, Charlotte
Augusta's sister, remains well represented today by her
daughter-in-law, Mrs. Orme Wilson, who is in her nineties,
very active and generally considered the doyenne of the
family. The most Astor blood outside Jack and his children
belongs to the children of Jack's older half sister, Alice.
Two of them live in the United States. Mrs. Eric Glandbard is considered the closest to an Astor that the Rhine-

beck area can claim today. Her older half brother, Ivan Obolensky, divides his time between New York and Grosse Point, Michigan. Two other Alice daughters live abroad.

For the most part, they all lead unobtrusive lives, their Astor connection faint, a thing of the past.

EPILOGUE

More than any other family, the Astors changed the nature of what may pass for American aristocracy. It was under their reign that money replaced blood as the principal criterion by which a man and his family were judged and placed in or excluded from high society. Before them, the crème de la crème came from two sources—the Dutch patroons who first settled New York and, later, the families who held vast tracts of land granted them by royalty. Self-made men were, with a few military and political exceptions, slightly repugnant, as though still damp with perspiration and perhaps faintly noisome. The original John Jacob Astor began the process whereby such aversion was overcome, not directly but after a fashion and after time. He did so by the overwhelming nature of his success, which made him impossible to ignore. Ignorant of the social graces, he was nonetheless powerful and interesting enough to receive invitations into most of the best homes, although he was not always invited back. More importantly, his children, given all the advantages of education

and upbringing denied John Jacob by his poor circumstances, grew up accepted or at least acknowledged by the
best families. And it became a long-standing Astor tradition that the male members improved the social standing
of the family by the marriages they made. Thus William
B. Astor, John Jacob's son, married Margaret Armstrong,
whose ties to such families as the Livingstons gave her impeccable social credentials. His sons would in their turn
continue to improve the Astor bloodlines, but it was the
Astor fortune that provided the entree, and by the third
generation it was Astor money just as much as the good
breeding of their wives that propelled the Astors to the
forefront of American society.

The source and timing of that money were probably important to the Astors' social success as well. Theirs was the
first of the great American fortunes to be made in the
United States, and at the time of John Jacob's death his
fortune was some ten times as large as any other in the
country. The control John Jacob exercised over the fur
trade in America during the first quarter of the nineteenth
century rivaled the great oil, steel, tobacco and powder
trusts of future generations in its strength. His company
was the largest business in the United States, but it would
be three quarters of a century before monopoly became
not only a dirty but also an actionable word. By that time
the Astors had long been out of trade. Their money was in
real estate, like so many of the great European fortunes
and unlike most of the vast fortunes in the United States.
The Rockefellers, Mellons and du Ponts built family fortunes through enterprise; the Astors, after the first John
Jacob and his son William, reaped profits generated by the
industry of others. Through the foresight of their forebears,
later generations owned land on top of which was to rise
the greatest city in the country. The Astors were essentially

powerless to stop or abet the process. They could only profit from it.

The Astors were fortunate, too, in that the basic demise of the family dynasty, brought on by Vincent's failure to produce an heir, came before the great social unrest and increasing influence of the radical fringes determined to upset establishment equilibrium, sure that a quick redistribution of wealth according to need would prove the social panacea that had so long been so elusive. True, Vincent was around to be attacked by the Nye Committee, but he was a peripheral case in those hearings. There were bigger fish to fry. The Astors were not, of course, universally admired. Journalists would periodically take some verbal swings at them, their wealth and the use to which it was being put. But, as Henry Adams wrote in his classic, *The Education of Henry Adams*:

"Newspapers might prate about wealth till commonplace print was exhausted, but as a matter of habit, few Americans envied the very rich for anything the most of them got out of money."

Others in subsequent generations would echo Adams' sentiments. Being really rich was probably better than being really poor during the years the Astors ruled wealthy society, but it wasn't necessarily all it was touted to be. Noel Coward, for example, was a man who spent plenty of time hobnobbing with money and its holders and came away sure he was better off than they. After one visit to the yacht of Niarchos, Coward talked about the "unscalable barriers of money and power" that rose between Niarchos and even his good friends. "I still hold to my conviction that the very rich lead most unenviable lives," he said. Another time, Coward reflected that "the life of the very rich is not for me, and although it is enjoyable to observe at close quarters for a brief spell, it is strangely deadening to the heart."

It is an intriguing phenomenon of the American system that success is honored and envied only up to a point. Individual initiative exercised in an atmosphere of individual freedom is the ideal action in the system. It is what has always made the wheels turn. But the flaw in the system is that there is no logical conclusion to which such action can be carried. The better you play the game, the richer and more powerful you become. Somewhere along the way you pass a point at which your wealth and power become not objects for admiration and, God willing, imitation, but threats. You become a mutant in the ecosystem with the potential for limiting the opportunity of others. You have gathered not so much more than your share as parts of the shares of others, and yet it is difficult to express gratitude or repay those from whom you have allegedly taken because, in your own eyes, you started at the same place everyone else did and simply ran a better race. The Astors should have been the victims of this phenomenon, but because they were more or less its first manifestation, they escaped. They escaped despite an arrogance and a general lack of public spirit that caused considerable caviling among the intelligentsia of their day. By the time the public consciousness had been raised against the abuses of extraordinary wealth, Vincent Astor was at the head of the American family and demonstrating a sympathy for and interest in the public weal that was not generally considered hereditary. By the time Vincent's approach to philanthropy was itself coming under scrutiny—the private foundation as tax dodge—Vincent had died. In any case, his foundation had not then abused and does not today abuse the special privileges granted foundations. Those who mourn what they see as the passing of foundations because of tax laws prom-

ulgated as a result of abuses deplore the loss of foundations like Astor's because they contribute in efficient and
innovative ways to the solving of the nation's problems, a
job that, without foundations, will be left virtually in its
entirety to the government. That is not an altogether comforting prospect to many.

The Astors are different from other American families of
vast wealth in another respect. In the histories of most of
these families can be traced the transition from accumu-
lation to conservation. One can see the spark going out as
the heirs to the family fortune begin to realize that, given
the tax laws, inflation and the growing size of the family, it
will take as much genius just to conserve the fortune and
leave as much to their children as they themselves inherited as it ever did in past generations to accumulate the
money in the first place. There is a tendency to adopt a
shoulder-shrugging attitude, for these young scions of
wealth are spoiled and know not how to apply themselves
to the solution of big problems. Indeed, most would deny
the existence of such problems, or at least the possibility of
their solution. There comes a simple resignation to the
ineluctable: Nothing lasts forever. That is especially true in
the United States. One of this country's proudest boasts is
that its citizens enjoy an upward mobility unparalleled in
history. However, unless it is to become very crowded at
the top, upward mobility implies an equal amount of
downward movement. That is what happens. True, a large
share of the nation's wealth lies in the hands of a relatively
small percentage of the population, but the people making
up that percentage change from generation to generation.
The Astors and the Vanderbilts have been replaced by the
Hunts and the Gettys. In most cases this process is gradual
and takes place over several generations. One can see it
happening in the traditional manner with the English

branch of the family. But the American Astors made the transition abruptly, in a single generation, Vincent's. Before Vincent, the American Astors were so wealthy that conservation was not something any of them gave much thought. There was plenty. There always had been and undoubtedly always would be. Vincent's father died before the institution of the graduated income tax.

Usually, inheritors somewhere around the third or fourth generation go into what might reasonably be likened to a stall in a college basketball game. The stall is ball-control strategy designed to protect a tenuous lead or keep a game between unequally talented teams close. But it is a strategy that can backfire easily, especially if it has been employed too early in the game. A team loses momentum and the aggressive rhythm it had while building its lead, or the talented opposition hits a few shots and the stallers miss. The lead can evaporate or the rout can start. The Astors never used the stall; they had run up such a big lead early in the game that the stall just wasn't needed. They left the court winners.

Of course the game is shorter in America than in Europe, in present times than in past. The Hapsburgs, the Bourbons, the Medicis, all had greater staying power than any of America's great families. Blood, it seems, is a firmer foundation than wealth on which to build a dynasty. America prizes its individuals, not its dynasties.

In most of America's great families one can find a series of great, larger-than-life people whose enterprise and ingenuity made the family what it was or is. This is rather dramatically untrue of the Astors. The founder of the American family was such a person, rough at the edges perhaps but big enough so that the edges mattered little. The only other two Astors who would reasonably qualify for inclusion in this category were Astors only by marriage.

(Mary Astor, the actress, was, by the way, not a member of the family. In fact, Astor was not her real name. She chose it, she said, because of its connotations of wealth and prominence.) The first of these women was Caroline, wife of William B. Astor, Jr., and the dominant figure in American society for the last quarter of the nineteenth century. In an era when women wielded needles and spatulas more than gavels or pens, Caroline was perhaps the most powerful woman in America. It was not exactly a utopia over which she reigned. As Colonel Mann described it in *Town Topics* in 1890, society was not flourishing. "In time, I believe society will outgrow its present vapid and aimless condition, passing from stupidity and ridiculousness into a state of dignity and true elegance." Colonel Mann's notion of dignity and true elegance, one suspects, was perhaps too self-centered ever to gain wide acceptance. He went on to call Mrs. Astor "a monument of profitless pride." She was not often so underrated. Society in the days before Hollywood, when entertainers were considered a little scandalous, provided the gossip and the dreams on which the public thrived, and Mrs. Astor was society personified.

The most famous Astor of the twentieth century was unquestionably Nancy Langhorne, Lady Astor, the woman who exchanged verbal barbs with Winston Churchill and was the first woman to serve in England's Parliament. She was a dynamic and irrepressible personality. The extent to which she was more than that or, conversely, the extent to which she was no more than a spoiled, willful poseur are subjects for which room to disagree must be allowed. Whether she would ever have been content to play the Perle Mesta role had her husband been able to retain his House of Commons seat is not clear. What is clear is that much of what Nancy Astor became she owed to Waldorf. Nancy must not be underrated; no woman who was all suf-face and no depth would ever have captured the friendships of so diverse and important a group as she did. On the other hand, history may be selling Waldorf a little short if his wife continues to receive the lion's share of the attention she demanded in her lifetime but may not deserve in retrospect.

While the temptation might be strong to blame the Astors, the fact is that their dearth of interest in the public welfare was more a product of the times than callousness or indifference. It was not until after World War I that any pressure was brought to bear upon the very wealthy in this country to acknowledge their debt to the society that had spawned them. The Vanderbilts were no more generous than the Astors in the nineteenth century. The great Ford, Rockefeller and Mellon foundations and family charitable contributions are products of this century. The original John D. Rockefeller was not a particularly generous man during the years he was building the gigantic Standard Oil combine. He did eventually give away somewhere between $500 million and $750 million in his lifetime, but the Rockefeller Foundation wasn't even founded until 1913, when he was seventy-four. Andrew Mellon's principal largesse, the donation of his art collection and the funds to build a museum (the National Gallery in Washington) in which to keep it, came in 1937, the year of his death. The foundation that bears his name was not even formed until 1969, with the combination of two family foundations whose total assets were about $700 million. Henry Ford started the Ford Foundation in 1936, but it was not until after 1950 that the foundation branched out from local philanthropy in the Detroit area. By the time these families were recognizing their societal debts Vincent Astor was alone representing the main line of the Astor money and was doing his best to keep up.

Before this time, the man who gave away great chunks of his money to benefit public causes was an exception. The most spectacular was unquestionably Andrew Carnegie, who gave New York Carnegie Hall in 1892, retired from the steel business that had made him one of America's wealthiest individuals in 1901 and spent the remaining eighteen years of his life giving away money, a total of about $350 million. He created a series of foundations and charitable institutions. Whereas the Astors can be considered among the major benefactors of the New York Public Library, one of the greatest institutions of its kind, Carnegie can be said to have been responsible for the nation's network of public libraries, having contributed to some 2,800 of them. It was Carnegie who said upon hearing that J. P. Morgan had died and left an estate of $68 million, not including a $50 million art collection, "And to think he was not a rich man!" It was William Jennings Bryan who said of Morgan, after hearing that Morgan had said America was good enough for him, "Well, whenever he doesn't like it, he can give it back to us."

Morgan was no slouch in the philanthropic field. He once took a look for just a minute or two at plans for expansion of the Harvard Medical School, pointed to three buildings, announced he would build those three and bade the openmouthed trustees a good morning. Those were, to coin a phrase, the good old days. The Astors were more interested then in their own pleasure than the comfort of the afflicted. There is a story told by an elderly gentleman now living in Greenwich, Connecticut, about how one Astor, who employed the same architect as this older man to build his New York home, allowed the servants to help with the functional design of the house, if not its aesthetics, the theory being that no one would know more about how the house needed to function on a practical level than the servants. According to the story, Mrs. Astor's only remark upon seeing the plans for her new home was, "They're wonderful! But where is the musicians' entrance?"

Those days are gone. Perhaps the last house like that was the one belonging to Mrs. Cornelius Vanderbilt III on Fifth Avenue. It was closed in 1945. Mrs. Vanderbilt is generally given credit for the classic line, delivered in England, "In America I take a rank something like your Princess of Wales." The lavishness is gone, too, from England. Several years ago the Duke of Devonshire described himself as but a caretaker, suggesting that the cheapest way for the government to maintain England's great estates was to allow the owners to live there. The duke remembered a prior generation in his family when it was recommended to his ancestor that the financial situation of the dukedom be ameliorated by the letting go of the second pastry chef. "Can't a fellow even have a biscuit?" the poor duke is alleged to have whined.

Among living persons, entertainers seem to have taken over a large portion of the charitable activities once reserved for the nation's wealthy social families. Jackie Gleason, Andy Williams, Glen Campbell and many others sponsor golf tournaments, the proceeds from which go to charity. Benefit performances are given for a host of causes. Athletes, who are paid like entertainers today, give time, name and money to everything from the United Fund to free seats at the ballpark for the local underprivileged young people. Bing Crosby once estimated his friend Bob Hope gave $20,000 a week to charity. Hope pays something on the order of $60,000 in country club dues annually and explains when asked why he still works, "I've got a government to support."

The Astor family—and most particularly Caroline Astor

—managed to mold an American aristocracy out of money, leisure and several generations of breeding up, but the question that now arises is whether America's peculiar brand of democratic capitalism and its untraditional aristocracy can flourish side by side. At the moment the concept of an aristocracy in the United States attracts minimal support. Elitism is a dirty word, and heredity is something to be overcome through education and environment. It is difficult to reconcile aristocracy and upward mobility, if the former is achieved by accident of birth while the latter represents individual effort.

Nonetheless, if aristocracy is struggling, so, too, are both capitalism and democracy. Capitalism is seen today as spawning the more-is-better syndrome, materialism and greed. Increasingly its natural directions and inclinations are being curbed by regulation as, in effect, we ask the government to protect us from ourselves. But the more we expect from government in the way of panaceas, the more surely will we be disappointed and frustrated, losing faith in the system. A democracy is not, in all likelihood, going to prosper when only half the eligible citizens participate in the process.

Chances are the aristocracy over which the Astors ruled through the second half of the nineteenth century belongs to a time that will never be recaptured. For the most part, it will be little mourned. At its best it promoted a certain aplomb, almost a dignity, and provided a stability of tradition and a recognition of the past. At its worst, which was also its most visible, it was tastelessly ostentatious, mindless and vacuous. But it may have been a step in the right direction.

Digby Baltzell, a University of Pennsylvania sociologist, argues that society needs both democratic and aristocratic forces at work or government winds up making all the decisions. He concedes that at the moment neither of these forces is very strong and in his classic mid-1960s book, *The Protestant Establishment,* contends that the class once dominated by Astors and Vanderbilts has deteriorated (actually, it has reverted) from ruling class to irrelevant exclusivity. What he is apparently saying is that the important people, who make the big government and business decisions, are no longer solely products of the White Anglo-Saxon Protestant process, and yet these new power brokers are forced to remain outside the inner social circles. Not that they mind much, but the point is that those inner circles are losing their meaning again, much as they did during Caroline Astor's time. Only this time the meaninglessness is obvious to everyone.

In other words, the society needs a flexible aristocracy within the confines of which the nation's leaders can know one another. It is Baltzell's contention that, without a ruling class, power reverts to government institutions that, because each institution is isolated in the social context, cannot make decisions, can only react to events, not influence or direct them. He points to the Nixon administration and Watergate, arguing that within that group were no common backgrounds, affiliations or codes of behavior, no peer pressure. The resulting chaos was almost predictable. It was not just coincidence, he would claim, that Archibald Cox and Elliot Richardson, two very proper WASPs, were alone in refusing to go along with administration machinations. The Old School Tie, according to this theory, is no insidious entanglement of wealth and privilege but a membership agreement that coerces members to behave within the parameters of a code of manners and ethics that everyone clearly understands. It is thus a useful, perhaps even essential, arrangement in our society. But only as long as it remains flexible enough to include those who arrive at the top by different routes than the perceived standard road of New England prep school, Ivy League university and family business.

The Astors understood and agreed with this arrangement. A few of them would even have gone along with the flexibility part. After all, if the ruling isn't done by those who have something to lose when the system collapses, the system may be encouraged to collapse. The status quo was for generations a status worth preserving in the Astor view. And, while the world without experienced the dramatic upheavals of the Civil War, the Industrial Revolution and both World Wars, the inner (or upper) circle inhabited by the Astors remained rather remarkably static and invulnerable to change.

The demise of the Astors in the United States should not be viewed as a social, economic or political phenomenon, for it has been really none of these. True, Vincent Astor displayed a social conscience that could not have been inherited, and the Astor Foundation would probably have been started in any event. But the real reason for the demise of the American Astors was the fate that took Colonel John Jacob's life before the birth of his second son and left his first son, Vincent, without children. One could almost say the American Astors are dying of natural causes.

BIBLIOGRAPHY

Books

Adams, Henry. *The Education of Henry Adams*. Houghton Mifflin, 1918.

Adams, Russell B., Jr. *The Boston Money Tree*. Crowell, 1977.

Aldrich, Margaret Chanler. *Family Vista*. Pamphlet distributing, 1958.

Amory, Cleveland. *The Last Resorts*. Harper & Bros., 1948.

——. *The Trouble with Nowadays*. Arbor House, 1979.

Astor, Brooke. *Footprints*. Doubleday & Co., 1980.

Astor, John Jacob IV. *A Journey in Other Worlds*. D. Appleton & Co., 1894.

Astor, Michael. *Tribal Feeling*. London: John Murray, 1963.

Astor, William Waldorf. *John Jacob Astor*. 1899.

——. *Sforza, a Story of Milan*. Charles Scribner's Sons, 1889.

Baird, Robert. *Transplanted Flowers or the Memoirs of Mrs. Rumpff and the Duchesse de Broglie*. 1839.

Birmingham, Stephen. *The Right People*. Little, Brown & Co., 1958.

Bristed, Charles Astor. *The Upper Ten Thousand*. 1852.

Burnham, Sophy. *The Landed Gentry*. G. P. Putnam's Sons, 1978.

Carleton, G. W. & Co. *The Parlor Table Companion*. 1877.

Chanler, Margaret Terry. *Roman Spring*. Little, Brown & Co., 1934.

Churchill, Allen. *The Splendor Seekers*. Grosset & Dunlap, 1974.

Collier, Peter, and Horowitz, David. *The Rockefellers*. Holt, Rinehart & Winston, 1976.

Cowles, Virginia. *The Astors*. Alfred A. Knopf, 1979.

Crowninshield, Frank. *The Unofficial Palace of New York*. 1939.

Curtis, Charlotte. *The Rich and Other Atrocities*. Harper & Row, 1976.

Elliott, Maude Howe. *This Was My Newport*. Mythology Co., 1944.

Friedman, B. H. *Gertrude Vanderbilt Whitney*. Doubleday & Co., 1978.

Halberstam, David. *The Powers That Be*. Alfred A. Knopf, 1979.

Harrison, Rosina. *Rose: My Life in Service*. Viking, 1975.

Hersh, Burton. *The Mellon Family*. William Morrow & Co., 1978.

Hershkowitz, Leo. *Tweed's New York: Another Look*. Doubleday & Co., 1977.

Howe, Julia Ward. *Is Polite Society Polite? and Other Essays*. 1895.

———. *Modern Society*. 1880.

Hoy, C. I. *John Jacob Astor: An Unwritten Chapter*. Meador Press, 1936.

Hubbard, Elbert. *Little Journeys to the Homes of Great Businessmen*.

Kavaler, Lucy. *The Astors*. Dodd, Mead, 1966.

Konolige, Kit and Frederica. *The Power of Their Glory*. Wyden Books, 1978.

Langhorne, Elizabeth. *Nancy Astor and Her Friends*. Praeger Publishers, 1974.

Lesley, Cole. *The Life of Noel Coward*. Penguin Books, 1976.

Lewis, R. W. B. *Edith Wharton: A Biography*. Harper & Row, 1975.

Lundberg, Ferdinand. *The Rich and the Super Rich*. Lyle Stuart, 1968.

McAllister, Ward. *Society as I Have Found It*. Cassell, 1890.

McLean, Evalyn Walsh. *Father Struck It Rich*. Little, Brown & Co., 1936.

Minnigerode, Mead. *Certain Rich Men*. G. P. Putnam, 1927.

Morris, Lloyd. *Incredible New York*. Random House, 1951.

Morton, Frederic. *The Rothschilds*. Atheneum, 1961.

Obolensky, Serge. *One Man in His Time*. McDowell, Obolensky, 1958.

O'Connor, Harvey. *The Astors*. Alfred A. Knopf, 1941.

O'Connor, Richard. *The Golden Summers*. G. P. Putnam, 1974.

Parton, James. *The Life of John Jacob Astor*. 1865.

Porter, Kenneth Wiggins. *John Jacob Astor: Business Man*. Harvard University Press, 1931.

Samuels, Ernest. *Bernard Berenson: The Making of a Connoisseur*. Harvard University Press, 1979.

Scully, Vincent J., Jr., and Downing, Antoinette F. *The Architectural Heritage of Newport, R.I.* Clarkson N. Potter, 1952.

Simon, Kate. *Fifth Avenue: A Very Social History.* Harcourt Brace Jovanovich, 1978.

Smith, Arthur Douglas Howden. *John Jacob Astor, Landlord of New York.* Blue Ribbon Books, 1931.

Sykes, Christopher. *Nancy: The Life of Lady Astor.* Harper & Row, 1972.

Thomas, Lately. *A Pride of Lions.* William Morrow & Co., 1971.

———. *Sam Ward: "King of the Lobby."* Houghton Mifflin, 1965.

Thorndike, Joseph J., Jr. *The Very Rich: A History of Wealth.* American Heritage, 1976.

Vanderbilt, Cornelius, Jr. *Queen of the Golden Age.* McGraw-Hill, 1956.

Van Rensselaer, May King. *Newport: Our Social Capital.* 1905.

———. *The Social Ladder.* Holt, 1924.

Wecter, Dixon. *The Saga of American Society*, with introduction by Louis Auchincloss. Charles Scribner's Sons, 1970.

Weymouth, Lally. *America in 1876: The Way We Were.* Random House, 1976.

Wharton, Edith. *The Age of Innocence.* D. Appleton & Co., 1920.

Other Publications and Periodicals

A significant portion of the research for this book was conducted among the periodicals at the New York Public Library, the New-York Historical Society, and the Newport Historical Society. Magazines such as *Vogue, Cosmopolitan, Town and Country, Harper's Weekly, Literary Digest,* and many others all contained useful articles in their back volumes. Colonel Mann's *Town Topics* was read extensively, especially in the decade from 1885 to 1895. The New York *Times* and the London *Times* were both helpful sources. Many other New York newspapers besides these two sources were consulted for specific stories they carried.

INDEX

Tracing th... ...liams *

John Jacob Astor II
(1791 – 1869)

John Jacob Astor III ══════ m. ═══ Charlotte Augusta Gibbs
(1822 – 1890)

William Waldorf Astor ═ m. ═ Mary D. Paul
(1848 – 1919)

Waldorf Astor   John Jacob Astor V
(1879 – 1952)   (1886 – 1971)

m.   m.

Nancy Langhorne Shaw ... Lady Violet Elliot Murray ... Nairne

William ...
As...
(1907...

m.

Sarah K...

William ...

Anna...

Wa...